D0229559

1001
MORE
RIDICULOUS
WAYS TO DIE

This book is dedicated to all my allies in heaven and comrades in hell.
Like most other things in my life, this book would not have happened without the support
of my wife. She makes every day worth living. This book would also not have happened
without the support of Steve Howe – a true brother. Another brother by another mother
who made a path for this work was Matt Adams.

Two other brothers who need to be mentioned are Kevin Allen and Alan Williams,
as the writing of this book has delayed me buying them the drink I owe them.

First published in Great Britain in 2013 by Prion
an imprint of the
Carlton Publishing Group
20 Mortimer Street
London W1T 3JW

A CIP catalogue for this book is available from the British Library.

ISBN 978-1-85375-903-1

Printed and bound by CPI Group (UK) Ltd, Croydon CR0 4TY

10 9 8 7 6 5 4 3 2 1

1001 MORE
RIDICULOUS
WAYS TO DIE

A comprehensive collection of humorous
true stories about the most ridiculous
ways people have met their maker

David Southwell

PRION

INTRODUCTION

'He who does not fear death dies only once.' – Giovanni Falcone

The last words of the great English actor Edmund Keen in 1833 are alleged to have been: 'Dying is easy. Comedy is hard.' Hopefully this book contains hundreds of stories proving Keen mistaken. When it comes to ridiculous deaths, comedy often goes hand-in-hand with tragedy.

Make no mistake. All death is a tragedy for someone. In writing this book I am not mocking the grief that comes from death. I have deep sympathy for all those left behind in mourning. How could I not? I have not lived a life without grief and loss myself. However, acknowledging the ridiculousness of some exits from this vale of tears seems to be more healthy a response to death than pretending it does not happen.

All the stories in this book happened, or at least have multiple reference points from credible sources. Many of the sources have been checked out firsthand in phone calls, e-mails and Skype conversations. Many have been sent to me by law enforcement officials from countries as diverse as Australia, Thailand and Sri Lanka. When it comes to a mordant sense of humour, no one does it better than a police officer. Though I have checked and rechecked the stories to ensure they happened, the lawyers thought it better for me to change the names and locations for some of them. Therefore a guy called Wayne dying in Atlanta might be called Bob and have died in Washington, but everything else is accurate, I promise. Lawyers, eh?

Some stories of ridiculous deaths that fly around on the Internet are little more than urban myths. Despite really wanting the story of the frogman scooped up in the water and then dumped out into a forest fire by a fire-fighting plane to be true, I found no evidence for it. When you drill down into the proper research detail of other famous death tales, such as Italian stripper Gina Lavola who suffocated whilst waiting to jump out of a cake, you soon find they did not happen. There is no death certificate nor inquest report because Gina Lavola never existed outside the imagination of the journalist who made her up for a story in the *Weekly World News*.

There never was an accountant called Ken Barger who accidentally shot himself in the head while groggily trying to answer a 4am phone call. There never was a clown called Yves Abouchar who drowned when a foam pie was thrown in his face. Preposterous, insanely absurd and ridiculous deaths happen everyday, but some of the tales reported as fact are just wonderful little stories people tell because they feel the need to laugh in the face of death.

Writing this book has convinced me of many things. Firstly it has shown me that reality is so strange it is beyond fiction to capture it. The dubious tales of comic death – whether made to entertain or serve as propaganda – never come close to the weird reality the world offers. It never comes up with something as insane as a man dying while trying to scare motorists into thinking that Bigfoot is out there. Never comes up with anything half as ironic as a man trying to cure his fear of death by staging a mock burial that actually ends up killing him for real.

It has also persuaded me that authors John Keel and Andrew Collins are right when they talk about a Cosmic Joker – some form of universal force which loves irony and playing with coincidence. What else can you do but laugh when you come across the story of skydiver Andrew Wing III, who died when he crashed into the wing of a plane during a jump? The conductor who died during a performance of Bach's *Come Sweet Death*? Surely the cosmos is having a laugh at us.

I feel like I have tempted fate so much by writing this book that my own death, when it comes, will be ridiculous enough for someone else to write about. While writing this book, my wife accidentally served me a supposedly healthy vegetable curry that contained small fragments of glass. As I pulled a chunk from my mouth, I could only think: 'Oh well, if I am going to die like this, it will make a perfect entry if they ever do a follow up to this book.'

The only sane response to both the inevitable and yet often random nature of death in my view is to live and love strong. To relish life and all its adventures. Whatever your faith, Seneca was right when he said: 'The day which we fear as our last is but the birthday of eternity.'

MAGNUM FORCE

John Wilson, 44, died when he was hit in the groin by a bullet that came through the ceiling of the motel room in Buffalo, New York, he was sharing in 1984. The killer bullet was not aimed by some irate partner, but by a drunken Kal Aram in the room above, who told the police he fired the gun 'at the TV because it was showing *Magnum P.I.*'

THE FLYING LAWNMOWER OF DEATH

In 1979, American football fans were enjoying the half-time show at a Jets-Patriots game at the Shea Stadium in New York. The entertainment was being provided by the Electronic Eagles Radio Control Association and during the show, one plane – made into the shape of a lawnmower – refused to respond to its controller and nosedived into the stands. It hit two Patriots fans in the head, injuring one so severely he died a few days later.

MY GHOST WIFE TOLD ME TO DO IT

Nonito Locaya, a 65-year-old widower from Quezon City in the Philippines, hung himself with a telephone cord from a wooden beam in his home. His reasons for doing so were somewhat strange. His sister said that minutes before, Nonito told her the ghost of his wife appeared, telling him to hurry up and join her in the afterlife. Before his sister left the room to make coffee, Nonito said: 'Look, it is my wife, I have to do what she tells me.' When she came back, Nonito was already dead.

A BAD CASE OF POOR PRIORITIES

Florida man Johnny Moore, 58, was so drunk that instead of getting medical attention for the gash in his ankle caused by a broken beer bottle, he put his foot in a plastic bowl so the blood did not spill on the carpet. He then kept drinking beer and watching a late night movie. By the time the film was finished, so was Johnny. His blood loss had proved fatal.

A SHITTY WAY TO GO

Poor Barry Ballard, 53, from Australia decided to take shelter under a shop awning whilst a storm raged in 2007. Unfortunately for Ballard, the owner of the shop had not taken care of the huge quantity of pigeon droppings that had built up in the awning. As the storm raged, the awning collapsed from the weight of pigeon poop and came down on Ballard, killing him.

EXORCISM EXIT I

In the twenty-first century, when rationalism and scepticism hold sway, the idea that anyone takes possession and exorcism seriously seems utterly odd. That people actually die due to such beliefs is beyond ridiculous. However, of all the myriad peculiar ways of leaving this mortal realm, death by insane exorcism is worryingly common.

In January 2013, 23-year-old Takuya Nagaya from Japan was head-butted and bitten to death by his 53-year-old father Katsumi Nagaya. Takuya's mother thought her son was possessed by a snake demon when he began to slither on the floor and talk about becoming a snake. Rather than calling for a mental health professional, she called her husband, who then spent two days beating and biting his son in an attempt to exorcise the alleged demon inhabiting him. When Takuya went limp for the final time from a particularly brutal head-butt, his parents took his body to hospital, where he was declared dead.

EXORCISM EXIT II

In June 2012, 35-year-old Karla Kuhl from El Sobrante, California smothered 53-year-old Patricia Medeiros with a pillow. Karla claimed that the killing was entirely accidental and happened whilst she was attempting to exorcise a demon from Patricia by beating her with a Bible. Given that both women had been romantically involved with the same man, police took a somewhat sceptical view of this explanation and arrested Kuhl for the killing.

HOME SURGERY DISASTER

Austrian composer Alban Berg, 50, died on Christmas Eve 1935. Earlier in the year he had been stung by a bee on the back which resulted in a carbuncle. In an absurdly ill-advised bit of home surgery, his wife tried to cut off the growth with a pair of scissors. Unsurprisingly, he died of blood poisoning due to an infection in the wound made by Mrs. Berg.

CARPETS SPELL CURTAINS

Margo Jones was one of the giants of 1950s American theatre. The director and producer left a lasting legacy when she died in 1955 at the age of 43. There is no doubt she would be better remembered today if not for an untimely death brought about in no small part by being house-proud. Jones died from exposure to carbon tetrachloride fumes after having the carpets cleaned in her Dallas apartment. I know some people think housework is important, but it is not worth dying over.

FOR BETTER, FOR WORSE

Russian husband and wife Aleksandr and Agafya Lagunov did everything together, even working on the same police force. Unfortunately, they also died together when Aleksandr tried to do a bit of DIY on the sewer system in their house in the Saratov region. Making a hole in the cover of the septic tank led to him being overcome by fumes and falling in. Agafya then tried to pull him out, but was also overcome by fumes. A cop colleague said: 'They were a close couple. At least they went together.'

DEATH, WHERE IS THY STING?

Some people are lucky. They crash their car into an electricity sub-station and stumble from their vehicle safe and relatively unhurt. Then there are the ludicrously unlucky, like 60-year-old Mariana Carmichael from Johannesburg who crashed her car into a sub-station in 2005, stumbled from the wreck and was stung to death by a swarm of more than a million bees, whose 10-year-old hive was built into the sub-station.

MAGICAL MORT I

Death caused due to a misplaced belief in magic is depressingly routine in many parts of the world. However, for those whose response to the certainty of death and the grim insanity that often surrounds it is laughter, at least deaths caused by failures in magic usually provide a big wallop of humour. A good illustration of this happened in Chitungwiza, Zimbabwe in January 2013 when six people died in an explosion during an attempt to kill a goblin. One survivor of the tragedy, traditional healer Clara Banda, claimed the explosion happened in an attempt to deal with a goblin that was causing problems for its owner Clever Kamuyedza. Clever had agreed to pay $15,000 to self-styled prophet and magician Speakmore Mandre for the ritual which ended with a house-destroying bang. Sceptical Zimbabwean police believe the actual cause of the tragedy was that Clever and Speakmore were attempting to extract the mythical munitions component red mercury from a stolen hand grenade.

MAGICAL MORT II

In some parts of Kenya, crime has reached such epic proportions, and faith in the police is so minimal, that residents have turned to magic as their first line of defence against theft. As is often the case with magic, death with a degree of macabre humour has resulted from spell-casting. James Okello, 28, became so panicked and afraid when he broke out in boils after stealing mangos from an orchard protected by witchcraft, that he felt the only way to free himself from the malign magic was to take his own life; hanging himself from one of the trees from which he originally stole the fruit.

MAGICAL MORT III

Dying over a sporting event is wrong. Dying over a sporting event where magic is allegedly involved is plain ludicrous. When a player was accused of using witchcraft during a football match between Congo teams Socozaki and Nyuki System in 2008, a riot broke out which claimed 13 lives. The problem started when the goalkeeper for Nyuki, who were losing the game, ran up the pitch and tried to cast a spell. This action enraged Socozaki fans, who began to riot, pelting the pitch and opposing supporters with stones. In a misjudged attempt to regain control, police fired shots into the air and tear gas into the stands, causing a fatal stampede.

MAGICAL MORT IV

Attempts at mad magic and death seem to go hand-in-hand, but then again, burying yourself before death seems to have a pretty close relationship with ridiculous ways of dying. In 2011, Russia suffered from an Internet meme that burying yourself would magically endow you with life-long luck. Two 35-year-old friends in the eastern city of Blagoveshchensk entered into a pact to bury each other to get the mystical bonus, but unfortunately for the one going first, luck ran out during the attempt. Though he was buried in an improvized coffin complete with air pipes, a bottle of water and a mobile phone, when his friend returned the next morning to clear away the 20cm of earth, the buried man was dead. Police investigator Alexei Lubinsky said: 'It is possible heavy rain overnight blocked the air supply.'

BEWARE OF THE BULL

In 1866, Irish strong man James Calhoun died when he attempted to lift a young bull above his head for a bet. He managed to lift the animal, but overbalanced. The beast landed on top of him, kicked him in the head, and killed him.

OH, THE IRONY I – DEAD AND BURIED

Alongside the Russian craze of 2011 of burying yourself overnight in an effort to gain supernatural luck, the Russian fondness for self-burial led to a death in an attempt to cure a man of his fear of death. In 2010, Alexander Shokin from the Volgoda region, persuaded a friend to bury him in a homemade coffin to try to help him overcome his fear of premature death. Unfortunately, the weight of earth collapsed the coffin, killing Mr. Shokin. Irony, like stupidity, seems to be fatal.

OH, THE IRONY II – CREMATORIUM BILL KILL

Dairy owner Tham Singh, 70, from Ghaziabad in India dropped dead from the shock of receiving a receipt for his own cremation. The receipt, numbered 89 and suggesting his dead body had been burned a week earlier at the Hindon Mokshasthali crematorium ground, so upset Mr. Singh that within minutes he was complaining of chest pains before undergoing a massive heart attack. Police were called to investigate whether the receipt was a vicious prank or a strange mistake. When Mr. Singh was cremated a week after his actual death at Hindon Mokshasthali, his family refused to accept the cremation receipt they were offered, as it too was numbered 89.

SPONTANEOUS HUMAN COMBUSTION I

Dying from something most scientists claim does not exist qualifies as a ridiculous way to die. Spontaneous human combustion – dying by burning without any apparent external cause – has been cited as the cause of death in more than 200 cases during the last 250 years, yet scientific opinion still holds that the phenomenon does not happen. Maybe one of the disbelieving scientists should have had a word with 76-year-old Irishman Michael Flaherty whose badly burnt body was found in his home despite the fact there was no damage to anything else in the property. West Galway coroner Keiran McLoughlin ruled the death as due to spontaneous human combustion because no other explanation seemed adequate for the freaky fatality.

NEVER WAKING UP AGAIN

What is the most appropriate thing to do at the wake of a friend who died from an overdose of the recreational drug GBL? For 28-year-old Jane Hill, who died on April 28, 2012, it was taking exactly the same industrial cleaner-based drug as had killed her friend John King. An ambulance crew collected Hill from the wake when she collapsed, but she died shortly after arriving at hospital. Some people just never learn.

CURSE OF THE GARGOYLE

Ann Newton, 58, died in a tragic but ridiculous accident in 2011, when the former schoolteacher from Penshaw slipped whilst refilling a bird feeder, and drowned in her 18in deep garden pond. Ann, who been drinking, was unable to get out the pond because as she fell in, her blouse snagged a grotesque wooden carving of a gargoyle that toppled with her into the water and pinned her down. Ann's partner, Norman Lunn said: 'Ann never liked the sculpture, she said it kept looking at her funny. She always wanted me to get rid of it. I'll still be keeping it in the garden. If I kicked it, it would just hurt my toe.'

BEWARE FLYING BEAR

Canada is one of the most beautiful nations in the world, its countryside stuffed to bursting with amazing wildlife. Unfortunately, therefore, fatal collisions between motorists and fast-moving deer are not uncommon. However, death by flying bear is both rare and somewhat absurd given that 91kg of hulking black bear is both slow moving and easy to spot or miss. However, in June 2011, a 25-year-old driver from rural Ottawa and a 40-year-old man in the passenger seat behind her, both died when she drove into a bear so fast that its massive body flew into the air, landing on the car, with fatal consequences.

THE DANGERS OF SELF LOVE

A 16-year-old from the Rubiato in the Goiás region of Brazil died from the overexertions of a night of continuous, compulsive masturbation. A medical examiner told the local newspaper he believed the teenager had masturbated 42 times over a 12-hour period, leading to death. The unfortunate boy's mother told the paper her son was addicted to 'touching himself' and was due to see a psychiatrist about his problem. A large quantity of pornography was found in the boy's room and an inspection of his computer showed that he had invited many of his classmates to watch his fatal masturbatory frenzy over the Internet.

BUM DEAL

Vanity is a vile trap. Former Miss Argentina Solange Magnano, 38, was so obsessed with keeping her fading looks as her modelling career ran out of steam that she opted to have gluteoplasty – surgery to insert buttock implants. Tragically, the mother of twins died from a pulmonary embolism during the operation. Fashion designer, Roberto Piazza, a close friend of Solange said: 'She lived the life of a goddess. Now she is dead because she wanted a firmer behind.'

SMOKING KILLS I – ALWAYS READ THE LABEL

Warning labels are there for a good reason – to prevent a tragic and unnecessary death. This is as true for hair care products as it is for the old cancer sticks. English hairdresser Jenny Mitchell, 19, had her life cut short when a spark from her cigarette lighter ignited the hydrogen peroxide she was carrying in her Mini Cooper. She had opened the car's window to ventilate it as she smoked, making a lethal cocktail of hair product chemical, oxygen and fire that led to a massive fireball. Seriously, people, read the bloody labels.

REAL BALLBREAKER

When a shopkeeper refused to let Yan Lien park her scooter outside his shop in April 2012, things got ugly, painful and deadly. The 41-year-old woman from Haikou, China, grabbed the shopkeeper's scrotum, squeezing it till he passed out from pain. Despite being rushed to hospital, he died from injuries inflicted by Yan.

IS IT A PLANE? IS IT A BIRD? NO, IT'S A CORPSE

On September 9, 2012, a body of a man fell to ground in the residential street of Portman Avenue in Mortlake, London. The unidentified dead man had fallen more than 610m when the wheels had been lowered from a jet coming in to land at Heathrow airport. He had been stowing away in the plane's landing-gear bay.

BELOW PAR I

Golfers are renowned for their colourful clothing. Given the number of golfing-related fatalities, it is a shame they are not more well-known for safety clothing. Even if the idea of golfers wearing protective helmets is remote, those running golf courses ought to think about providing them to their employees. In a tragic scene that seems to have drifted out of a cartoon and into fatal reality, maintenance man Maurice Hayden was pulling weeds at a Mayfair Country Club course in Florida when he was struck in the temple by a golfer's tee shot some 27m away. Someone, very possibly Maurice, really ought to have seen that coming. Fore!

COOK-OFF KILL-OFF

In September 2008, fork-lift truck driver Jim Smith died from heart failure after eating a bowl of super hot chili. Keen amateur cook Smith had made a bet with his girlfriend's brother over who could make and eat the hottest chili. Clearly Smith won, because shortly after eating his own dish, he suffered cardiac arrest. Smith's recipe seems to have involved the infamous Bhut Jolokia, also known as the ghost chili.

KILLER COFFEE

There is always some idiot who jokes about needing an 'injection of coffee'. Thanks to Brazilian trainee nurse Rejane Moreira Telles, we now know exactly what a coffee injection does. It kills. In 2012, just three days into her job at a Rio de Janeiro clinic, Telles injected 80-year-old Palmerina Pires Ribeiro with milky coffee whilst administering an IV drip. The coffee went straight to the poor patient's heart and lungs with fatal results. Telles was charged with involuntary manslaughter and went on television to explain what happened. 'The drips were next to each other,' she said. 'I injected coffee and put it in the wrong place. Anyone can get confused.'

A RUBBISH WAY TO GO I

Several homeless people die in the United Kingdom each year, crushed to death in garbage trucks, because in a desperate attempt to keep warm they spend the night sleeping in bins. Tragically, Sean Wickes, 24, from Yorkshire, did have a home to go to when he climbed into an industrial bin at 4.45am after a night on the town in February 2013. His body was found at a recycling plant in Leeds the following day.

KILLED BY DEATH I – KILLER COFFIN

English heavy metal band Motörhead once wrote a song called *Killed By Death*. It seems they were onto something more than a witty pun given the number of times the business and trappings of marking death seem to end up leading to ridiculous ways to die. A typical example of this phenomenon happened in November 2012 in the Brazilian state of Rio Grande do Sul. Marciana Silva, 67, was killed instantly whilst travelling in the front of a hearse on her way to her late husband's funeral when his coffin broke loose and hit her in the back of the neck.

KILLED BY DEATH II – TOMBSTONE TAKE DOWN

In October 2008, a 77-year-old man was killed in the St. Gregoire cemetery in Buckingham, Quebec when a tombstone fell on top of him. According to policewoman Isabelle Poirier, he had gone to the boneyard at night to dig at the site of his parents' grave. 'He was digging a hole around the tombstone's foundation when the block fell on his back.' Am I the only one thinking of vengeful spirits?

THE DEVIL DOESN'T LOOK AFTER HIS OWN

Computer games are designed to be addictive. However, maybe some games are a little too good at setting out to be time vampires. Shalin Chuang, 18, booked a private room at a Taiwanese Internet cafe in July 2012. He then proceeded to play *Diablo III* for 40 hours straight. Chuang was found slumped over a PC by a cafe attendant. Taiwanese medical examiners believe sitting for such a prolonged period caused a blood clot. *Diablo III* is clearly a hell of a game.

UP, UP AND DEAD

A revered man of God ascending into the heavens. What could possibly be wrong with that? An awful lot if your chosen way of flying into the sky is attaching more than a thousand helium balloons to a chair. Bonkers Brazilian priest Adelir Antonio de Carli – also known as Padre Baloneiro – was well-known for trying to raise funds via balloon-related stunts. To gain funds for a truck-drivers' spiritual rest stop, de Carli attempted a sponsored cluster balloon ride in 2008. Unfortunately, the balloons not only allowed de Carli to gain an altitude of 6,000m, but carried him out towards sea. The priest used his mobile phone to try to get instructions on how to work the GPS unit he was carrying so he could guide rescuers to his location. Unfortunately, that was the last call he made and neither prayers nor the unused GPS device helped him out. The lower part of his body was eventually found 100km out at sea by an oilrig support vessel some three months later.

BAD WAY TO BECOME A LEGEND

Chuang might have saved himself from a ridiculous death if he had paid attention to the death of a fellow Taiwanese gamer earlier in 2012 which had already achieved legendary status on the Internet (The Devil Doesn't Look After His Own, page 15). In February, 23-year-old Chen Rong-yu was found dead in a New Taipei Internet cafe after having played *League of Legends* for 23 hours non-stop. Chen may have been an ace online monster killer, but according to the doctor who performed the post-mortem, his body could not fight the damage done by dehydration and exhaustion caused by his marathon of gaming.

AN INVENTIVE WAY TO GO I

New Zealander Michael Roiall was a keen amateur inventor who ended up creating the means of his own ridiculous death in August 2012. The 34-year-old was experimenting with a helmet he had designed to allow him to control appliances in his home remotely. However, Roiall had clearly not invented a safety feature to stop the helmet depriving him of air, as he was tragically found suffocated by a family member. Somehow, I doubt we will be seeing his remote control helmet on *Dragons' Den* anytime soon.

MURDEROUS MAMMARIES

For some it might be the ideal exit from the realm of life, for others being smothered to death by your girlfriend's ample breasts is just a ridiculous way to go. A 51-year-old man from Hermiston, Oregon, was rushed to hospital in January 2013, where he was pronounced dead. Police later arrested his 50-year-old girlfriend Anne-Marie Forkel for causing his death by lying on him with her chest in his face. Another man and three other women were at the scene of the death. Not surprisingly, like Forkel and the victim, police found them all to be intoxicated.

AN INVENTIVE WAY TO GO II

Science and ridiculous death often walk hand-in-hand through the avenues of human stupidity because, as the demise of 25-year-old Ukrainian Vladimir Likhonos shows, just because you are scientifically-minded does not mean you are not a complete idiot. Likhonos, a chemistry student at the Kiev Polytechnic Institute, was discovered dead in his room in 2009 with the lower part of his face blown off. He had died when a stick of chewing gum had exploded in his mouth. This was not your usual joke shop trick candy, but Likhonos's own creation of gum coated with explosive. Subsequent police investigation never made it clear why Likhonos was coating gum with explosive material, nor whether he chewed on his own deadly invention by accident or as an experiment that went ludicrously wrong.

DEATH BY CHOCOLATE

If you grew up reading Roald Dahl, you'll already know that chocolate factories can be dangerous places. Unfortunately it seems that reality lived up to fatal fiction for 29-year-old Vincent Smith Jr. Smith was working at the Cocoa Services Inc plant in New Jersey in July 2009 when he fell into a vat of 49°c hot chocolate. Before his colleagues had a chance to rescue him, he was killed by an unexpected blow to the back of his head from the automated paddle mixing the chocolate. At least no Oompa Loompas were involved in the tragic accident.

FROM HIGH TO LOW

As Bill Hicks said, Why don't those high on drugs who think they can fly start by taking off from ground-level? Tom Copeland, 24, took the then legal drug Ivory Wave in August 2010 and then proceeded to run around the cliff tops of Dorset while stretching his arms sideways and making plane noises. Sadly, but not surprisingly, Copeland's body was soon found floating in the sea. It was not thinking that he could fly whilst high on drugs that led to Copeland's death, just the running around on cliffs whilst high that did it.

A VERY BLACK FRIDAY I

From the broken economy to the degradation of the environment, consumerism is blamed for many ills afflicting our planet. It may also be blamed for the tragic death of Jimmy Overby. On Friday November 28, 2012, the day known to US retailers as Black Friday and a focus for sales activity, more than 200 shoppers rushed into a Wal-Mart store in Long Island. Overby was working to take the store's doors off the hinges when he was trampled by the surge of shoppers so desperate to pick up a bargain in the sale that they missed the poor man dying under their feet.

DEATH DUMP

Deaths on New York's subway system are relatively common, but January 13, 2013 saw one of its more ridiculous ones. The body of an unidentified man was recovered after he fell from the space between two moving subway cars. The reason he was in the space between carriages? He was taking a dump.

A RUBBISH WAY TO GO II

Compulsive hoarding helped claim the life of Joy Jordan, 59, from Kent in January 2012. Piles of paper 2.4m high fell onto her hob whilst she was cooking. The rubbish in the house, at least 1.5m deep in every room, made escape impossible and she died from smoke inhalation. It took firemen three days to recover her body. One of them told the coroner at her inquest: 'We had to crawl through the tops of doorways to get into the room. Our backs touched the ceilings. Every room was full of rubbish and bags of human excrement.'

DEAD WRONG ON THE OLDEST LIVING MAN

Sogen Kato was thought by municipal officials to be the oldest living man in Tokyo. However, when they paid an unexpected visit to him in July 2010 to celebrate his supposed 111th birthday, they found not a long-lived citizen but a mummified corpse, which experts believe had been dead for more than 30 years. Police ended up investigating Kato's family for fraudulently receiving millions of yen in pension payments for a long-dead relative. One official said: 'We were not suspicious for many years, as the family said he had retired to his room, like a living Buddha, who would not see anyone. Yet when he did not take his award for his 111th birthday, we began to think something was wrong.'

GOING BERZERK

Dying from playing computer games is not a twenty-first century phenomenon. The first fatality from the addictive excitement of wiggling a joystick, pressing buttons and blasting things to shit is alleged to have occurred in 1974. However, one of the earliest substantiated deaths from video gaming happened at Friar Tuck's Game Room in Calumet City, Illinois in 1982. The game being played was Atari's Berzerk and the sheer excitement of managing to get his name on the arcade game's high score list twice caused Peter Burkowski to suffer a heart attack. The deputy coroner in the case said the stress of gaming was a factor in his death.

BAD HAIR DAY

A night out clubbing ended in tragedy for 34-year-old Londoner Liv Parkes. Getting home at 6am she collapsed and died from anaphylactic shock. Her body had reacted to the latex glue she used to fix her hair extensions. A pathologist told her inquest that it was probably not until she began sweating on the dance floor that traces of glue seeped into her bloodstream.

TOP 10 RIDICULOUS DEATHS FROM HISTORY – 620 BCE TO 1063 CE

10. Draco, the revered Athenian law-maker and creator of the first written law code enforced by courts, was allegedly killed in 620 BCE in an act of celebrity adoration. Draco was smothered to death by the gifts of cloaks thrown onto him by appreciative citizens when Draco visited a theatre.

9. At the 564 BCE Olympic games, the champion pankratiast – a sport involving a blend of boxing and wrestling – Arrichon of Philalia, killed himself to maintain his title. Whilst in an opponent's stranglehold, his coach shouted: 'What a fine death if you do not submit at the Olympia!' Arrichon then kicked his opponent whilst casting his body to the left causing his opponent to yield whilst simultaneously snapping his neck. Arrichon was made champion posthumously.

8. Wrestler, warrior and friend of Pythagoras, Milo of Croton, was an all-round strong man reputedly able to lift a bull above his head. However, over-confidence in his strength was Milo's undoing circa 500 BCE. Whilst attempting to split a tree asunder with his bare hands, his hands became stuck in the crack he had made. Whilst rendered defenceless, he was attacked and killed by a pack of wolves.

7. Theagenes of Thasos was one of the most famous boxers and athletes of his day, winning laurels at many games, including the Olympics in 480 BCE. Sadly for this book, he died a completely normal death, upon which his admiring fellow-citizens erected a statue in his honour. According to the Greek writer Pausanias, one man had a grudge against Theagenes and took a stick to the statue, beating it repeatedly and causing the statue to fall over and kill him. The horrified citizens of Thasos tried the statue for murder, found it guilty and threw it in the sea.

6. Euripides was one of the greatest writers of tragedies in the ancient world, but his death in 406 BCE has more of the touch of comedy about it. Most scholars discount the idea that he was torn apart by frenzied female worshippers of Dionysus, going with the story that whilst a guest of King Archelaus I, he took a walk in the woods of Macedonia in search of inspiration. During this, he was attacked by a pack of the king's hunting dogs, who mistook him for a boar and pulled him to death.

5. Zeno of Citium was a key Greek thinker and founder of stoic philosophy. At the age of 72 in 262 BCE, he tripped whilst leaving his school, breaking his toe. Taking possibly an illogical response to this, Zeno struck his fist on the ground, shouted out at death: 'I come, I come, why dost thou call for me?' and then promptly died on the spot by holding his breath.

4. Qin Shi Huang, the first person to call himself Emperor of China, brought about his own death in 210 BCE. Wanting to live forever, the Emperor swallowed several pills of mercury. Unsurprisingly, rather than gaining eternal life, he was soon dead from mercury poisoning.

3. Eleazar Avaran, also known as Eleazar Maccabeus, is regarded as a hero in Jewish history. However, his death at the battle of Beth-zechariah in 162 BCE was not only heroic, it was imbued with a full-on dose of ridiculous. Believing a war elephant to be carrying the enemy king, Antiochus V, Eleazar rushed under the beast and thrust his spear into its belly. This caused the now dead pachyderm to fall on top of him, crushing the life out of him.

2. According to Pliny the Elder, Lucius Fabius, a Roman senator in the second century, died from choking. The cause? In Pliny's words: 'a single hair in a draught of milk'.

1. Béla I, known as the Champion or the Bison, was King of Hungary from 1060 to his death in 1063. His short reign is most well-known for the bloody quelling of pagan revolts against his rule. Cursed by the pagan magicians amongst those he suppressed, Béla died when his large wooden throne canopy collapsed on him.

BEWARE GREEKS DRESSED AS BOARS

Dressing up in animal skins and roaming your local forest during hunting season is so ludicrously and obviously dangerous, you would have to be a monumental moron to do it. However, this fact did not stop 49-year-old Christos Constantinou donning goats' skins for camouflage whilst he and other family members went hunting for wild boar in the Greek woodland of Corinthia in December 2009. Not surprisingly, a crouching Christos was mistaken for a wild animal and shot dead by two of his own family. An inevitable Greek tragedy, given the fatal flaw of gross stupidity.

SUICIDE SET-UP

Some suicides have a flair for the dramatic. Few people intent on suicide put as much thought into it as Guatemalan lawyer Rodrigo Rosenberg. He not only hired assassins to ambush him, but set the whole thing up in an effort to frame his county's President, Alvaro Colom. Rosenberg recorded an 18-minute speech, which was uploaded to YouTube after he had been 'murdered' in May 2009. In it, he said: 'If you are watching this message, it is because I have been murdered by Alvaro Colom.' He went on to claim his life was threatened because he was going to expose the corruption by the President and the President's wife. Unsurprisingly, the video caused a massive scandal that almost brought down the government of Guatemala.

However, thorough investigation by an independent UN commission showed that Rosenberg hired the assassins who shot him whilst he cycled in Guatemala City. Rosenberg had been depressed since the murder of a lover, and appears to have seen taking his own life as his chance to bring down a political elite he hated. As suicide schemes go, it beats putting your head in an oven for conspiratorial complexity.

CLOWNING AROUND I

A phobia can be defined as an irrational fear of something. Given the details of one ridiculous death from 1854, coulrophobia – the fear of clowns – might not be irrational. Death registry records in San Francisco relate that in the January of that year, 13-year-old William Snyder died. Cause of death: 'Being swung around by the heels by a circus clown.'

WHAT A COCK-UP I

Men can be very sensitive about the size of their penises. Some men can also be as rabidly macho and aggressive as the worst anti-male propaganda would suggest. Put these facts together and you have the potential for deadly disaster. Add some racial prejudice into the mix, and it seems almost certain something fatal will occur.

Whilst at a urinal in a Durban bar in September 2008, an Indian South African commented to a white South African using the next urinal that his penis was bigger because he was an Indian. When the two men went back into the bar and discussed the incident with their respective friends, a serious of racial slurs was shouted and a brawl ensued. Five Indian men then left the bar, returning shortly to open fire with shotguns and automatic pistols, killing three white drinkers instantly. Two lessons here. First, racism sucks. Secondly, whatever the size of your genitals, it is never a good idea to strike up a conversation about them in a toilet.

WHAT A COCK-UP II – THE GREAT LEVELLER

From ancient times, writers and philosophers have proclaimed death as the great leveller. However, the great minds of ages past probably never foresaw the ludicrous circumstances surrounding the death of Argentinean construction worker Eduardo Aguilero, 36, from the city of Catamarca. At work on a building site, he got into an argument with a workmate over who had the biggest penis, leading to Eduardo brandishing a drill. In retaliation, his co-worker hit him in the head with a 120m metal spirit level, killing him instantly.

THE DOWNSIDE TO SCIENCTIFIC PROGRESS

Science can do marvellous things, including genetically altering plague bacteria to the point where they are so weak they can be safely studied by human scientists. Unfortunately for plague specialist Malcolm Casdaban from the University of Chicago, weakening them enough for him to handle just made them more deadly, as he had a common genetic mutation found in those of European descent whose ancestors had survived plague in the medieval period. Whilst the mutation gifts stronger resistance to naturally occurring plague strains, they make you very susceptible to genetically engineered weak strains. Oops.

SASQUATCH SHOCKER

When people ask me which of the 1001 deaths in this book I think is the most ridiculous, it will most likely be that of 44-year-old Randy Lee Tenley from Kalispell, Montana. Randy died after being hit by two cars on Highway 93 in August 2012. What makes Randy's death truly ridiculous and not just another tragic pedestrian killed by automobile statistic is what he was wearing when he died and how it helped cause the collision.

Walking alongside any major road is risky, but doing so dressed in a specially tailored ex-military camouflage suit in the hope of perpetuating a Bigfoot hoax is dangerous and, frankly, insane. Disguised as a Sasquatch, Randy leapt into the road in front of a passing car. However, his camouflage suit worked all too well, and the poor teenage driver couldn't see him until it was too late. Despite swerving, she hit Randy, knocking him down and into the path of a car coming in the opposite direction, which provided the coup de grâce.

One of the Highway Patrol Troopers involved in the case told me: 'Randy Lee was a damn fool. Hiding along Highway 93 and trying to scare people with his Bigfoot hoax nonsense was just pure wrong thinking. You'd hope a grown man would have better things to do with his life than run around scaring kids in cars.' Quite.

DRINKING AND DIVING

Paris is sometimes called the city of a 100 bell towers. Often neglected by tourists, these are a manifestation of Paris's history and character. Many suicide victims have decided to leap from them across the centuries. However the tower of Notre Dame de Bonne holds a stranger story. Late one night in 1876, a drunken grocer decided that he would break into the church, climb the bell tower and sleep off his booze-fuelled excess there instead of going home to his wife. According to the authorities, the early ringing of the bells woke the unfortunate man and in a disorientated state, he toppled to his death. Ding-dong, the grocer is dead.

DRINKING AND NOT DRIVING

As the previous story shows, choosing wisely where to sleep off a drinking binge is important. Whilst most people have the good sense not to climb to great heights to recover from a bender, I would also advise not drinking 13 pints and then going to sleep in a car outside your house as Martin Jencks, 33, of Leeds did in 2009. After more than 24 hours of seemingly sitting very still in his Ford Focus, a worried neighbour called the police, who discovered his dead body. An autopsy suggested that Jencks was so drunk that he had fallen asleep in a position that led him to be immobile for more than 12 hours, sparking the deep vein thrombosis which killed him.

50 SHADES OF DEAD I

Ohio bear-wrestler Sam Mazzola, 49, was no stranger to death or newspaper coverage. Well-known locally for keeping all sorts of exotic animals in cages that really were not suited to their welfare, Mazzola obtained national infamy when one of his bears escaped and badly mauled a neighbour. Another of his bears killed the teenager employed to feed it.

Whilst a lack of proper restraint for a bear caused one tragic death, over-use of restraint led to Mazzola's own absurd demise. His body was found spread-eagled on his bed, tied down with handcuffs and chains. He was wearing just a leather mask with its eyes and mouth zipped shut and a two-piece metal sphere over that. An autopsy showed that Mazzola had choked on a sex toy, which he had been helpless to remove from his throat. Police ruled that it was an accidental death and that the teenage boy paid to leave him tied up like that had no idea how the sex roleplay would spin so badly out of control.

SWIFT JUSTICE

Metal theft is one of the booming crimes of the twenty-first century. However, it is often a deadly business for thieves. In 2009, two men were killed when they broke into an electricity sub-station in South Wales and triggered a fire safety device that flooded it with carbon dioxide as they tried to strip it of copper wire. Experts believe they would have been dead with seconds.

DEATH O'CLOCK

Clock repair sounds like it should be relatively safe. However, such preconceptions go out the window if you are talking about the S. Haler Elgin 400-day anniversary clock. Withdrawn from sale in the 1980s due to a design flaw that sometimes meant it failed to safely maintain the clock's powerful spring, the timepiece is known in horology circles as the 'German time bomb'. It is a shame that Italian Adolfo Accardo did not know that the clock given to him to mark his retirement went by this reputation. In 1978, he attempted to wind his gift a year to the day after he had retired, only for it to explode, shattering its dome and sending glass and metal shrapnel into Accardo's face. His widow said: 'He did not even like the clock. He wanted his colleagues to buy him a watch when he retired, not the silly clock that killed him.'

DEATH BY COMPUTER

In the first volume of 1001 *Ridiculous Ways To Die*, I chronicled how the machines' war against mankind officially began on January 25, 1979 when Robert Williams became the first man to be killed by a robot. Now however, computers are getting in on the act and we are making it easy for them to slaughter us by giving them guns! In 2007, a computer-controlled anti-aircraft gun which also reloads itself – the Oerlikon GDF-005 – went haywire in South Africa. Instead of its radar systems targeting low-flying missiles or aircraft, it locked onto nearby soldiers, opening fire and killing nine of them.

BETWEEN ROCK AND A HARD PLACE

Taking illegal substances sold to you from the backrooms of seedy shops or by street vendors is never a good idea. This is as true for aphrodisiacs as it is for recreational drugs. When you further note that the street aphrodisiac is made from hardened poisonous toad venom, you would think people would have the sense to steer clear. Oh no. Mankind rarely does the right thing when it comes to sex. The drug, which goes by names as varied as Jamaican Stone, Rock Hard and Chinese Rock, has caused hundreds of Americans to be rushed to hospital with heart problems and has killed several men in New York City alone.

One was Roy Booker, 35, who swallowed a lump of resin made from a toad of the Bufo genus. After two days of agonizing stomach pain, he admitted himself to hospital where he died from disrupted heart rhythms caused by the drug. Dying because you need a little help in the trouser department is sad; dying because you are so desperate for action you will swallow toad venom ranks as a ridiculous way to go.

WHEN FARTS GET FATAL

At times it seems alcohol is the most dangerous substance on the planet. Amongst its many properties is the ability to take any petty argument or bad feeling and turn it into a reason for deadly violence. If there had not been alcohol at the party Bob Saxon, 21, attended in Seattle in January 2011, it is unlikely the teasing he was suffering over his excessive flatulence would have gotten so out of control. Also, if Saxon had not been drinking beer, he might not have even been so windy.

Tired of an evening of seemingly non-ending fart gags at his expense, Saxon stormed out of the party returning with three knives with which to stab his tormentors, including 21-year-old Rick Harrison, who died from his wounds. Police charged Saxon with murder, assault and carrying a deadly weapon. They probably could have got him for having an offensive anus as well. Dying over a fart gag – it really is the bottom of the ridiculous death barrel.

OUT WITH A BANG

Alcohol can lead to some absurd and deadly scenarios, but when you mix some homemade firearms in with the booze, it is impossible to imagine things ever ending well. Quite why 39-year-old Mark Morris ever thought making a homemade cannon was a good idea is beyond me, but unfortunately making the cannon was far from the worst idea he ever had. One night in March 2012, under the influence of a large amount of alcohol, Morris decided to test the effectiveness of his DIY mortar powered by the gunpowder from fireworks, by shooting it into his trailer park home in Alabama. Unfortunately his girlfriend, daughter and three other adults were in the trailer when he blasted away. The only surprising thing is that the only person to die from Morris's stupidity was his poor girlfriend.

CROCODILE TEARS I

Despite what a certain infamous song proclaims, it is clear that suicide is often far from painless. In fact, some suicides go to ridiculous extremes in search of painful ways of ending the anguish in their lives. One such was Tiphawan Jisathra from Thailand. In September 2012, depressed by financial problems, she walked to the popular tourist destination of Samut Prakarn crocodile farm just outside Bangkok and fed herself to its many-toothed residents. She was seen by workers at the farm, but they could do nothing to save her. The excruciating end of Jisathra was not the first time a suicide had occurred at Samut Prakarn. A suicidal tourist had done exactly the same in 1990, and in 2002 Somjaj Sethboon swam towards the crocodiles and embraced one of them after the 300 beasts in the pool initially showed no interest in devouring her. Sethboon had been drinking whiskey and arguing with her husband, whom she suspected of infidelity.

CROCODILE TEARS II

If you do not have a crocodile park nearby, but are still intent on ending your life in one of the most agonizing ways possible and are lucky enough to live in Africa, why not just wade into a crocodile-infested river to end it all? That is what depressed South African farm worker David Lubisi did in April 2011. Local police, alerted to Lubisi's painful plan, searched the Lepelle river, but managed to find only one of his legs. A police officer told me: 'He had domestic problems, but we do not know why he decided on such a painful death. It probably would have taken several minutes for a crocodile to kill him – either from blood loss or drowning. It is certainly not the way I would choose to take my own life.'

CROCODILE TEARS III

Given that crocodiles are one of nature's most excellently designed predators, you might think than non-suicidal members of humanity would have the common sense not to venture into their territory unless absolutely necessary. You might think that, but renowned South African explorer Hendrik Coetzee did not. In 2010, despite knowing full well the danger, he decided to lead two American tourists on a kayaking trip through the Congo's Lukuga River – one of the world's most crocodile-infested and volatile whitewater rivers. Coetzee was pulled from his kayak by a crocodile as his two comrades scrambled to the shore. The last entry in Coetzee's journal reads: 'I had the feeling I might be doing something I should not. I pushed through the doubt and when I finally shot out the bottom of the rapid I was happy I did. It was just paranoia after all.' Yes, Coetzee, just paranoia and a bloody hungry croc.

MUSHROOM MASSACRE

Truffles taste so good they almost make an argument for intelligent design all by themselves. They also command a price that makes wallets burst into tears, and where there is money there is ridiculous death. In fact, across two weeks in August 2010, 18 truffle hunters managed to massacre themselves in Italy's alpine region.

A combination of hot weather and an unusually high number of thunderstorms produced the perfect conditions for a bumper crop, leading hordes of truffle hunters to head into the mountains at night. Among the dead was Durante Brambani. Friend and fellow hunter Bernardino Cremaschi told police: 'We were scrabbling on rocks and slipping. Durante did not want to use the torch even though we were close to a cliff edge, as he did not want other hunters to see where we were. He found a truffle, but I told him to leave it as it was too dangerous to reach. He went for it and was telling me, "Shut up Bernardino! I've got it!" as he slipped and went off the edge.'

Gino Cornelli, head of Italy's Alpine Rescue service commented: 'There is too much carelessness. Truffle hunters don't give a damn about the rules and unfortunately this is the result. It is ridiculous.'

OH, THE IRONY III – GHOST OF A CHANCE

On August 27, 1891, a train came off the tracks on a high bridge near Statesville, North Carolina. This event has led to a ghost story that on the anniversary of the incident each year, the sound of screeching wheels, screams and an almighty crash may be heard. On the 119th anniversary of the wreck in 2010, a dozen ghost hunters gathered on the bridge in the early hours of the morning hoping to hear something.

What they heard was the sound of an actual train coming at them. Unable to jump from the bridge without risk of death, the ghost hunters began to run the 150ft back to safety. Unfortunately, 29-year-old Christopher Kaiser did not make it. He is now allegedly haunting the bridge. The haunting hunter now hunted by the very ghoulish ghost obsessives he used to number amongst.

TO BE OR NOT 2B

A self-inflicted death is by its nature tragic, yet so often it seems to run alongside absurdity. Window cleaner Jeffrey Burton, 57, stabbed himself to death with a giant novelty pencil in 2010. His bloody body, wearing just underpants and covered in stab wounds to the groin, was found next to the over-sized pencil. The coroner at his inquest said: 'It is a mystery to me. If you were choosing to take your own life, that's not the way you would do it. It can't have been a single stab wound. He seems to have worked on it. The pencil was blunt.'

THE SWEET SMELL OF DEATH

Like many people, Russian businessman Arseny Kozlov of Saratov was worried his BO would cause offence. Arseny became so obsessed with the issue he would use a whole can of anti-perspirant per day. When he unexpectedly dropped dead, a post-mortem discovered that poor Arseny had been killed by his clean living due to a build-up of butane in his system. If only he had read the first 1001 Ridiculous Ways To Die he might still be alive today, as it detailed how deodorant addict Jonathan Capewell managed to poison himself the same way. Be safe – BO.

IT'S ONLY THE END OF THE WORLD AGAIN I

People have been predicting the end of the world since at least 634 BCE, when some Romans got very worried about a prophecy concerning 12 eagles. From medieval Popes to 2012 doomsayers, a lot of false prophets have led to a loss of life. Whatever your faith, if you cannot see that it is ridiculous to die either because you think the world is going to end or because it has not ended when you expected, the world just might be better off without you.

American Baptist preacher William Miller predicted that Christ would return to sweep his chosen to heaven on March 21, 1844. He convinced thousands, too. When the day came and went without any discernible signs of the second coming, it became known as the Great Disappointment. However, for the family and friends of one Millerite, it was a lot more than disappointing, as he jumped off his barn at midnight expecting to be scooped up and saved by the returning Jesus. Needless to say, it was not Jesus scooping up the mess he made of his body.

IT'S ONLY THE END OF THE WORLD AGAIN II

In 999, Pope Sylvester II predicted the end of the world on January 1, 1000, leading to riots across Europe that claimed dozens of lives. In 1524, so many astrologers predicted that a great flood would happen on February 1 that more than 20,000 Londoners fled to high ground in the surrounding countryside. Competition for hill space was so great that a mass brawl broke out, which claimed four lives.

In the same year, German astrologer Johannes Stoeffler of Tubingen University predicted the start of a new great flood on February 24. Some citizens in the city took him seriously and made rafts. When a great storm happened to occur on the 24th, more than a hundred people died fighting to try to obtain space on the craft. The rain stopped the next day.

BEING HEALTHY CAN KILL YOU

Many Americans use neti pots – which look like small genie lamps – to irrigate their sinuses with salt water. It is claimed to help with a range of chronic sinus problems. However, according to the Louisiana Department of Health, this health trick killed a 50-year-old Louisiana man and a 20-year-old woman in 2011 because they used tap water in their neti pots instead of distilled water. According to officials, both died from the brain-eating amoeba *Naegleria fowleri*, which infects people by entering through the nose. Whilst it might be safe to drink the water in Louisiana, it is not OK to pour it up your nose through a magic lamp.

BEWARE DRUNK ELK

In 2008, Swedish man Ingemar Westlund found the body of his wife Agneta next to a lake in the village of Loftahammer. Police arrested Ingemar on suspicion of murder and kept him in custody for 10 days. The case against him was dropped only when forensic investigators found moose hair and saliva on the dead body. Police now believe Agneta was attacked by an elk, not her husband. Whilst elk are usually shy and run from humans, they undergo a complete change of personality, becoming dangerously aggressive, after they have eaten fallen fermented apples.

TV RATING HITS

Most TV executives would sell their souls for high ratings, but Brazilian politician and TV presenter Wallace Souza was willing to go to an even more extreme length for a large audience share – he was willing to murder. In 2009, Brazilian police arrested Souza for hiring hitmen to kill five victims to help increase the ratings for his true crime show. Having arranged the hits, it was easy for Souza to get the scoop and rush to the scene of the murders before even the police did. Whilst awaiting trial for wasting lives in such an outrageous way, Souza died of a heart attack in his cell.

CRIME COUPLE ALL AT SEA

British couple Peter Clarke and Sharon Arthurs-Chegini liked to think of themselves as a modern-day Bonnie and Clyde as they robbed, swindled and conned their way through Britain and Europe to fund the cocaine and champagne lifestyle of which they boasted. On the run from the police since 2005, the criminal couple had a habit of stealing luxury yachts – possibly not the best move, as neither of them were master mariners. In May 2006 they stole a yacht from a Portuguese resort and headed out to sea. They probably should have checked that the boat was stocked with a little more than a few bottles of bubbly. The boat was found in September, adrift off the coast of Senegal. On it were the decomposing bodies of Clarke and Chegini. There was also a diary kept by Sharon charting how they had not eaten in weeks and had only recycled urine to drink. One entry read: 'I dream of my mum's steak pie, I dream of her sausage and mash.' Some of their victims may feel the couple got their just lack of desserts.

KILLED BY DEATH III – CURSE OF THE HEARSE

A hearse is not the most obvious vehicle to take a joyride in, but that did not stop a 19-year-old from Northern Ireland stealing one in 1997. What did stop him was the street light he smashed into at high speed whilst being pursued by police. The hearse was completely wrecked, meaning it couldn't be used to transport the body of the reckless thief who died in the crash.

ON THE SLAB

South African construction worker Ishmael Makone was killed instantly in 2009 when he chipped away at the pillar supporting a massive concrete slab directly above him. He was crushed by tonnes of rubble, and it took several days to recover his body from the cab of his mini excavator. What makes his death even more ridiculous is that neighbouring office workers had been watching him work for three days, and speculating that he would get crushed if he was working underneath the pillar when it came down. It is harder to know who the bigger idiots were: those watching Makone who did not warn him or the man himself for not seeing what was so clearly inevitable.

SUICIDE FOREST DRIVES MAN TO TAKE HIS LIFE

Aokigahara Forest in Japan has some of the most beautiful views of Mount Fuji it is possible to imagine. Unfortunately, the place known locally as the Sea of Trees is more famous as Japan's suicide forest. Hundreds of people come to it each year to end their lives, despite signs that adorn many of the trees telling people to ring a counselling hotline and get help instead.

The sheer number of deaths had an unfortunate impact on local man Fujimoto Katsuo. Walking there one day in 2009, he came across two suicides. According to friends, Katsuo was so upset by seeing two bodies in one day he became depressed and began to question 'what the point of life was if such sadness existed in the world'. On his next visit to the forest, Katsuo took his own life, leaving an ironic note saying he could not go on: 'when people come to such a beautiful place and see only death'.

DEADLY DISTRACTION

Riding a motorcycle can be a dangerous business, but it becomes deadly when there are idiots like Claire Ward in charge of cars. Ward ran her car into poor John Bush in June 2008. Hunt told police she ran the red light and ploughed into Bush at 8okm because she was distracted by painting her nails at the time. In the following court case for reckless homicide, the jury were shown accident scene photos of the dashboard of her car covered in streaks of dark red nail polish.

RIDICULOUS DEATHS ARE AS OLD AS THE HILLS

Lest anyone thinks the tales of ridiculous death they see in the news about soldiers going into battle believing they cannot be shot because they have been blessed by the Holy Spirit is a new or purely African thing, let us have a quick history lesson. The Camisards were French protestant guerrilla fighters who took to the rugged hills and caves of the Cevennes region of France in the 1700s like a Christian Taliban. Not only did they place mystically blessed grain amongst the pewter shot of their guns in the belief it ensured they would always hit their targets, some wore charms into battle, believing it made them invulnerable to musket fire. It did not. History records a number of their ambushes going spectacularly wrong as Camisards rushed towards their enemy, certain of their protection, only to be mown down.

KILLED BY DEATH IV – EXPLODING CASKET

The process of microbial decay in a human body can give rise to surprising levels of methane gas. Sometimes the gas will just bloat a body, but in an enclosed coffin or tomb, a dangerous build up of gas can occur in what is known in mortician circles as exploding casket syndrome. Many modern caskets have valves in them to allow the burping out of gas to prevent lids being blown off. Unfortunately this safety feature was not around when Guerino Muggia worked as a cemetery and mausoleum supervisor in 1968. The 44-year-old Italian was killed when a casket exploded with such force it blew a crypt door off, which struck poor Muggia in the head.

THE ROAD OF DEATH

You'd think a road known locally as 'the road of death' and christened 'the world's most dangerous road' by Inter-American Development would be a place to avoid unless you really needed to travel along it. Especially if you knew it claimed an average of 300 lives a year. Oh no. Some idiots adore danger. The North Yungas Road now actually attracts tourists, despite its 600ft drops, tendency to crumble, narrowness, lack of guard rails and the extreme weather conditions often encountered on it.

One such absurd danger tourist was Englishman Alex Hooper, who wanted to cycle down an unbroken 64km downhill stretch of it. Hooper was observed by one motorist going in the opposite direction attempting to film his descent with only one hand on the handlebars of his bike. Unsurprisingly, Hooper never completed his downhill death trip, careening off the road and falling hundreds of feet to his end.

GET WITH THE PROGRAM

The relatives of deceased idiots are often quick to blame anyone or anything, but the idiot for the insane antics which killed their loved ones. Often the thing blamed with the scantiest of evidence is a movie or computer game. However, in some cases, the relatives may have a point. In 1993, the film *The Program* was released. In it, the young hero proves his nerves of steel by lying down at night in the middle of a busy road as traffic hurtles passed him in both directions. In October that year, 18-year-old Michael A. Shingledecker Jr. from Pennsylvania lay down in a road at 1am and was instantly hit and killed by a pickup truck. On the same night in Long Island some 640km away, 17-year-old Michael Macias lay in the road and was soon hit by a car.

Shingledecker's mother blamed the film, which her son had seen a few days before. Whether the film influenced the deaths cannot be proven, but one thing is certain – if you lie in the middle of the road at night, you are a fool on the highway to hell.

WORKED TO DEATH

A lot of us have complained about our bosses working us to death. However, in Japan the physical reality behind the expression happens so often there is even a word for it – karoshi. In 2006, the state labour bureau ruled that one of Toyota's chief engineers had been officially worked to death by making him do 114 hours per month of overtime in the six months before he died of a heart attack. It is not the first time Toyota have been officially judged to have killed by karoshi. In 2007, 30-year-old engineer Kenichi Uchino collapsed at work. The authorities blamed the car company for making him work 80 hours per month overtime – most of it for no pay – in the previous six months. Dying for a job truly is a ridiculous way to go. Remember Japan, work to live, not live to work.

THE WORM THAT TURNED

Everyone has a breaking point. German Kurt Bayer, 75, reached his after his nagging wife had made him sleep in the garden shed for 48 years. In March 2012, he snapped and took an axe, killing the old battleaxe shouting: 'This will shut your moaning up!'

KINGDOM COMES TO GROUND

Tennessee man Gary Kingdom was not a criminal mastermind. Well-known to police as a burglar and drug user, he set out one night in 1995 to rob a house, accompanied by his Rottweiler, Lobo. Before climbing up a ladder to gain entry to the second-storey window of a property, Kingdom secured Lobo's lead to the ladder. When the homeowners returned home unexpectedly, they spooked Lobo, who ran towards them, bringing down the ladder and Kingdom, who was dead before the police arrived.

TOP 10 RIDICULOUS DEATHS FROM HISTORY
– 1286 TO 1649

10. The courtiers of King Alexander III of Scotland advised him not to visit his wife in Fife on her birthday in 1286 because of foul weather. The king ignored them and, whilst travelling, became separated from his guides. Lost and in the dark, he led his horse straight over a steep coastal embankment. The bodies of both king and horse were found the next day on a beach with their necks broken.

9. Charles II was King of Navarre from 1349 to 1387 and was known to his subjects as Charles the Bad. His unpleasant but wonderfully ridiculous death is a lesson from history that both the Grim Reaper and absurdity have no regard for status. He was swaddled in brandy-soaked bandages in an attempt to alleviate his rheumatism when a female servant accidentally dropped a candle on Charles. Terrified, the girl fled, leaving the King to be burnt alive in his own palace.

8. James II of Scotland keenly promoted the use of the latest artillery in his armies and was something of an expert in cannons. Ironic, then, that when he died in 1460 whilst besieging Roxburgh it was due to one of the cannons he had imported from Flanders – known as 'the Lion' – exploding beside him.

7. There have been some really unsuitable Popes throughout history. Pope Paul II, famous for allowing horse races to be run in the Papal state and owning a collection of 54 silver shells with pearls in them, was not exactly a pious character. Therefore it is unsurprising that some contemporary accounts of his death in 1471 record him as having died from a stroke whilst being sodomized by his page boy.

6. King Charles VIII of France, known as 'the Affable', died in 1498 due to his gallantry. Bowing to his wife to let her go first into watch a game of real tennis, Charles stood up and hit his head on the low lintel of a door, causing him to fall into a coma from which he died nine hours later.

5. Pope Alexander VI most likely died from poisoning. The real mystery is whether it was by the hand of his own illegitimate son Cesare Borgia, who was poisoned at the same meal in August 1503 but survived due to his better health, or whether the Pope accidentally dosed himself when attempting to poison his son and one of his cardinals.

4. György Dózsa was a mercenary granted permission by Pope Leo X in 1514 to raise an army to fight the Ottomans. However, Dózsa used his peasant army to lead a rebellion against Hungarian landlords. The rebellion failed, and to mock his ambitions to be king, he was killed by being forced to sit on a smouldering iron throne whilst holding a burning orb and wearing a red-hot iron crown.

3. Humayun was the second emperor of the Mughal empire in the sixteenth century, ruling most of modern-day Pakistan and Afghanistan until his death in 1556. Alongside being a mighty ruler, he was a scholar of occult science. Whilst coming down a flight of stairs carrying a pile of books, Humayun heard the call to prayer, automatically knelt, caught his feet in his robe and tumbled to his death.

2. James Douglas, the 4th Earl of Morton, was one of the regents of Scotland whilst King James VI was in his minority. During his time in charge, Douglas introduced 'the maiden' – a form of guillotine – into Scotland as an efficient method of execution. Somewhat ironic, then, that when he fell out of favour in 1581 and was executed for murder, it was death by his own killing machine.

1. Sir Arthur Ashton was a Royalist commander in the English Civil War during the Siege of Drogheda in 1649. Not for Sir Arthur a heroic military death. Captured by Parliamentarian soldiers, he was beaten to death with his own wooden leg in the mistaken belief that it contained hidden gold coins.

CALLING SHERLOCK HOLMES

You have to admire some suicides: clever, determined and as mad as a box of frogs on its way to Psychoville. In July 2008, 55-year-old business executive Thomas Hickman drove his jeep through New Mexico till it ran out of gas. He then walked into a field, carefully taped over his mouth and attached a revolver to several helium balloons. Hickman then shot himself in the back of the head. When his body was discovered, police originally thought he had been abducted and murdered, but when the balloons and gun was found snagged in a nearby tree, they managed to piece together the elaborate suicide. Authorities believe he came up with the baroque plot in an attempt to ensure insurance companies paid after his death despite the suicide clause in life insurance policies.

OUT OF HIS TREE

On a list of things worth dying for, you will never usually find the word 'Frisbee'. A possible exception to this might have occurred if Thomas Thorpe, 23, of California had been writing the list. In 2008, an inebriated Thorpe climbed a tree in a park to retrieve a Frisbee. Climbing trees whilst in a state of drunken bravado rarely ends well and in Thorpe's case, it ended him when he toppled out of the tree.

SMOKING KILLS II – SMOKING MAD

Smoking can kill you in so many different ways. Florida cops received a 911 call to attend the home of Jake Jamieson in 2009 after neighbours complained of hearing a violent argument. Inside they found the dead body of his roommate Pasco Gillan. Jamieson admitted putting Gillan in a stranglehold whilst the pair rowed over a pack of cigarettes. They must have been smoking mad to fight to death over some not so Lucky Strikes.

NOT BOXING CLEVER

Miami man Jason Maynard kept his gun in his underwear drawer. One rushed morning in 1986, Maynard threw the contents of the drawer onto the floor as he searched for something to wear. This caused the semi-automatic handgun to go off, hitting him in the back of the neck, killing him instantly. His girlfriend, who was in the bedroom at the time told police: 'Jason was late for work, he was throwing clothes everywhere. I think he forget the gun was in the drawer with his boxers.'

BEEHIVE YOUSELF

If you've got a beehive in your home that you think is dangerous, what do you do? Calling a pest controller would probably be wise, but for Louisiana man Pat Stone in 1988, his solution was to burn it out of his house. He first emptied one can of hairspray onto the bees's home and then decided to turn another into a DIY flamethrower. The result was an explosion, a fire and a dead amateur exterminator.

SANDWICH SHOCKER

Shane's Sandwich Shop in Jacksonville, Florida must have been very tempting to burglar Tim Dixon. He was so keen to break in that in December 2009, he stripped off all his clothes to make himself thinner, threw them down a vent and then tried to crawl down after them. Unfortunately, even naked, he was not small enough to wriggle through the enclosed space. Dixon became trapped and died from asphyxiation, his body discovered above the fat fryer at 6am the next morning, when employees opened up.

TROLLIED

How drunk do you have to be to tie a shopping trolley to a fire truck? How drunk to then climb into the trolley in an attempt to hitch a ride when the truck pulls off? We know the answer due to blood tests done on Oklahoma man Gary Perez in 1987. He was found to be eight times over the legal limit when his mangled body was recovered after the shopping trolley worked loose and smashed into a parked car.

STOPPED DEAD IN HIS TRACKS

Christopher Allen, 44, robbed the Ocala Florida Citizens Bank in January 2010 of $1,805 and sprinted out the door. Unfortunately, his getaway came to an unexpected stop when he was gripped by a massive heart attack just a few yards into his dash from the law. A medical examiner blamed the stress of carrying out the robbery and the exertion of running away for bringing about Allen's death.

SMOKING KILLS III – TIME TO QUIT

If smoking has already made you so ill you need an oxygen tank in your home to help you breathe, you really should take the hint and quit. However, Bernette Scott, 55, was so addicted to cigarettes that not only did she keep on smoking, she even lit up whilst taking oxygen. Bad idea. The resulting explosion and fire claimed her life and burnt down her family's Arkansas home.

JACKASS STRIKES AGAIN

I have lost track of how many ridiculous deaths absurd TV show *Jackass* has helped inspire across the years. In idiotic death terms, it is a serial killer. In 2008, Cameron Bieberle, 18, from Orange County, Florida died whilst imitating one of the programme's stunts – being pulled at speed in a shopping trolley whilst holding onto a SUV driven by friend Michael A. Smith. The cart hit a speed bump, overturning and sending the foolish teen into the air and an early grave.

EXTERMINATED I

When homeowners in Davidson County, Tennessee returned to their property in 1992 after having had to vacate it whilst it was fumigated, they found the body of 34-year-old Kevin J. Matthews. He had attempted to burgle their home despite the warning signs on the lawn letting him know it was filled with a cloud of toxic gas. Matthews' only precaution had been to place a bandana over his mouth. All the dumb crook managed to stuff into a backpack before being overcome by toxins was a Game Boy and a handful of Rolling Stones CDs.

GETTING INTO A SQUEEZE

Films and TV shows in which people either break in or out of somewhere by sneaking through a ventilation shaft are a staple of poorly written pop culture. Maybe the 82kg burglar found dead in the ventilation shaft at the 411 All-Star Sports Bar in Hollywood, Florida in July 2008 had taken inspiration from something he had seen on screen. If he did, he clearly did not muse on the fact that fiction never portrays an obese man successfully making use of a ventilation shaft. By the time the unidentified man's body was discovered due to an unpleasant odour, police estimated it had been in the shaft for four days. A Hollywood cop said: 'The bar was closed and there was no money on the premises. It was a ridiculous way to go for stealing a few drinks.'

WHAT ARE THE ODDS?

Two lifelong friends, 64-year-old Stanimir Dmitrovic and 66-year-old Slavko Banzle, regularly enjoyed a coffee together in Nevade, Serbia. One day whilst sipping on their drinks in May 2008, they both began to suffer chest pains at the exact same moment, before both collapsed and died of heart attacks. The authorities, unable to believe this absurdly unlikely coincidence-tested both men for poison, but were forced to conclude that the Grim Reaper had decided to go for the two-for-the-price-of-one deal that day.

UNGRATEFUL AND DEAD

It was a case of out of the frying pan and into the fire for ungrateful 37-year-old Steven Andrew Hirschfield. Except in his case, it was out of deep water and into the line of fire. The Los Angeles man had fallen into San Diego harbour whilst drinking on a cruise ship in July 2008. Harbour Police rescued Hirschfield from drowning, but when they pulled him onto their launch, he went berserk, taking one officer's taser gun and beating him with it, forcing another officer to shoot Hirschfield fatally in the chest.

A NEW MEANING TO 'POP' YOUR CLOGS

New Zealand coroner David Crerar said drinking large quantities of Coca-Cola was a 'substantial factor' in the death of 30-year-old Natasha Harris in 2012. The mother of eight regularly drank up to 10 litres of the fizzy drink per day. Crerar calculated that drinking 10 litres of Coke amounted to more than 1kg of sugar and 970mg of caffeine. This meant Harris was twice over the recommended safe caffeine limit and consuming 11 times the suggest sugar intake. Her family said at the inquest: 'Natasha would go crazy if she ran out … she would get the shakes, withdrawal symptoms, be angry, on edge and snappy.' Coca-Cola said in response: 'We are disappointed that the coroner has chosen to focus on the combination of Ms Harris' excessive consumption of Coca-Cola, together with other health and lifestyle factors, as the probable cause of her death. This is contrary to the evidence that showed the experts could not agree on the most likely cause.'

DYING FOR A PEE I

A Polish tourist on a trip to London to improve his English in July 2008 might have saved his own life if he had been able to ask for directions to the nearest toilet. Instead, whilst at Vauxhall Station, he decided to urinate onto the train tracks, unaware that one of the rails was electrified. His stream of urine connected with the current, electrocuting him.

DONE IN BY DEEP SHAG

When Texas police first found the body of multi-millionaire Virginia E. Mayes in her mansion in 1982, they thought they had stumbled onto the scene of the perfect murder. The first autopsy suggested Mayes had died from suffocation, but it gave no indication of any possible suspect. However, after a 10-month investigation, experts finally worked out what happened – Mayes had simply fallen and suffocated in the deep shag of her luxury carpets.

SMOKING KILLS IV – DYING FOR A SMOKE

If a 52-year-old commuter making a late night journey home on London's Tube had waited just another 10 minutes to arrive at his stop, it's likely the unidentified man would have lived to die of lung cancer another day. However, he was so desperate to smoke during a trip in June 2011, that he forced open the emergency door so he could step outside to smoke in the gap between carriages. Unfortunately he slipped whilst the train was moving at 80km, fell onto the track and was decapitated.

WHAT A COCK

I am a bad man: I cannot help thinking that some of the victims of ridiculous death got exactly what they deserved. Jose Luis Ochoa, 35, regularly entered birds into illegal cockfights in California. At one of the despicably cruel bouts in February 2011, a rooster sliced Ochoa in the leg with the knife that had been attached to it for the fight. Due to the illegal circumstances, he delayed getting medical attention and the wound in his calf eventually caused him to bleed to death.

POLITICIAN WITH A GUN CONTROL ISSUE

Judging by the number of ridiculous deaths which come from within its borders each year, Thailand is a strange and, at times, overly lethal place to live. In August 2012 it produced an outrageous story which I might have struggled to believe if it had come from anywhere else. Senator Boonsong Kowawisarat was at a restaurant with four friends when he tried to adjust the position of his Uzi machine gun pistol in its holster. He kept the 9mm on him at all times for self-defence out of concern for terrorists or attacks from political opponents. Unfortunately for his fellow diners, he managed to accidentally fire the gun whilst it was still in its case, killing both his ex-wife and personal secretary. Police charged Boonsong with causing death by negligence.

ONE HELL OF A CURE FOR HICCUPS

US Army soldiers Patrick Myers Private First Class (PFC) and Isaac Young PFC were watching football and drinking beer with a friend in September 2012, when Young got the hiccups. In an attempt to cure his friend of the problem, Myers began to wave a gun in Young's face whilst threatening to shoot him. According to Texas police, the extreme scare tactic backfired when Myers accidentally discharged his gun, permanently curing Young's hiccups by fatally shooting him in the face.

SLEEPWALKING TO HELL

Sleepwalking can get you into all sorts of outlandish situations, but sleepwalking in the wrong place at the wrong time of year can get you killed. Timothy Brueggman, 51, from Haywood, Wisconsin, went sleepwalking one night in January 2009. Wearing only his underwear and a fleece shirt, Brueggman walked out in -20°c temperatures, making it only 174m from his home before succumbing to hypothermia. Local police deputy Tim Ziegle commented: 'How in hell can a guy walk out in 20-below zero and not wake up?'

IT'S ONLY THE END OF THE WORLD AGAIN III

Comedian Bill Hicks once told me in an interview: 'There is nothing more obscene than the pornography of doom.' Bill was dead right. When London was rocked by an earthquake on February 8 and then again on March 8, 1761, doomsaying soldier William Bell whipped the city into a frenzy, proclaiming the world would end in another earthquake in 28 days. Thousands fled the city and on the appointed day, thousands took to boats in the Thames, hoping that water would be a safer place to become apocalypse. Unfortunately one vessel was so overcrowded it sank, drowning 18 people. The day after the world did not end, Bell was thrown into London's infamous Bedlam asylum.

IT'S ONLY THE END OF THE WORLD AGAIN IV

No one seems to learn the lessons of history, not even Londoners who are usually a savvy bunch. So many people believed a prophecy allegedly made by Elizabeth I's magician Dr. John Dee, that the Thames was thick with panic boats again. According to the hoax prophecy, Dee predicted the end of the world on March 16 or 'possibly a day or two between' and that 'London's rich and famous town/Hungry earth shall swallow down'. No one drowned this time, but one idiot, convinced the end was nigh, swallowed arsenic to meet his maker ahead of the expected rush.

MUSHROOMING MORTALITY

I despise mushrooms. I believe them to be the work of the devil. Others adore the vile things. However, in November 2012, one 'caregiver' at the Golden Age Villa retirement home in Loomis, California foraged in the grounds of the home and used the mushrooms to make the residents a special soup. The soup was so special it contained several poisonous fungi and killed residents Barbara Lopes, 86, and Teresa Olesniewicz, 73.

WHO ATE ALL THE FARMER?

When Terry Vance Garner went to feed his 318kg pigs on his farm at Riverton, Oregon in September 2012, he never expected to be on the menu himself. However, he fell whilst in their enclosure and when his family went to find him several hours later all that was recognizably left of him was his dentures.

WHAT A BUMMER

A 28-year-old office worker in the Chinese city of Guangzhou died in 2010 after the gas canister in his swivel chair exploded. The explosion sent shrapnel into his bottom, resulting in death from blood loss. According to the Chinese press, death by exploding chair was an increasing problem in China, having claimed the life of a 14-year-old in Jiaozhou the previous year.

48

LOOK BEFORE YOU LEAP I

It is impossible to feel sorry for some suicides. The right to any sympathy ends the moment you selfishly take not only your own life but that of some poor, unsuspecting soul. Whatever stress and heartbreak you are suffering from, would it hurt you to take a few seconds and look before you leap to your death? No, it would not, but so many of them just do not take the time to bother. Thoughtless wasters.

Case in point: 62-year-old widow Raymonde Demares took a death leap from the 12th-floor of her apartment block in Brussels in March 2010. If she had only taken a few seconds to look before she leapt, she could have avoided landing on and killing 72-year-old Herman Lingg, who was on his way into the building.

LOOK BEFORE YOU LEAP II

Suicidal widows crushing inoffensive souls to death with the fatal flinging of themselves from buildings is more common than you might think. May 2010 saw depressed widow Josefina Venizela plunge out of the window of her 12th-floor apartment without giving due consideration for those below. Her fall killed her and poor Luisa Almendares, 56, the cleaning lady for the adjacent apartment block, who was innocently taking out the rubbish at the time.

LOOK BEFORE YOU LEAP III

Not all widows who fall and kill others are suicides. Widow Helen Lam fell from the balcony of her 27th-floor apartment in Hong Kong's Ma On Shan district in March 2009 when she slipped whilst hanging out washing. The fall killed her and 50-year-old Chan Kwai-mui, a cleaner on her way to work.

IT'S ONLY THE END OF THE WORLD AGAIN V

Those who take their religious teachings to absurd extremes have been blighting humanity for thousands of years. At least the members of the Red Death cult were focussed on killing each other instead of those who did not share their faith. Centred in the Russian town of Kargopol in 1900, the cult outlawed marriage, rewarded those who enjoyed sexual intercourse by smothering them with a red cushion, and instructed a member who had met the recruitment target of bringing 12 others into the group to commit suicide. Believing that the world would end on November 1, 1900, 864 of its members decided the best way to please God was to set fire to their homes whilst still in them. By the time the authorities realized what was going on and put a stop to it, more than a hundred of them were dead.

DEATH HAS YOUR NUMBER

In China, the number 8 is regarded as being lucky. Licence plates and telephone numbers with 8 in them are hotly fought over. Whilst the telephone number 0888 888 888 would be regarded as the luckiest ever in China, in Bulgaria it has become known as the 'number of death'. A worker at Bulgarian mobile phone network Mobitel, told me: 'We withdrew the number from use after everyone who had it seemed to die. Maybe there was a curse on it.' The last three holders of the number did all meet gruesome ends. Mobitel's CEO Vladimir Grashnov died in 2001 from radiation poisoning by a business rival. The number then went to mafia boss Konstantin Dimitrov, who was murdered in 2003, when it was passed onto Konstantin Dishliev, an estate agent who was shot dead at an Indian restaurant in Sofia in 2005.

EXTREME PUPPY LOVE

The love people can have for their pets is special. For C.N. Madranraj and his wife Tarabai, maybe their love for their dog 'Puppy' was just a bit too special for their own good. When the 13-year-old pooch died in 2007, they held a huge funeral feast for the dog and then went home and hung themselves. They left a note explaining they could not go on living without their pet.

EELY PAINFUL DEATH

Some deaths are just so wrong on so many levels, that any faith you hold in humanity is shaken. A 59-year-old chef in China's Sichuan Province was rushed to hospital in with lower body pain, but died within minutes of admission. An autopsy showed he died after an Asian swamp eel had been eating his bowels. Police investigating his death discovered that the live eel had been inserted into the man's rectum by a group of friends when he had passed out drunk. Why the alleged friends just could not write on him with marker pens like most people, I do not know.

HEY TEACHER, LEAVE THAT KID ALONE

Detention, lines, being sent to the principal's office – these are all accepted methods of punishing a student. However, teacher Hu Daofa from a school in China's Shandong Province, decided to punish 14-year-old boarding school student Zhang Jixing in December 2009 by sending him outside in -10°C degrees. Hu then went out drinking for the night, forgetting about his punished pupil, which is a shame because Zhang was discovered the next morning frozen to death in the gutter.

IT'S ONLY THE END OF THE WORLD AGAIN VI

Alleged Seventh Day Adventist prophetess Margaret Rowan predicted the world would start to end on February 13, 1925. This news proved so distressing to two of her followers that they decided to end their lives with poison rather than face the prospect of Rowan's predicted seven years of storm, plagues and hellfire. If they had lived to see her prophecy fail, they might have also made it to 1927 and had the chance to see Rowan go to jail for conspiring to murder someone who dared to call her powers of prophecy fraudulent.

THE MORON FROM MORON

Most of us have the sense to remember that only Father Christmas has the power to safely climb down chimneys to gain entry into homes without the need for a conventional door. Would-be burglar Luis Fernandez clearly thought he could do a good Santa impersonation when he tried to break into a holiday home in the Spanish town of Moron de la Frontera. The moron from Moron became stuck in the chimney and died after several days deprived of food and water. He was discovered at least a month after his death when the owner of the house returned and found a decomposing arm sticking out into the fireplace.

THE FUTURE'S NOT BRIGHT

Wearing sunglasses at night in the name of alleged coolness marks you out as a grand idiot. You want proof of this? Nineteen-year-old Thai Thanes Boonprasob had been warned by friends and family that his habit of wearing Ray-Bans™ at night whilst driving his scooter was dangerous. The reckless youth, wedded to the idea that shades after dark made him look edgy, died instantly when he ran his motorcycle into a wall. Authorities said he could not see where he was going because post-sundown, the sunglasses cut out more than 80 per cent of available light.

MURDER ON THE DANCE FLOOR

A life in organized crime carries some obvious dangers, but 24-year-old Bulgarian Emil Dobrev found a particularly ridiculous way of letting his career as a gun-carrying thug end his days. In February 2008, after a hard day at the coalface of criminality, Emil went to a nightclub and enjoyed several slugs of the strong Bulgarian spirit rakia. Emil then took to the dance floor, where his energetic jigging caused the pistol he had in the pocket of his jeans to accidentally discharge into his thigh. Not wishing to seem weak in front of his criminal colleagues, macho Emil refused to go to hospital and carried on drinking. He was later found dead in the club toilets due to blood loss caused by shooting his femoral artery.

DIDN'T SEE IT COMING

A lot of people in Thailand regularly use fortune tellers known as mor doo (seeing doctors). It is such an accepted part of Thai culture that even top politicians are quite happy to be seen consulting them. Noo Laoyang of Northern Thailand consulted mor doo Malee Noppadol to learn of her romantic prospects. When the fortune teller told her 26-year-old client she would never marry nor have children, Noo beat the mor doo to death with a walking stick.

MURDEROUS MONKEY

Tree climbing can be dangerous, monkeys can be dangerous. Climb a tree with monkeys in it and you have a potentially deadly and ridiculous combination. The mangosteen fruit is popular in Malaysia and 34-year-old Mohamad Muthia was so keen to pick some fresh that he thought nothing of climbing a tree which was occupied by a monkey with the same idea. The competition between man and animal for the same sweet natural resource led rather unexpectedly to confrontation. Mohamad's friends watched as he attempted to push a monkey away from him, only to be slapped in the face by a simian paw, causing him to lose his balance and tumble to his death.

MURDER BY BRA

Guns, knives and axes are all commonly regarded as deadly weapons, yet seemingly innocuous everyday objects can be lethal if wielded in a certain way. However, being killed by a bit of lingerie has more than a touch of the ludicrous about it. A Russian pensioner from Zakamensk, a small Russian town near the border with Mongolia, was brutally murdered when she refused to give her 26-year-old neighbour money to buy vodka. According to local police, the younger woman was so incensed by the refusal and being told to 'live a less debauched life', that she whipped off the bra she was wearing and strangled the old lady.

DOWN THE SWANNY

Most of us know the folk adage that 'a swan can break a man's arm'. Given the number of swan-related deaths recorded, it might be more helpful if the maxim went: 'a swan can kill a man'. If anyone should have known just how vicious and dangerous swans could be, it was 37-year-old Anthony Hensley who was employed by a Chicago company that used swans to keep geese away from apartment complexes. Tragically, the swan handler was knocked out of his kayak by one of the swans he was caring for and attacked by the bird until he drowned in a pond. As swan songs go, it has the redolent whiff of the absurd.

IT'S ONLY THE END OF THE WORLD AGAIN VII

French astronomer Camille Flammarion caused panic across the world in 1910 when he claimed that the return of Hailey's Comet in the May of that year could 'impregnate the Earth's atmosphere with cyanogen gas and possibly snuff out all life'. In the rush to cash in, spurious anti-comet poison pills were sold and sales of gas masks soared across the world. Whilst the comet's tail did not kill anyone with its allegedly impregnating gases, 53-year-old Antoinette Renard died in Belgium from suffocation whilst wearing an anti-comet gas mask she had bought by mail order.

LENIN'S LAST LAUGH

Communism may be dead in the states of the former Soviet Union, but it still casts a long and occasionally lethal shadow. A drunken 21-year-old making his way from bar to bar in the Belaruslan town of Uvarovichi decided he would swing on the outstretched arm of a 6m high plaster statue of Lenin. Unfortunately for the drunk, Lenin was not pointing the way forward for Socialism, he was pointing to a ridiculous way to die. The arm collapsed, hitting the unfortunate young man fatally on the head.

BLIND MAN'S BLUFF

A 65-year-old from Newport in South Wales who spent a decade faking blindness despite being able to see perfectly well, came to a ridiculous and possibly appropriate end. Geoffrey Haywood used a cane and talking watch, but his brother told an inquest into his death that the blindness was purely psychological. 'I'd put Christmas dinner in front of him and he would say, "Where's mine?", but if someone dropped money he would pick it up straight away. He used it as a way to get people to feel pity for him.' Haywood died from drowning after falling into a flooded ditch. The coroner said: 'Either he did not see or did not want to see the ditch, slipped and drowned.'

DEAD DOG LEADS TO DEATH

Such was the love of 47-year-old South African plumber Rob Emslie for his dog Sheevah that after she died, he wore the bitch's lead around his neck as a mark of respect. Before you get dewy-eyed with sentimentality, it's worth pointing out the consequences of wearing a 3m nylon lead. One night, Rob got into his car and shut the door without realizing the end of the lead was trailing outside. As he reversed away, the lead became ensnared in the car's axle, snapping his neck instantly. Are dogs really man's best friend?

IT'S ONLY THE END OF THE WORLD AGAIN VIII

In 1974, astronomers Dr. John Gribbin and Stephen H. Plagemann published the best-selling book *The Jupiter Effect*, which predicted that a planetary alignment on March 10, 1982, would cause all sorts of world-devastating catastrophes, including a massive earthquake in California. However, the only person who experienced a fatal 'Jupiter effect' was 44-year-old John McDonald, who was attending one of the many parties in California held to celebrate the end of the world on March 9. He was described by fellow party-goers as drinking too much because he said: 'The world ends tomorrow. There will be no hangovers.' An intoxicated McDonald tumbled down some stairs to his death as he attempted to leave the party.

SAFETY KILLS

You cannot deny that being killed by something designed to save your life ranks high on the ridiculous scale. In November 2010, 59-year-old John Railton crashed his car in Gosport, England. His car's airbag inflated and helped save him from immediate death in the multiple vehicle pile-up. Unfortunately for Railton, a sliver of glass pierced the bag, releasing a cloud of noxious fumes and powder. Inhaling this caused him to develop bronchial pneumonia and pulmonary fibrosis, which ended up killing him within two months.

IS EXERCISE REALLY GOOD FOR YOU?

Many of us harbour a secret suspicion that exercising in an effort to look good is actually rather unhealthy. Someone who rather seems to prove the point is the late Mick Denmark, from Bournemouth. In May 2012, the 29-year-old waiter was found dead on his weight-lifting bench with a 40kg barbell across his neck. A bottle of bourbon was found next to his body and a post-mortem showed he was more than three-and-a-half times over the drink drive limit. Rather unsurprisingly, the post-mortem also showed he had died from compression of the neck.

GREEN THUMB

This book provides ample evidence that as soon as you add alcohol, even the most mundane of activities can become deadly – even something as sedate as gardening. Thai school gardener Wansadej Konghul had been drinking on the job when he decided to eat a centipede that had bitten him on the thumb as a drunken act of revenge. However, the poisonous centipede had the last laugh. About 20 minutes after swallowing the insect, Wansadej began to vomit. Co-workers suggested he lie down in the tool shed and when they checked on him two hours later, he was dead.

OH, THE IRONY IV – GETTING FIT FOR DEATH

Most people who die whilst playing a computer game are sedentary individuals whose idea of living an active life is making several trips to the refrigerator. That was not the case for 25-year-old Tim Eves from Norfolk, England. Tim led a full, active life and was regarded by everyone who knew him as fit and healthy. Tragically, he died from a rare heart disorder triggered moments after playing a jogging mini-game on his Wii Fit – a game system designed to help its users become fitter and live longer.

GETTING THE CHOP

Rows often turn violent when guns are to hand. Shooting someone dead over an affair with your wife is wrong, but almost understandable. However, some differences of opinion that end in a fatal shooting are so ridiculous you cannot help but laugh. In September 2012, John Cunningham, 43, of St. Louis grabbed a shotgun and fired at his uncle Lessie Lowe, 44, during a heated argument. Lessie died from the blast. The cause of the row? John called the meat they were preparing to barbecue pork 'steaks' whilst Lessie called them pork 'chops'. As Porky Pig might say: 'That's all folks!'

THE WEDDING THAT WENT OFF WITH A BANG I

In most countries, we celebrate the happy event of a wedding by charging our glasses and raising a toast to the couple. With one or two notable exceptions, it is a safe and sensible way of marking the occasion. However, in some countries the traditional way of celebrating is firing a volley of bullets into the air. Deaths from this activity happen so often they have almost moved out of the ridiculous category and into the commonplace. However, one terrible event which happened in October 2012 is so ludicrous it is worth recounting. Despite firearms being banned at Saudi Arabian weddings, guests at a marriage in Abqaiq shot their guns into the sky and brought down an electric cable, killing 23 of them instantly.

JOUST STUPID

We have grown accustomed to deaths from road rage, but there is something shocking and ludicrous about hearing of a death from disability scooter rage. Two Arkansas women forced to use disability scooters to get around due to their morbid obesity got into a heated row in the frozen food aisle of a supermarket. The women began to scooter joust, repeatedly charging into each other's scooters and screaming at each other until one charge forced a scooter to overturn. Its occupant died on the way to hospital from head trauma whilst the victorious jouster was arrested for manslaughter.

YOU PLANK

Just when you think the world will run out of ridiculous ways to die, you can rely on a new Internet meme to inject a bit of novel stupidity into the business of death. The online fad of planking – being photographed lying face down with your arms at your side mimicking a wooden plank whilst in an incongruous place – has become very popular in the past few years. Known in some parts of the world as 'playing dead', planking went from merely stupid to deadly when 20-year-old Australian Acton Beale gave it a try. He decided to impersonate a plank on the seventh floor balcony of a Brisbane building. Acton lost his balance whilst playing dead, tumbled off the balcony and plummeted to his death. In English slang, a 'plank' is a massive idiot.

BIFF! POW! SPLAT!

If being photographed planking was not stupid enough, a new Internet meme emerged in 2011 – Batmanning. Popularized by a group of students from Purdue University in Indiana, Batmanning involves hanging upside down by your feet with your hands by your side, being photographed and posting the evidence of your stupidity on the Net. Its name comes from the famous caped crusader and the habits of bats. Within months of it becoming popular, the fad claimed its first life when after an afternoon of binge drinking, a 20-year-old student from Leicester suspended a ladder between two fences and got into position to be photographed. Despite being only a few inches above the ground, he slipped and the subsequent fall broke his neck.

TOP 10 RIDICULOUS DEATHS FROM HISTORY – 1747 TO 1869

10. Simon Fraser, the 11th Lord Lovat, had a grim last laugh at his execution on Tower Hill in 1747. A stand full of spectators waiting to see him beheaded collapsed, killing 20 of them, much to the amusement of Fraser. Some have tried to argue that this event is the origin of the phrase 'laughing your head off'.

9. Fatal blows on the head seem to run in the blood of the Hanoverian dynasty. Prince Frederick, the eldest son of George II, died in 1751 before he could ascend to the throne. At the time, his death was widely attributed as the result of being hit on the head by a cricket ball during a game at Leicester House.

8. Elvis was not the first king to die on the toilet. In 1760, King George II of England died whilst straining to relieve constipation. He fell from the toilet and smashed his head on a cabinet, triggering an aneurism which killed him.

7. One of Austria's lesser composers, Johann Schobert, managed to kill not only himself but his wife, four friends, three of his children and a maidservant in 1767 by insisting that it was as safe to eat poisonous fly agaric mushrooms as it was to eat ordinary mushrooms. It was not.

6. American patriot and revolutionary James Otis Jr. was the man who coined the immortal phrase 'Taxation without representation is tyranny'. Otis also said to his sister: 'When the Almighty in his providence shall take me out of time, it will be by a flash of lightning.' So how did Otis die? He was struck by lightning whilst he stood outside a friend's house in 1783.

5. American sea-captain and explorer John Kendrick died in 1794 when the British ship *Jackal* fired a friendly 13-gun salute at Kendrick's ship to welcome him to Honolulu. Unfortunately, one of the cannons was still loaded with grapeshot, smashing into Kendrick's table on deck, killing him and several of his crew.

4. Gouverneur Morris was an American statesman and founding father of the United States. He authored large sections of the constitution and was one of its signers. Surely such a man as this could not have died in a ridiculously stupid fashion? Well, dear reader, in 1816, Morris died after sticking a piece of whale bone through his urinary tract to relieve a blockage he thought was there. Gouverneur Morris – a statesman and a dick.

3. Italian tenor Americo Sbigoli died in January 1822 whilst performing Pacini's opera *Cesare in Egitto*. Straining too hard to match the style of the tenor who had first established the role, Sbigoli ruptured a blood vessel in his neck and died.

2. French author and literary giant Honoré de Balzac puts most modern caffeine addicts in the shade. His regular taking of 50 cups of thick, black Turkish coffee a day lead to stomach cramps, high blood pressure, an enlarged heart, ulcers and straight-out caffeine poisoning, all of which combined to kill him in 1850.

1. Amateur Anglo-Irish scientist Mary Ward managed to achieve a notable but deadly first in 1869. A passenger in an experimental steam car invented by her cousins, she decided to stand up in the car to get a better view and was thrown from it as it turned a corner. She fell under the wheels, dying within moments and becoming the first recorded fatality in a car accident.

LAST TRAIN TO DEADVILLE

Freighthopping, or train jumping as it is sometimes called, has a long and notorious history in America. First gaining popularity during the Civil War, illegally sneaking into a freight car either at a rail yard or by jumping onto a moving train allowed hobos to travel for free across the length and breadth of the United States. Although less common today, there is still a thriving 'hopping' community.

Among these was 25-year-old Christopher Artez and his partner Medeana Hendershot, 22. The pair had criss-crossed America by hopping, despite being warned by officials of the danger of what they did. In December 2011, the bodies of the pair were found in a load of coal delivered by train to Florida's Lakeland power plant. When the train had arrived, the cars' bottoms opened up, dropping the coal onto a waiting truck several stories below. It is thought the pair were sleeping on top of the coal when the train arrived. Post-mortems showed Artez had died from being buried alive in the coal whilst Hendershot had died from the blunt trauma of coal dropping onto her. Artez's mother Susan explained the pair had hopped a train to Florida to be somewhere warm for the winter. She was philosophical about his ridiculous and preventable death saying: 'If he had to die so young, at least there was a moment where he was on top of the world.'

DIVINE JUSTICE? I

Thief Robert Adoyo stole a collection box from a church in Nairobi in September 1987. He ran straight from the scene of his crime and into the busy street outside, where he was hit by a bus as he tried to cross the road.

DIVINE JUSTICE? II

Metal theft is one of the fastest rising crimes in the twenty-first century. It is a dangerous crime, but trying to steal copper cable supplying power to a church is, just possibly, tempting fate too much. It certainly was for one 48-year-old thief whose body was found in the parking lot of a church in Gary, Indiana in July 2012. He had been electrocuted whilst climbing a utility and fell to his death.

YEW SILLY MAN

Antoni Kyracou, 24, was found dead in his Covent Garden home by his mother, Tracey McGowan, in May 2012. He was smiling serenely, music was still playing on his headphones and beside his deathbed was a cup of seeds and leaves from a yew tree. Ms. McGowan told the subsequent inquest: 'My son was interested in an ancient practice in which yew seeds were consumed at a time when Jupiter and Venus where in alignment. There was a tribe of people who took yew seeds at that time to travel to the afterlife and then come back.' Clearly the planets were not aligned or Antoni was not in the right tribe, because whatever afterlife he travelled to, he has not and will not be coming back from it.

IT'S ONLY THE END OF THE WORLD AGAIN IX

Who is responsible for the deaths that result when someone begins preaching about the end of the world? The doomsayer or the dumb followers who fall for it? In 1992, South Korean cult leader Lee Jang-Rim began to prophecy that the world would end on October 28 that year. After four suicides and one death by fasting resulting from the apocalypse hysteria inspired by his religious nonsense, the authorities stepped in. On the appointed day, more than 1,500 riot police barred windows and closed all exits to the roof of the cult's temple to prevent any mass suicide by the 1,000 followers who had gathered in expectation of the end of time.

TRACKS TO TEARS I

When an inebriated Dean Bradbury rang his girlfriend to tell her he had missed the last train from London's Stratford Station in August 1996, he explained he would be walking home. However, he forget to mention the route he would be taking – following the train tracks. Bradbury managed to walk more than 4.8km and through at least one other station before stumbling onto one of the electrified rail tracks. The most surprising thing is that he managed to make it that far given he was four times over the legal drink drive limit at the time.

TRACKS TO TEARS II

If you are going to do something as monumentally stupid as walking along train tracks whilst intoxicated, adding to the already incredible level of danger is just plain ridiculous. However, that did not stop Gary Arnold Harris from not only drunkenly walking the line near Norfolk, Virginia, but doing it whilst listening to music on his personal stereo headphones. The music was so loud Harris did not hear the train that came from behind, hitting him and dragging his body more than 91m along the track.

IT MAKES YOU SICK

I have been on some riotous stag nights. I have been chained to a celebrity dwarf and drunk far more than is good for me, but I have never been on a stag night that has ended in tragedy. This may be a statistical anomaly given how many fabled last nights of freedom seem to end in tragedy. Mark Cave, 27, fell to his death from the fourth storey of a holiday apartment complex in Ibiza whilst on a stag do in September 2012. Cave had been leaning out of the window to vomit at the time of his fall.

LACK OF CARE PROBLEM

A 96-year-old woman died at a Welsh care home when her carer reversed her wheelchair into a lift shaft after she made the mistake of assuming the lift was there. Carer Carole Conway, who survived the 6m fall in 2012, said: 'I did not look inside before I stepped in, I just assumed it was there. The lift was playing up – we always had problems with it.'

LACK OF DRINK PROBLEM

Drinking too much is not good for you. It may kill you slowly, it may kill you quick, but too much alcohol is a killer. In the end, the drink problem for Stan Morton of Yorkshire was not the five-to-six bottles of vodka he drank each week, but stopping drinking them. Put on a cold turkey dry out cure by a counsellor in March 2011, Stan's body went into such extreme alcohol withdrawal that he went into a fit of convulsions and died within 12 hours of attempting to be sober.

ISN'T IT IRONIC?

There is a vicious rumour abroad that Americans lack a sense of irony. This is completely untrue. Take the case of Philip A. Contos, 55, a keen motorcyclist who was taking part in a 48km ride from Syracuse to Lake Como in New York in support of changing the law so motorcyclists could choose for themselves whether on not to wear safety helmets. Like many of the other riders that day, Philip chose to go without a helmet, something he may well have regretted when he lost control of his Harley-Davidson and went over the handlebars. He suffered a blow to the head and died instantly. Investigators said if he had worn a helmet, he would still be alive.

THE ODDS ARE AGAINST YOU

A man in his 20s died from cardiac arrest when a 9m long betting shop sign fell on him in January 2013. The sign belonged to the William Hill betting shop in London's busy Camden area. One witness to the accident said: 'It could have been me or anyone else walking. I guess his number was up.'

iDEAD

Robert Gary Hones was jogging at Palmento Dunes in South Carolina when he was struck and killed by a plane making an emergency landing on the beach in March 2010. Police investigating the scene of the crash commented: 'We suspect the victim was hit as he was unaware that the plane was descending. We don't think he heard it, as he was listening to his iPod.'

EXTERMINATED II

A Ukrainian man brought about a family tragedy when he tried to get inventive with some DIY pest eradication in June 2010. The 71-year-old man from the city of Dnepropetrovsk thought it would be a good idea to attach a hosepipe to the exhaust of his Soviet-era ZAZ Zaporozhets car and use the fumes to kill the plague of rats in his basement. After running his car for a while, he went down in the basement to see if his idea had worked. He was overcome by the build-up of fumes and collapsed dead. When his 72-year-old wife went to check on him, she was also overcome and killed, as was their 29-year-old granddaughter. Their bodies, but no dead rats, were discovered by another granddaughter.

GAME OVER

The main hobby of Chris Staniforth, 20, was playing 12-hour straight sessions of the computer game *Halo* on his Xbox. However, the marathon game nights took a terrible toll on poor Chris when he developed deep vein thrombosis – a condition more usually associated with passengers on long-haul air flights who are forced to sit in the same position for hours. Whilst he spent an evening blasting aliens in June 2011, a clot formed in his left calf before travelling to his lungs, triggering a pulmonary embolism. Chris's father, David, did not blame the game, but urged fellow gaming addicts to be aware of the dangers of sitting for long periods.

PILL PERIL

A patient at a Scottish hospital died after he took a tablet from his bedside cabinet thinking it was a painkiller, but instead swallowed a disinfectant tablet meant for the patient's baths. Hospital officials said the fact the two types of tablet looked so similar was 'regrettable.' Yes, I would bloody say so!

WHAT A BOOB

Think it is only idiot criminals who die ridiculously by trying to enter a home through the chimney? Oh no, some of the cleverest people do dumb things. Californian doctor Jacquelyn Kotarac would not take no for an answer when an ex-boyfriend refused to see her when she turned up at his home in September 2010. Whilst he slipped out the backdoor, she slid down the chimney. Unfortunately her chest size prevented her from descending and she became stuck and suffocated. Her body was discovered three days later when a house-sitter noticed an odd smell coming from the fireplace.

IT'S JUST NOT FAIR

Teenagers throw worse tantrums than toddlers and some of them can be fatal. When Arizonan Hughstan Schlicker, 15, was banned from using the Internet by his father in 2008, he did not just storm to his room, slam the door and play music extra loud. Instead, he took his dad's shotgun and blasted it into his father's face. Asked by police why he did it, he told them that not being able to access MySpace felt like: 'I was stabbed by a knife in the chest ... no matter how hard I pulled, I couldn't pull out the knife.'

BIGFOOT FAECES FATALITY

Chinese scientist Yu Gong devoted most of his career to searching for the Yeren – a Chinese equivalent of Bigfoot. According to colleagues, it was his obsession for proving the creature existed that led to his death in a car crash in January 1996. A fellow Yeren hunter said: 'Yu was so sleepy from staying up five nights in a row hunting that he was exhausted and could not keep his eyes open. It was not bad luck he crashed into a tractor, but tiredness from looking for Yeren faeces.'

WHAT A LEMON

A 16-year-old from the Indian city of Satara died whilst trying to impress his friends by swallowing and then regurgitating a lemon in 2008. He had successfully performed the trick twice earlier in the day, but on the third attempt, the lemon became stuck and he choked to death.

THE SQUIRREL OF DEATH

I like squirrels. I used to have a tame one that would come whenever I called out: 'Bobby La-La!' However, some people see them as nothing other than tree rats with bushy tales. It is likely that 61-year-old builder John Mason from Birmingham in England was in the hater camp. He died after falling from a ladder in 1996. Colleagues told his inquest that the tumble occurred because he was trying to fend off an attack from a squirrel he had disturbed in a gutter.

DAY STARTS WITH A BANG, ENDS WITH A ROAR

Guatemalan gun salesman Paco Cazanga, 32, was distraught when a bad day at work in 1995 ended with him accidentally shooting a potential client whilst demonstrating a pistol. Cazanga was so upset that he threw himself into a local zoo's jaguar pit. Firemen used fire extinguishers to force the jamboree of jaguars back, but Cazanga died from his injuries.

MAGICAL MORT V

We know that as a breed, politicians are unrelentingly stupid. We only have to look at the mess they have made of the world to realize this. Yisa Anifowose, leader of the Odua's People's Congress in Nigeria, was even more terminally dumb than most of his ilk. Having bought a magical charm he thought would make him bullet-proof in September 2011, he thought the wisest way to test it was to ask his friend John Taju to shoot him in the chest at point-blank range. Taju obliged, resulting not in the bullet falling harmlessly away as Anifowose expected, but the world having one less political idiot to worry about.

ANY OLD IRON

James Arbuthnot, 41, was so determined to drown himself by walking into the sea off Lancashire in 1953 that he attached 18 irons to a chain on his body. However, struggling with the weight caused him to die from a heart attack before he even reached the water.

SUICIDE SOLITAIRE

Despite already being an inmate on death row at San Quentin in 1930, William Kogut was so eager for his punishment that he constructed a pipe bomb in his cell, using a hollow leg from his bed stuffed with torn-up playing cards. At the time, the red ink of cards contained nitrocellulose, which can create an explosive mixture when wet. Kogut sealed one end with a broom handle, added water before warming the bomb on his cell's heater with the open end pressed against his skull. The resulting explosion forced the pieces of card into Kogut's skull with enough force to kill him. Impressive.

NOT SUCH A CLEVER WAY TO GO

Professor Kurt Gödel was a genius – a logician, mathematician and philosopher, whose intellectual prowess earned him the respect of some of the most famous thinkers in the twentieth century, including Einstein. However, in his later years, Gödel became so paranoid that a foreign power was trying to poison him, he ate food prepared only by his wife Adele. When she was hospitalized for six months, Gödel refused to eat anything, starving himself to a weight of 60lb before his death in 1978.

EXTREME TRAIN SPOTTING I

Brazil has a thriving train surfing culture – if 'thriving' is defined as resulting in almost 150 deaths since 1990. Known as surfistas, the mainly teenage boys get a thrill trying to stay on top of a moving train whilst dodging overhead electrical cables and bridges. Knowing when to duck is an essential surfista skill. Shame, then, that Roberto Barbosa, 17, seemed to lack it. In 1998 he was decapitated by a train signal whilst surfing on a São Paolo train. Whatever happened to the good old days of train spotting?

EXTREME TRAIN SPOTTING II

If being a *surfista* was not a stupid and deadly enough hobby for Brazilian train lovers to adopt, the incredibly stupid can also elect to become a *pinguente*, or 'hanger-on'. *Pinguentes* do not do anything as conventional as ride atop a speeding train's roof. Oh no. *Pinguentes* get their thrills by hanging onto the underside of a train carriage and riding a few inches above the track. Unfortunately for 18-year-old Alfredo Costa from Rio, someone had left a tool-box on the track the day he decided to try his hand at the world's most dim-witted pastime. Whilst the train easily cleared the obstruction, Costa did not.

HEROICALLY STUPID

Some deaths might result from doing something ridiculously stupid, yet also retain an air of nobility. A case in point happened on July 20, 1981. Edward Allen Kirwan dived into the Celestine Pool in Yellowstone Park's thermal spring area to rescue a friend's dog called Moosie. The pet had run off into the death-trap when released from its leash. Onlookers told Kirwan the spring reached temperatures of 93°C and warned him not to jump in. He then said: 'Like hell, I won't!' and dived under. Somewhat predictably, neither he nor Moosie survived.

MAGICAL MORT VI

We have already seen that allegedly magical charms have a somewhat disappointing track record in suspending the laws of physics when a gun is fired at someone wearing one. In comparison, how do concoctions of magical herbs prepared by a juju man do at deflecting certain death? Just as badly is the answer, as 23-year-old Aleobiga Aberima from the Ghanaian village of Lambu found out in 2001. Despite having spent two weeks continuously smearing his skin with a magic herbal potion, it took just a single bullet from a fellow villager's rifle to kill him and prove that no magic herb does the work of a good, old-fashioned ballistic vest.

ROLL IN THE HAY

For former member of rock group Electric Light Orchestra, Mike Edwards, a drive in the country turned deadly in September 2010. Edwards was killed when a giant bale of hay rolled off of tractor down a hill, crashing through a hedge to land on top of his van, causing him to swerve into the path of another vehicle.

WORLD CHAMPION DUMB

Between 1999 and 2010, Finland hosted the World Sauna Championship, a globally televised event in which people competed to see how long they could endure sitting in a sauna. Why, you ask, did the event stop in 2010? Good question. That year, Russian competitor Vladimir Ladyzhensky and five-time Finnish champion Timo Kaukonen both entered a sauna with a temperature in excess of 93°c. After six minutes both men had passed out. Ladyzhensky was dead and Kaukonen was rushed to hospital with 70 per cent of his body covered in third-degree burns. Organizers later said that as they could not find a way to return the sport to its 'original, playful character' they would not be continuing with the event.

DEADLY WARCRAFT

In 2007, Zhang Wei from northern China died of heart failure after spending a full week playing *World of Warcraft* during his nation's national holiday period. He weighed 150kg, but authorities said it was clocking in the marathon gaming hours and not his weight that triggered his death. A medical official said: 'Death resulted from an embolism caused by spending so long seated in front of the computer. First his Internet addiction made him gain weight, then it killed him by making him sit throughout the whole holidays.' However, neighbour Xu Yan sympathized with Zhang, saying: 'The holidays are a boring time. The only options are TV or computer. What else can you do when all the markets, karaoke bars and cafés are closed?'

TOO MUCH OF A GOOD THING

Too much of anything can kill you, but if you have to choose something to fatally overdose from, surely there are better things than carrot juice? Not for Basil Brown, a 48-year-old health nut from England who in 1974 managed to guzzle 38 litres of carrot juice in just 10 days. The beta-carotene in the carrots impacted on his body's conversion of vitamin A, leading to him having 10,000 times the recommended daily amount of the vitamin in his system. First his poisoned liver turned him very yellow, then at the crunch, very dead.

OH, THE IRONY V – GOD CAN KILL YOU

North Carolina university student Ariane Noelle Patterson sent a tweet from her phone celebrating her 21st birthday in January 2012. It read: 'Thank you God for another year of life.' Ariane, who was on #teampurity and #teamJesus, collapsed and died from a heart attack just a couple of hours later whilst in a religion class.

WHAT A TWEET I

Whilst the preceding tragic death was rendered ridiculously ironic by social media, Twitter helped make the death of aspiring rapper Ervin McKinness AKA Inkyy, just plain ridiculous. After a night of heaving drinking, the fool sent a tweet admitting drunk driving which read 'Drunk af going 120 drifting corners #Fuckit YOLO' (you only live once). Less than 20 minutes later, Inkyy had proved himself right, living his once by smashing his SUV into a wall, killing himself and his passengers. #RIP #whatawaste #damnidiot

CURTAIN CLOSER

American opera singer Richard Versalle had enjoyed an international career, singing on some of the world's finest stages. The 62-year-old tenor was performing in the premiere of Janácek's The Makropulos Case at New York's Metropolitan Opera in January 1996. His character was halfway up a 6m ladder and had just sung the line: 'You can only live so long' when Versalle had a heart attack and fell to the stage dead. The show did not go on and there were no refunds.

DOUBLE CURTAIN CALL

Maybe opera is cursed. Austrian conductor Felix Motti died whilst leading a performance of *Tristan und Isolde* at the National Theatre in Munich in 1911 at the moment his wife sang the line 'O death-doomed head, O death-doomed heart'. His ghost was said to haunt the building, something German conductor Joseph Keilberth might have wanted to keep in mind whilst conducting the same opera at the same theatre in 1968. Keilberth collapsed and died moments after conducting Tristan's aria 'Let me die, never to wake'.

KILLED BY DEATH V – DEAD AT THE WHEEL

There is nothing unusual or odd about dead bodies being in hearses when they are safely contained in coffins. However, citizens in Beverly Hills called the police in August 2012 when they saw the body of a woman slumped in the front seat of a white Lincoln Continental customized into an oversized hearse. The hearse was drifting between lanes of traffic. The driver, 59-year-old Garlandine Garvin, had died from natural causes whilst taking a body to a viewing.

CROCODILE TEARS IV

Camping is a bad idea. Civilization has achieved hot water, central heating, duvets and refrigeration. Voluntarily living in a tent and spitting in the face of all that is an insult to humanity. If camping is a bad idea, camping in an area you know to be densely populated with crocodiles is absurdly bonkers. However, that did not stop 39-year-old Lee McLeod spending a night camping beside the McArthur River near Darwin, Australia. Not surprisingly, McLeod's head and torso was eventually found in a harpooned croc. In possibly the best comment I have ever heard from a policeman in 20 years as a journalist, a Darwin copper told me: 'Yep, Dave, we think the bloke was a pillock too.'

OH, THE IRONY VI – CONDUCTING HIS OWN DEATH

Maybe opera is not cursed, it is just that conducting is a particularly dangerous and often fatal business. It certainly was for 59-year-old music teacher Carl Barnett. Whilst conducting at an Oklahoma school in 1974, he died from a heart attack mid-piece. The piece he was conducting? Bach's *Come Sweet Death*.

DEAD AS A DOG

Xavier Mertz was a renowned Swiss polar explorer. When the Antarctic expedition he was on in 1913 was down to just a few days' food, he decided that his team would kill six out of their group of 10 sled-pulling Huskies. Mertz was prepared to eat every part of the dogs, which in retrospect was a very stupid thing to do. He consumed all of the dogs' livers – which contain high concentrations of Vitamin A – and died not from the cold but from Vitamin A poisoning.

X MARKS THE FATAL SPOT

Wilhelm Rontgen discovered X-rays by accident and gave them that name because he had no idea what they were. Common sense would seem to dictate that when dealing with the unknown, a certain amount of caution would be in order. However, common sense was far from common among the early pioneers in this field, and several of them died from radiation poisoning. One of these was Elizabeth Fleischman Ascheim who, with her husband, ran the first X-ray laboratory in San Francisco. Not only did she take no precautions during her work, she often deliberately exposed herself to X-rays to prove to nervous patients that they were perfectly safe. They weren't. She soon developed a frightening skin condition and despite one arm being amputated, she died of cancer in 1905, at the age of 46.

CURSED

Actors are a superstitious lot, and no play makes then twitchier than Shakespeare's *Macbeth*, or as they call it, the Scottish play. Many of them believe it is cursed. It certainly has been the cause of a few ridiculous deaths. One legend that has been shown to be false is that Hal Berridge, the first boy supposed to have played Lady Macbeth died in rehearsals – but in 1735 English actor Charles Macklin was so outraged by poor reviews for his performance in the lead role, he got into a scuffle with another actor and killed him. In 1849 in New York, fans of two rival actors who were both playing Macbeth in the city, American Edwin Forrest and Briton William Macready, got into a brawl outside the Astor Place Opera House, which descended into a riot that killed 24 people. Most ridiculous of all, on his opening night performance as Macbeth in 1947, English Harold Norman uttered the line: 'Lay on, MacDuff!' before accidentally impaling himself on his fellow actor's sword and dying from peritonitis.

THERE'S NO FOOL LIKE AN OLD FOOL

Some people do not know when to quit. Despite having lost several family members of the Great Wallendas daredevil circus act in tragedies which occurred because they chose not to perform with a safety net, Karl Wallenda was determined to keep working – even at the age of 73. In 1978, he attempted a tightrope walk between the two towers of the Condado Plazo Hotel in Puerto Rico whilst carrying on the family tradition of no safety net. Winds in excess of 48km/h and misconnected guide ropes meant Karl took a dive of 37m to his death.

THE LUCK OF THE WALLENDAS

As we have already seen, the Wallenda circus family never seemed to be one of the luckiest. Karl's sister-in-law Yetta Wallenda died in 1963 when she tried to adjust a foot strap whilst 14m up a pole and without a net. Just 18 months after this tragedy, the Wallenda troupe was trying to form a seven-man human pyramid when it collapsed, killing two of them and paralyzing another Wallenda for life.

DIVINE JUSTICE? III

Despite solid photographic evidence emerging after he had been cleared of the brutal rape and murder of his partner Brenda Schaefer, double jeopardy rules meant Mel Ignatow could not be retried for her murder – even with a confession of the killing at his later trial for perjury. During the sadistic killing, Ignatow had blindfolded and gagged Schaefer, before binding her hand and foot to a glass coffee table. A decade after the murder, Ignatow tripped in his apartment, smashing his hand and head on a glass coffee table. He bled to death before he could raise any help.

GREEN WAS DEAD RIGHT ABOUT SUVs

According to some members of the Green Party in the USA, SUV drivers are going to kill us all with their unnecessary gas-guzzling. Unfortunately, Green Party member and candidate for US Senate Natasha Pettigrew was proved correct about the dangers of SUVs and the morons who drive them. In September 2010, she was hit by an SUV whilst cycling. The driver, Christy Littleford, thought she had hit a deer and did not even bother to stop.

THE CURSE OF EDDYSTONE I

Eddystone lighthouse, off the coast of Cornwall, has been a life-saving aid to navigation for hundreds of years. The current lighthouse was designed and built by James Douglas, and has been operational since 1882. It is, however, the fourth lighthouse to have been built on the site. The first Eddystone lighthouse was completed in 1699 by Henry Winstanley. Built out of timber and granite, it was considered immensely strong in its day, well able to stand up to the fiercest of storms. Winstanley had great confidence in his creation, and when a particularly severe storm brewed in November 1703, he insisted on being inside the lighthouse so that he could test its performance. Unfortunately for Winstanley, the storm tested his lighthouse to destruction; it collapsed, killing all inside.

THE CURSE OF EDDYSTONE II

The second Eddystone lighthouse was built by John Rudyard in 1709, and survived for nearly 50 years. Death came to Eddystone II in 1755, when the light set fire to the roof of the lighthouse. The three keepers – including 94-year-old Henry Hall – tried to fight the fire by throwing buckets of water at it, but had to take refuge on the rocks whilst the lighthouse burned. Whilst he was looking up at the blaze, a piece of molten lead fell from the roof and landed in Hall's mouth, burning its way through his insides and killing him. The lead is now in the National Museum of Scotland.

BE CAREFUL WHAT YOU WISH FOR

Germany is not known for its contribution to rock music. However, one of its better bands from the 1960s was the Lords, a beat group whose gimmick was that all of its members called themselves Lord. The group's singer, Lord Ulli, gave an interview in 1966 saying: 'When I die, I'd like to drop dead from the stage.' On a 40th anniversary reunion tour of the band in 1999, Lord Ulli got his wish. He tripped whilst performing their hit "Over In Gloryland" – a ditty about the joys of being called to heaven by the über-Lord himself – and fell from the stage and smashed his head.

A VERY BLACK FRIDAY II

In further proof that the American retail madness known as Black Friday is aptly named and we ought to be worrying about consumerism, not capitalism, comes a double dickhead death. In 2008 at a Toys 'R' Us in California, two men shot and killed each other. The wives of the men had begun fighting each other in an argument over grabbing bargains, when in front of their horrified children, both men pulled guns. One decided to flee, but when he was shot at whilst running away, he retaliated, leading to a cash register shootout and two dead bodies.

TOP 10 RIDICULOUS DEATHS OF WELL-KNOWN PEOPLE – DEAD FAMOUS

10. Hollywood actor Tyrone Power should have listened to his wife and others. They advised him for health reasons not to film the epic movie *Solomon and Sheba* in Spain in 1958 and not to do his own stunt and fight sequences. Disregarding their concerns, he died from a massive heart attack whilst filming a duel sequence with fellow actor George Sanders.

9. *Kabuki* actor Bando Mitsugoro VIII was so revered in Japan the government officially declared him a national treasure. Such was his reputation that when he ordered an illegally large portion of toxic fugu fish liver in a sushi restaurant in 1975, no one felt able to refuse him. Despite claiming he could handle the poison, he died after suffering seven hours of convulsion and paralysis.

8. Oscar-winning actor David Niven's first wife, Primula, died at a Hollywood party held in her honour in 1946. Whilst playing a game of hide and seek, she mistook the entrance to the cellar for a closet door and fell down a darkened flight of stairs to her death.

7. Golden Age of radio comedian and Hollywood actor Harry Einstein AKA Parkya Karkas died after coming off stage at the Friar Club of Beverly Hill during a roast of Lucille Ball and Desi Arnaz in 1958. He slumped in Milton Berle's lap, causing Berle to shout, 'Is there a doctor in the house?' The crowd erupted in laughter at what they thought was a joke.

6. Albert Dekker was a Hollywood actor who went on to become a member of the California State Assembly. His screen work got him a star on the Hollywood Walk of Fame, whilst he earned a reputation as a courageous opponent of commie-bashing Senator Joseph McCarthy. However, when he was found dead in his bathtub in 1968, he became the poster boy for ridiculous sex play death. He was naked, kneeling with a noose looped around the shower's curtain rod, blindfolded, gagged and handcuffed. Written with red lipstick on his body were choice words such as 'whip', 'slave', 'cocksucker' and 'make me suck'. The coroner ruled it an accidental and entirely self-inflicted death.

5. What do you do when you were once famous as 'America's highest paid model' earning $25,000 a year in 1932, had a picture deal with RKO, dated Howard Hughes and now no one knows your name? For Gwili Andre, the day after her 51st birthday in 1959, the answer was simple. Pile up all the old stills, press cuttings, promotional items and reels of your films, light them to make a huge pyre and then burn yourself to death on it.

4. What makes the death by drowning of Hollywood actress Natalie Wood in November 1981 more than a little ridiculous and to some, suspicious, was that Wood was a renowned, intense and lifelong sufferer from hydrophobia – a fear of water. Quite how she managed to end up falling into the water from a boat on which she, her husband Robert Wagner and Christopher Walken had been enjoying a trip is a bit obscure, but it turns out she was right to be afraid of the old H_2O.

3. Comedian and actor Dick Shawn died on stage in San Diego in 1987. He collapsed from a heart attack whilst performing a routine about nuclear attack. Thinking it part of the act, the audience burst into laughter and kept laughing even when CPR was performed on Shawn.

2. Today Marcus Garvey is regarded as Jamaica's first national hero and internationally known as one of the inaugural and most effective proponents of black nationalism. However, in 1940, Garvey was recovering from a stroke in London when he read several mistakenly published obituaries of himself. None of them was flattering and one even claimed he died 'broke, alone and unpopular'. The shock and revulsion at reading them brought about a second stroke, which killed him.

1. Actor David Carradine was best-known for his roles in the hit 1970s show *Kung-Fu* and as Bill in the *Kill Bill* films. In 2009, he was found suffocated in a hotel closest in Thailand. He had tied his hands above his head and placed a rope around his neck and genitals. Coroners ruled out suicide and suggested that, just as with Albert Dekker and Michael Hutchence in 1997, it was a terrible case of auto-erotic asphyxiation sex play gone wrong. Horribly, horribly wrong.

OH, THE IRONY VII – FUNERAL MARCH

French conductor Jean-Marc Cochereau died in January 2011 whilst conducting a rehearsal of Beethoven's *Eroica* with the Orleans Symphony Orchestra. His fatal collapse happened during the "Funeral March" section. The orchestra's spokesperson, Catherine Mounier, said: 'I think, honestly, that is the death he would have wanted.'

IT'S ONLY THE END OF THE WORLD AGAIN X

After World War II, Hector Cox made quite a name for himself as one of the most eccentric orators at London's famous Speaker's Corner in Hyde Park. On Sunday June 27, 1954, he deviated from pontificating about the Egyptian Book of the Dead and announced that the world would end within 24 hours. His prophecy came true for Hector. His body was discovered the next day with a kitchen knife plunged through his heart. His death was ruled as suicide.

TAR-RIBBLE WAY TO GO

Some moped drivers can be real assholes. However, Chinese Wang Wei, 23, made a mistake when he cut up a truck carrying several tonnes of boiling tar in Yuhuan in August 2012. The truck swerved to avoid him, overturned and sent a wave of tar that entirely engulfed Wang. Within a minute, the weight and heat of the tar had done its work and there was one less idiot on the roads.

STAIRWAY TO HEAVEN

They are used by millions of travellers everyday, so most of humanity has become blasé about the dangers of escalators. In March 2012, 88-year-old Sophia Klose fell whilst on an escalator at the Long Island Rail Road station. Her clothes became caught in the machine's teeth, leading to her being choked to death by her own dress. Remember, escalators are just as dangerous as you thought they were when you were a child.

DEATH CHAIR

A morbidly obese man from Bellaire, Ohio died in March 2011 after becoming fused to the fabric of chair he had not moved from in two years. The man lived with his girlfriend and a roommate, who allowed him to stay seated for so long. A city official said: 'The room the man lived in was beyond filthy, beyond deplorable. It's unbelievable that somebody lived in conditions like that.'

CRAPPY WAY TO GO

A family tragedy happened in May 2012 on the Maryland dairy farm of Jim Walton. The 48-year-old farmer went to suck some manure from a two-million gallon manure pit, when he fell into it. Two of his sons tried to rescue him, but also took a tumble in the crap and drowned in the effluent alongside their father.

BUG HOUSE BANQUET

If the world ends, I would not be surprised if it was not consumed in apocalypse set off by morons. The earth is plagued by them. I mean, what sort of idiots set up a cockroach eating contest and what sort of fool enters one? Well, that would be the Ben Siegel Reptile Store in Florida and 32-year-old Edward Archbold. Unfortunately for Archbold, who downed dozens of live roaches to beat 30 other contestants to the grand prize of a python, he choked to death on the bugs.

KILLER KARAOKE I

I do not take part in karaoke myself because I have a voice like a hundred crows being strangled. Avoiding karaoke is a wise choice, especially if it is being carried out by any member of the Yun family from Xian, China. Singing over terrible pop songs turned deadly in August 2012 when two uncles of a four-year-old boy became so outraged that the child was allowed to sing and sing without giving anyone else a turn, that they began to curse the child. His father, Mr. Yun, became embroiled in a brawl with the two men and when they had him on the floor and were kicking him, Yun's nephew ran into his nearby noodle shop. Returning with a cleaver, he proceeded to hack the two attackers to death.

KILLER KARAOKE II

Further evidence that karaoke can be a killer comes from a 2008 shooting spree in the Songkhla Province of Thailand. Weenus Chumkamnerd, 52, killed a neighbouring doctor and seven guests at her karaoke party after they repeatedly sang the John Denver song "Country Roads". Chumkamnerd said: 'When I began shooting, nobody pleaded for their life because they were all drunk. I warned these people about their noisy karaoke parties. I said if they carried on I would go down and shoot them. I had told them if I couldn't talk sense into them, I would come back and finish them off.' Other neighbours say the shooting started after guests belted out dozens of renditions of "Country Roads" one after the other.

OFF WITH HIS HEAD

Dr. Hitoshi Nikaidoh was a surgeon at the St Joseph Hospital in Houston. In 2007, as he stepped into an elevator at the hospital, the doors closed, pinning his shoulders. The doors refused to open, despite attempts by Nikaidoh and a lift passenger to free him. The lift then began to move up, decapitating the unfortunate doctor. It later turned out that earlier maintenance work had left the elevator without working safeguards.

HOTEL HELL

Dan Andersson was a Swedish author and poet whose work is still read and enjoyed in his native land. In 1920, a 32-year-old Andersson travelled to Stockholm for a job interview and stayed in room 11 at the Hotel Hellman. Unfortunately, before his stay, the room was sprayed with hydrogen cyanide to tackle a bedbug problem. Insufficiently aired, the room was toxic and Andersson soon succumbed to poisoning, as did an insurance inspector in another room.

SWAN SONG

Actress Edith Webster died from a heart attack whilst playing her death scene in the play *The Drunkard* at a Maryland theatre in November 1986. She had just sung the song "Please Don't Talk About Me When I'm Gone". The audience applauded as she died, thinking the convincing death was all part of the performance.

HYDRANT TO HEAVEN

A car crash in Oakland, California spelled doom for 24-year-old Humberto Hernandez in June 2007. However, it was not a car that hit and killed him, but a 91kg fire hydrant which was propelled into the air by extreme water pressure and the impact of the Ford Escape crashing into it. A deputy sheriff commented: 'The water pressure meant it went like a bullet and he was just unlucky to be in its path.'

MOTOR MADNESS

Most Englishmen have a soft spot for an Aston Martin car. Even later models like the DB7 conjure up a romantic image of power, success and luck with the ladies. For me, those images of the DB7 have been tarnished by the death of Gerald Mellin, 54, in August 2008. In a misguided attempt to get back at his younger wife who had left him, he sent her a text saying: 'Congratulations XXX', then tied one end of rope to a tree and the other to his neck. He then got into his DB7, put his foot down and experienced its ability to do 0–60mph in 4.9 seconds by decapitating himself. What would Q say?

EXERCISED TO DEATH

Chris Mason, 41, pleaded guilty to reckless homicide in 2009 for exercising her 73-year-old husband James Mason to death in Chardon, Ohio. She really didn't have much choice, as the court was shown a video in which she could be seen dragging her husband around the pool by his arms and legs. The video also recorded 43 occasions when she refused to let her husband stop exercising or get out of the pool, despite him resting his head on the side and gasping for breath.

I GUESS COYOTES HATE FOLK MUSIC, TOO

Before Canadian folk singer Taylor Mitchell ran into three coyotes whilst hiking in the Cape Breton Highlands National Park in Nova Scotia in 2009, no adult human had ever been recorded as having been killed by the animals. However, it was no consolation or help to Taylor to be first in the record books on this front. She was in the process of being eaten when a group of hikers came across her and scared the beasts away. However, despite being rushed to hospital, she died from her injuries. One of the songs on Taylor's debut album was called "Secluded Roads" – ironic, as that is exactly what she should have stayed away from.

KILLER KARAOKE III

The song "My Way" has led to so many fights and deaths due to poor karaoke versions in the Philippines, that most bars in the country have had it removed from their machines. Just one of the many "My Way" killings occurred in 2007. Security guard Romy Baligula shot 43-year-old Robilito Oretega in the chest for ruining the Sinatra classic with his out-of-tune singing.

KILLER KARAOKE IV

When karaoke turns deadly, it is not always because of the singer's choice of song. In December 2008, Malaysian karaoke fan Abdul Sani Doli refused to hand over the microphone to allow other patrons of the bar in Borneo the chance of murdering some popular ballads. In retaliation, three of them murdered Abdul, beating him to death.

THE SHOT NO PHOTOGRAPHER EVER WANTS

Carl McCunn was a celebrated wildlife photographer. In March 1981, he paid a bush pilot to land him at a remote lake in the Alaskan wilderness. He thought he had arranged for the pilot to pick him up five months later, but he hadn't. When he was not picked up in August, he wrote in his diary: 'I think I should have used more foresight about arranging my departure. I'll soon find out.' It soon became clear to McCunn he had forgotten to arrange a pick-up. By November, as the snow fell and he began to starve, McCunn had given up all hope of rescue and so shot himself with his rifle after writing in his diary: 'They say it doesn't hurt.'

RADIUM KILLED THE GOLFING STAR

Eben Byers was a famous socialite, athlete, ladies' man and amateur golfing champion. When he damaged his arm in a fall in 1927, he was prescribed Radithor – a patent medicine made from dissolving high concentrations of radium in water. During the next few years, Byers consumed vast amounts of Radithor, up to 1,400 bottles, believing it greatly boosted his health. However, by the time he stopped drinking it, he had accumulated so much radium in his bones that he had holes in his skull and had lost most of his jaw. When he died in March 1932, the *Wall Street Journal* ran the headline 'The Radium Water Worked Fine Until His Jaw Came Off'.

DEADLY SLIP DOWN

We would all like to think that when it comes to avoiding death, a doctor's office would be one of the better places to be. Unfortunately that was not the case for 76-year-old Edward Juchneiwicz. He was being transported from his nursing home to his doctor's by stretcher in an ambulance in 1991, and whilst the ambulance attendants talked to the doctor's staff, they took their mind off Mr Juchneiwicz. This slip of concentration allowed his stretcher to roll down a slope, overturning in the process and killing him.

LOOK BEFORE YOU LEAP IV

Writing this book has taught me many things, not least of which is that suicidal widows never look before they leap. In September 2009, Neus Espina, a 54-year-old widow from Viladecans, Spain, decided to end her life at 5.45pm. As is always the case, the inconsiderate woman did not look before taking the plunge from her third-storey balcony and landed on top of a 50-year-old man who lived in the neighbouring town of Gava. Espina died instantly, her poor victim was pronounced dead shortly after being taken to hospital. As those widows won't look down, we all need to be looking up a bit more often.

KILLED BY DEATH VI – STUNG TO DEATH

The funeral of the wife of Jaam Singh Girdhan Barela in September 2009 was a doubly tragic affair. The pyre burning his wife's remains in the Indian village of Nava Bilwa disturbed a nest of bees. As mourners fled the scene under a storm of stings, Barela refused to leave until he had performed the necessary rituals for his dead love. The result of this act of devotion was Barela being stung to death. Death really does have a sting – and the blackest, most ironic sense of humour.

TWO IN THE EYE FOR GREAT MUSIC

Johann Sebastian Bach was one of the greatest musical geniuses of all time, leaving behind a vast body of work that will live forever. Towards the end of his life, his eyesight began to fail and in his quest for a cure, he put himself in the hands of one John Taylor. Unfortunately, Bach did not check Taylor's credentials first. In those pre-Internet days, it might have been hard for Bach to find out that Taylor had blinded hundreds of patients when practising in Switzerland, but surely the fact Taylor described himself as the 'Ophthalmiater Royal – personal eye-surgeon to the Pope and King of England' and travelled in a coach covered in painted eyes would make most people think 'quack'? Regrettably for music-lovers through the ages, Bach submitted to Taylor's ministrations and died of complications shortly afterwards.

Not content with this, Taylor went on to snuff out another musical voice when he blinded George Fredrick Handel. Cosmic justice then caught up with him as he went blind himself, dying in poverty. One hopes that cosmic justice hasn't finished with him, and that he's in his own special hell, being forced to listen to the music of Justin Bieber for all eternity.

BELOW PAR II

Golf is a game that can induce either a Zen-like sense of inner calm or the ugliest sort of rage. Guess which of those modes was responsible for the death of 16-year-old golfer Jeremy Brenno at the Kingsboro Golf Club in Gloversville, New York in 1994? After he missed a shot at the sixth, Brenno smashed his 3-wood into a bench to vent his frustration. However, the club's shaft broke, bounced up and fatally pierced his heart.

BELOW PAR III

Brenno is not the only golfer to have been killed by one of his own clubs. In 1951, keen golfer Edward Harrison was playing a round at the Inglewood Golf Club in Kenmore, Washington. During the game, he shattered the shaft of one of his clubs, piercing his groin and severing the femoral artery. Bleeding profusely, he staggered 91m along the course before dropping down dead.

BELOW PAR IV

Even when not being used on a course, golf clubs can be deadly. Jimmy Newham, 15, found one lying in the streets of Edison, New Jersey in 2005. Newham thought he would test his swing by hitting a fire hydrant. Big mistake. The 5-iron fractured and part of the shaft rebounded into his neck, killing him.

DUCK!

Gustav Kobbé was one of the early twentieth century's most renowned music critics. He was also, as his death shows, something of an idiot in practical matters like survival. Whilst out sailing around Long Island in July 1918, Kobbé looked up to see an early hydroplane was losing altitude whilst heading towards his boat. Instead of sliding into the water or just ducking, Kobbé stood up straight so he could dive off his vessel. Big mistake. Standing up put Kobbé's head into contact with one of the plane's wings, killing him. Had he ducked, the plane would have passed safely overhead.

NUCLEAR MELTDOWN

If US Congressmen are doing their job right – admittedly a highly unlikely event – testifying before a Joint Congressional Committee ought to mean a tough grilling in an attempt to get the truth. However, for leading physicist Kip Siegel, the stress of facing questions from the Joint Committee on Nuclear Power was just too much. He died mid-session whilst defending his company's groundbreaking experimental work on laser-controlled fusion.

WHAT ARE THE CHANCES?

American composer John Barnes Chance died in his Texas back garden in 1972 due to a combination of tent, dog and electricity. Keen camper Chance was airing a tent in his yard whilst constructing an electric fence to keep in his dog, who had a habit of running into the road to chase cars. As Chance worked, the dog played in the yard, knocking the tent and causing one of its poles to fall and make contact with the fence, electrocuting its owner. Chance's death is either a case of absurdly bad luck or one of a clever, murderous hound who would go to any length for his car-chasing fix.

A POX UPON THE NAME OF SCIENCE

Whilst I tend to look at scientists as brave pioneers at the frontier of knowledge, you have to wonder if some of them are not just being a little too clever for their own good. Having eradicated the smallpox virus from naturally occurring by 1977, the world should have been safe from the killer disease. Unfortunately for medical photographer Janet Parker in 1978, her darkroom was above a laboratory being used to study smallpox and the virus spread through a service pipe. Parker's ridiculously tragic and avoidable death led to the scientist in charge of the laboratory, Professor Henry Bedson, taking his own life.

DEADLY BEAUTY I

Maria, Countess of Coventry was a famous society beauty in the mid-eighteenth century. The fashion of the day dictated that ladies should have pale skin, so Maria was liberal with the make-up. Unfortunately, her cosmetic of choice was based on white lead, which caused the eruption of sores on her face. These she covered with a thicker layer of make-up, which simply made the problem worse. Eventually, so much lead entered her bloodstream via the sores, that Maria was fatally poisoned. She was 27 years of age.

DEADLY BEAUTY II

One rival of the Countess of Coventry was the courtesan Kitty Fisher. She came from humble origins, but made her fortune the way only a beautiful woman can, the Earl of Coventry being just one of the lovers she took. She was painted by Joshua Reynolds, owned diamonds worth many thousands of pounds, and once ate a thousand-guinea banknote on a slice of bread-and-butter for breakfast. Though she conducted a running feud with the Countess of Coventry, she seems to have learned nothing from her, as she too succumbed to lead poisoning via her cosmetics. Her dying wish was to be buried in her best ball gown.

UP IN SMOKE

Finnish film actress Sirkka Sari was attending the wrap party for her third film – Rikas tyttö – in 1939 when a planned romantic liaison went awry. She and a male companion made their way on the roof of the Aulanko Hotel where the party was being held. Mistaking a ladder to a chimney for a ladder to a balcony, Sari climbed up. Unfortunately she slipped, fell into the chimney and went straight down to the hotel boiler's furnace below.

ICED

In December 1903, police officer Charles Daniels was making his rounds in the village of Cassopolis, Michigan. Snow and ice were thick on the ground, so he took care not to fall. Unfortunately for Daniels, snow and ice were thick in the air as well. A 4.5kg icicle crashed down from a building next to where he was standing and removed the top of his head. Ouch.

SMOKING KILLS V – CIGAR FATALITY

Austrian composer Anton von Webern survived the Nazi regime despite its initial view that he made 'degenerate music'. This is probably down to von Webern coming out as a keen supporter of Adolf Hitler during World War II. In 1945, with his country occupied by the Allies, von Webern left his home so he could smoke a cigar without bothering his grandchildren. An American soldier, seeing the red tip of his cigar and incensed by the violation of curfew, shot him.

A DOG'S DINNER

Marie Prevost was a silent film star who never made it in the talkies due to her thick Bronx accent. This left her on a downward personal and career spiral. In 1937, police broke down the door of her apartment after neighbours complained about the incessant barking of her dachshund. Police discovered that Prevost had drunk herself to death, surrounded by 16 empty bottles of whiskey and an I.O.U. to Joan Crawford for $110. She had been dead for at least a week and her dog had been very hungry. Those parts of Provost that the dachshund had not eaten were cremated at a service attended by friends such as Douglas Fairbanks Jr. and Clark Gable.

GLUTTON FOR PUNISHMENT

Julien Offray de la Mettrie was an eighteenth century French doctor and philosopher credited with being the first to come up with the metaphor of a man being a machine. His philosophy led him to prize all forms of hedonism, especially gluttony. In 1751, the French ambassador to Russia gave a feast for La Mettrie to thank him for curing him from an illness. La Mettrie decided to show the strength of his constitution and power of his gluttony by eating the largest amount of pheasant pâte and truffles ever eaten by a man. Whether he succeeded or not is unclear, but La Mettrie stuffed himself to the point where he became violently ill, dying from his over-consumption. Too much fuel for the tank of the machine man.

SKELETON NEEDED KEY

In 2002, the skeleton of 47-year-old artist Richard Sumner was discovered in a remote part of the Clocaenog Forest in Wales. He had been missing for three years. An inquest into his death heard that Sumner had tried to take his own life and had handcuffed himself to the tree and then thrown the keys out of reach in an attempt to ensure he could not change his mind and try to get help. The technique worked a bit too well, as pathologist Brian Rogers said the position of handcuffs and marks on the tree suggested Sumner had probably changed his mind, but could not reach the key.

OH, THE IRONY VIII – DYING FOR IMMORTALITY

Canadian composer Claude Vivier was stabbed to death in his Paris apartment by a young male prostitute in 1983. Sad, but not ridiculous. However, on the table was his last unfinished and somewhat prophetic manuscript for a piece called *Do You Believe In The Immortality of the Soul?* The music he was writing stopped at the line: 'Then he removed a dagger from his jacket and stabbed me through the heart.'

GOING OUT WITH A BOMB

In 1981, Maltese farmer Paul Gauci found what he thought was a large and heavy tin can in a field and decided to weld it to a pipe to make a mallet, as you do. Unfortunately for Mr. Gauci, his cylindrical tin was actually a German butterfly bomb left over from World War II, which went off as soon as he took his blowtorch to it, killing him and destroying most of his farmhouse.

FEET OF CLAY

Robin Putney from London committed suicide because he was convinced that his feet smelled too badly. Putney would sometimes spend entire days washing his feet, but had nevertheless convinced himself that people avoided him because of his foot odour. Unable to take it any longer, he leapt to his death from the roof of a multi-storey car park. Podophobia – the irrational fear of feet – is estimated to affect one person out of every thousand.

FIRE ONE ... FIRE TWO ... OH CRAP

HMS Trinidad was a Royal Navy submarine. In March 1942 she was escorting Arctic convoy PQ13 when she became involved in a running battle with German destroyers. Although she sank the destroyer Z26, one of her torpedoes had a faulty gyro, causing it to run in a perfect circle and hit HMS Trinidad, resulting in the deaths of 32 men.

FIRE ONE ... FIRE TWO ... OH CRAP ... AGAIN

USS *Tang* was an American submarine that had a distinguished record operating in the Pacific during World War II. She was credited with sinking 24 enemy ships, earning her captain, Richard O'Kane, the Congressional Medal of Honor. Unfortunately, the last torpedo she ever fired described a circular course and hit the *Tang* a devastating blow. Of the crew of 88, only five survived. These were picked up by a Japanese destroyer, which had earlier rescued survivors from ships the *Tang* had sunk previously. Not surprisingly, these men subjected the surviving crew from the *Tang* to a severe beating.

MAKE MINE 1,468,000 LITRES

In October 1814, an accident at the Maux & Co Brewery in Tottenham Court Road, London caused a vat of beer to rupture. A domino effect swept away several other vats, and a tidal wave of beer estimated at 1,468,000 burst out onto the streets. The foaming tsunami destroyed two neighbouring houses and seven people were drowned. Instead of coming to help, a vast crowd gathered with pots, pans, teapots, and bottles in the hope of getting a free drink. After the tragedy, the company's major concern was not compensating the victims' families but recovering the duty that had already been paid on the beer.

WIPE OUT

Worth Bingham was an heir to the Bingham newspaper dynasty, and despite having a playboy reputation, was also a fine journalist in his own right. In July 1966, he placed his surfboard horizontally across the backseats of his convertible and headed for the beaches of Nantucket. As he drove, one protruding end of the board hit a parked car, spinning the board around and killing Bingham instantly by crushing his neck.

GAME SHOW SLIP UP

Hong Kong pop star Wong Ka Kui was appearing on popular Japanese game show *Ucchan-nanchan no yarunara yaraneba* to promote his latest single in 1993. Taking part in the games, he slipped whilst crossing a wet platform, smashed his head and went into a coma. When even being played his own songs did not wake him, life support was switched off.

25 FEET TOO FAR

Sam Patch was an American daredevil known as the Yankee Leaper, who made his living diving off high platforms in front of crowds. This passed for entertainment in some parts of nineteenth century America. After failing to raise much money by jumping from 30m into the Genesee River in November 1829, he tried again the next week, but from a height of 38m. This drew a crowd of 8,000, who were able to watch him misjudge the fall, hitting the water at the wrong angle and breaking his neck. His body was eventually recovered, entombed in ice, the following March.

FATAL FIELD

Almost any sport can be dangerous. However, you would expect that one involving the chucking of possibly lethal weapons would engender a full-on respect for the health and safety aspects of track and field. Yet clearly health and safety went amiss at a Dusseldorf athletics event in August 2012. Dieter Strack, 74, was measuring a javelin throw when he was speared in the throat by another javelin thrown by an over-eager 15-year-old competitor.

DRIVEN TO DISTRACTION

We know that drinking and driving is a bad and often deadly idea, but how about driving whilst having sex? The death of Andrew Coronada in March 2011 probably puts the kibosh on anyone thinking that copulating whilst motoring is a goer. As his semi-clothed female passenger bounced up and down on his lap, Andrew lost control and crashed his car into a utility pole in San Antonio, killing him and leading to his passenger's hospitalization.

HALT, WHO GOES THERE?

Colonel David Marcus was an American-Jewish soldier who volunteered to serve in the nascent Israeli army in 1947, and who played a key role in breaking the siege of Jerusalem in 1948. One day before a UN-sponsored cease-fire, he and his men were billeted near Abu Ghosh. In the middle of the night, Marcus got up to relieve himself in a field. Because he was wrapped in a bedsheet, an 18-year-old sentry mistook him for an Arab, and shot him dead. With friends like that, who needs foes?

FOR WHOM THE TACO BELL TOLLS

Diane Durre, 49, was crushed to death when a gust of wind brought down a 23m Taco Bell sign onto the top of her truck, crushing her to death in North Platte, Nebraska. She and her husband had agreed to meet another couple directly under the sign at 12.30am on the fateful day in April 2009. Her husband escaped with only a broken finger.

WHAT A WHOPPING BIT OF BAD LUCK

Ariane Allen, 39, was parking her BMW at the corporate headquarters of Burger King in September 2011, when she hit an already parked SUV. Allen got out of her car to check the damage but left her vehicle in reverse gear with the driver's door open. Her BMW then reversed into her with fatal consequences.

WHOA, NOAH!

In the days before CGI, Hollywood had to try to do stuff for real for the sake of our entertainment. Often it went ridiculously and fatally wrong, possibly never more so than on the set of the 1928 epic Noah's Ark. During the filming of the Great Flood itself, the volume of water was so overwhelming that it washed away the extras – including a young John Wayne – killing three and resulting in one needing a leg amputated.

CROC ON PLANE!

Forget the awful film *Snakes on a Plane*, which could only kill you with boredom. Put a real crocodile on a plane and you have a deadly problem. This is exactly what happened in August 2010, when a passenger on an internal flight within the Democratic Republic of Congo smuggled a live crocodile onto the plane with the intention of selling it when he landed. When the croc got loose, it caused a panicked stampede by passengers, which skewed the L-410 Turbojet's centre of gravity, leading to a crash that killed 21.

BEDDING DOWN FOR ETERNITY

Several deaths in this book show the importance of choosing a good place to sleep off a hard night of partying. However, it staggers even my jaded palette to know that someone thought it would be a good idea to fall asleep in a bus lane. However, that is exactly what Craig Williams, 35, did in the early hours of July 30, 2012. After a night of heavy socializing, he took a bus to the Ocean Terminal in Edinburgh, disembarked and decided to bed down in the bus lane. In an incident that everyone but Mr. Williams saw coming, his sleeping body was later run over by a motorist who thought it safe to use the bus lane at 2am when there were no buses running.

BEWARE THE CASSOWARY

Given that the cassowary bird can run at speeds of 49km and each of its feet ends with three curved claws used by New Guinea tribesmen as spear points, you would think no one is stupid enough to pick a fight with one. However, when Philip McClean and his two brothers found a cassowary on their farm in Queensland in 1926, they decided to beat it to death with clubs. Big mistake. The bird knocked Philip to the ground and then kicked him in the neck, fatally severing his carotid artery.

TOP 10 RIDICULOUS DEATHS AT THEME PARKS – WE ARE NOT AMUSED

10. In 2011, a 34-year-old Tokyo resident fell 7.6m from a roller coaster at the Tokyo Dome City amusement park. The man was riding the Maihime – a roller coaster whose cars spin round as they roll along the track. According to reports, the safety bar of the car he was in did not click into position due to the size of the obese man's stomach and he was too embarrassed to point it out to the safety attendant.

9. If taking a ride at an amusement park is dangerous, so is working at one. In October 2010, a cleaner a Disneyland Paris was trapped under a boat when the It's A Small World Ride was accidentally turned on whilst he was cleaning it. The 53-year-old man was taken to hospital, where he later died.

8. If you have a weak heart, it is not a good idea to ride a roller coaster. This blindingly obvious bit of common sense was ignored by Ken Brown at an Ohio carnival in 1986. The 37-year-old refused to listen to his wife's warnings, telling her: 'I know my heart can handle it.' Famous last words given the shock of the ride led him to suffer a massive coronary.

7. If your job title is safety attendant and one of the things you are meant to check is that a roller coaster train is safely empty, it is an absurdly big foul-up not to notice that a passenger is trapped in a car. Yet in 1980, a worker at an amusement park in Missouri failed to spot a passenger unable to get out at the end of the ride. The train was sent to a service area with a low ceiling, jamming the trapped rider's head between his seat and a wooden beam, killing him.

6. Given that amusement parks can be deadly enough during the day when fully staffed, you would have to be a resounding idiot to think breaking into one after dark to use the rides was a good idea. Step forward Michael A. Rathgeber, who got into Asbury Park in New Jersey after hours, and proceeded to use one of its 19m slides. It was not a joy ride for Rathgeber, who managed to lacerate his liver on the way down and bled to death.

5. I am of the opinion that anything with an exclamation mark in its official title is always potentially a killer. Walt Disney World's Indiana Jones epic Stunt Spectacular! is based on the stunts from *Raiders of the Lost Ark* and involves a lot of pyrotechnics, so what could possibly go wrong? For 30-year-old stuntman Anislav Varbanov, what went wrong in August 2009 was a tumbling roll that led to a fatal head injury.

4. Lori Mason-Lorez, 40, was described by Californian authorities as 'larger than the average human being'. In 2002, the 132kg woman fatally fell out of the Perilous Plume Ride at Knott's Berry Farm amusement park. Due to her size, Mason-Lorez took the ride's 35m, 75-degree drop at nearly 80km without an adequately working safety harness.

3. Doing dumb things in Disneyland is just as likely to get you killed as it is in the outside world. In 1983, 18-year-old Philip Straughan of Albuquerque, New Mexico drowned in the Rivers of America segment of Disneyland Resort when he and a friend tried to row off Tom Sawyer's Island in a rubber boat they had stolen from a 'cast members only' area of the attraction.

2. In cartoons, if a character is run over, they usually just get up to suffer some other slapstick fate. Tragically for Walt Disney World worker, Javier Cruz, being dressed as Pluto did not help him. In 2004, he tripped over his costume's over-sized feet and fell fatally into the path of the Beauty and the Beast float in the Share a Dream Come True Parade.

1. Carousels look safe, just brightly painted wooden animals designed to be ridden by children as the carousel sedately rotates. Obese Spaniard Olinda Crespo might have saved her life if she remembered the 'designed for children' element. In 1984, she rode on a child's carousel in southern France. However, her overweight frame was too much for the wooden beast she was riding and it collapsed under her, causing her to fall from the carousel and break her neck.

GETTING THE BIRD

Alan Stacey was an Essex-born Formula 1 driver with a daredevil streak. However, it was not recklessness that got him killed during the Belgium Grand Prix in 1960, it was getting a bird in the face. Driving his Lotus at a speed of 193km/h, Stacey connected with a low-flying bird, causing him to lose control on a curve, smashing into first an embankment and then a 3m thick hedge.

IT'S RAINING CATS, DOGS AND ROCKETS

In December 2008, the Chinese military fired a silver iodide shell into an oncoming hailstorm threatening tobacco crops in Inner Mongolia, in the hopes of turning it into harmless rain. However, one of the shells failed to explode and hurtled down into the home and body of Wang Diange, killing him. When his family found Wang dead and their home ablaze, they blamed lightning. It was not until a piece of the rocket exploded as he was being cremated that the true story came to light.

TRAGIC TRASHING

Canadian estate agent Maria Pantazopoulos, 30, died when her 'trash the dress wedding shoot' went tragically wrong. Trashing the dress is a trend where the bride is photographed after the wedding ruining her bridal outfit. Don't ask me why, I'm a man. Pantazopoulos decided she wanted to be shot trashing the dress by swimming in it at Dorwin Falls in Quebec in August 2012. However, the large gown became heavy and began to drag her under. Photographer Louis Pagakis jumped in to try to save her, but it was too late. The waterlogged dress had already pulled her to a watery grave.

TIGER TEASER

Some suicides are not content with the tried and tested methods. No, they need something more dramatic as an exit. You certainly have to hand it to cleaner Nordin Montong. Walking into the white tiger enclosure at Singapore's zoo, banging a pail with a broom and puffing out your chest, inviting the tigers to eat you is dramatic. It is also incredibly stupid and painful. It took four minutes for two tigers to kill Nordin by inflicting more than 90 cuts and bites.

MAGICAL MORT VII

A misplaced belief in magic is often a recipe for death. It certainly led to the suicide of Rejoice Chishava, a 33-year-old charity worker from Harrogate, Yorkshire in 2007. Chishava was so afraid of not sending the money requested in chain letters from witchdoctors that she got into financial difficulties. When she was so in debt she could no longer keep up paying to keep the evil spirits away, she hung herself to escape from the fear of bad magic. The coroner at her inquest called the witchdoctors 'garbage'. Spot on, sir, spot on.

A DISH CLEARLY NOT FIT FOR THE GODS

Jaliya Karunasekera was preparing hundreds of portions of dried-fish curry for a religious ceremony at a temple in Kadulwela province, Sri Lanka in 2004 when he fell asleep on the job and tumbled into the huge bubbling cauldron. Despite attempts to pull him out, he died in the dish he was preparing.

NO FISHERMAN'S FRIEND

A Brazilian man, fishing with friends on a beach in Icapui in November 2012 when he caught a small sole. He then bet his friends that he could keep the wriggling creature between his teeth for a complete minute. Unfortunately he lost. The fish quickly slipped between his teeth and down his throat, choking him to death. Icapui police chief Carlos Alberta said: 'It was a silly thing to do, but he didn't deserve to die because of it.'

MAGICAL MORT VIII

Religious tensions between Buddhist and Muslim communities in southern Thailand were so strong in 2007 that many Buddhists sought magical Jatukan amulets to protect them from violence. When the Nakhon Si Thammarat temple announced it would be selling them, a crowd of more than 10,000 camped out to buy them. As the amulets went on sale, a stampede broke out, which ended up crushing a 50-year-old woman to death. Obviously she was not wearing a Jatukan amulet at the time.

BEN HURT

Back in the old days when Hollywood tried to make things look convincing by actually doing them, the makers of the 1925 version of Ben-Hur, MGM, decided to film a real chariot race in Rome. Unfortunately things turned out to be far too akin to the reality of historical chariot racing when the wheel of one of the chariots broke, sending its driver 9m into the air before crashing down to his death on a pile of wood. The stunt might have been convincing, but it was not used in the film.

EXTREME TREE HUGGING

Welsh computer engineer Kevin Kirkland, 44, drank seven pints of lager and a vodka and coke on a night out with a friend in December 2009. At the end of the evening, having said goodbye to his pal, he decided to strip naked, fashion a pair of handcuffs out of rope and tie himself to a tree. He also attached a cord to the base of his penis. He was found next morning, suffering from hypothermia and with his wrists bleeding where he had made desperate attempts to free himself. Despite being rushed to hospital, Kevin did not survive.

50 SHADES OF DEAD II

British motorsport mogul Robin Mortimer, 58, was found dead in the Belgium sex dungeon of the self-proclaimed 'most perverted dominatrix in Europe'. Found wearing a leather gimp mask, chain and ball-gag, Mortimer had paid Mistress Lucrezia (real name Ira Van Denderen) and Mistress Juno (Vicky Vanherle) £600 to abuse him. He died from choking on nitrous oxide, which he was using as an anaesthetic to be able to withstand the pain of Lucrezia's torments, which in the past had included sewing zips onto her willing male victims.

DYING FOR A PEE II

At some time, all of us have been desperate to pee. All of us have been tempted to go somewhere we should not for a bit of relief, but you have to be incredibly drunk or stupid to think climbing down off a train platform to urinate by the electric rail is a good idea. Zachary McKee, 27, had been drinking when he clambered onto the tracks of the Chicago subway to pee. He slipped and ended up on the third rail, electrocuting himself. Earlier he had tweeted a picture of a bar and the words 'All u can drink, play ball.' More like all you can drink, play dead.

DIGGING YOUR OWN GRAVE

If there was a world record for stupidity in trying to break world records, Sri Lankan Janaka Basnayake, 24, would be a strong contender. Enlisting the help of family and friends, he buried himself in a 3m deep trench sealed with wood and soil in March 2012. He had been hoping to obtain the world record longest time buried alive, having managed a personal best time of six hours previously in practice. Unfortunately for Janaka, there is no record for longest time buried alive before suffocating.

MURDER MOST FELINE

Chinese billionaire Long Liyuan, 49, was murdered by local official Huang Guang whilst the two men shared a dish of slow-boiled cat meat stew. Huang poisoned the cat hotpot with extracts of the herb *Gelsemium elegans*. A third man dining with the pair was poisoned, but did not die due to not eating much because the cat 'tasted more bitter than usual, despite us knowing it had been freshly killed'. Huang was later sentenced to death for the murder and for embezzling money from Long.

A REAL BLOODSUCKER

Somwathie De Silva, a 36-year-old woman from the Sri Lankan city of Negombo stabbed her partner to death in 2003 after he became reluctant to let her feed on his blood. Police said: 'The victim had gone along with her belief she was a vampire for months and regularly let her cut him and feed on his blood, but he had told friends she was too greedy and was not going to let her have so much.'

HUNG OUT TO DIE

A 38-year-old man from Bradford died when he fell into a clothes horse as he hung out his washing to dry. Brian Depledge asphyxiated after he tripped and toppled backwards into the rack, trapping his neck between his rungs in 2011. The coroner at his inquest described the death as an accident against all odds and that there was 'a greater chance of being killed by lightning or a meteorite' than by a clothes horse.

POLICE STING OPERATION

Sarath Bandara was a Sri Lankan policeman attached to a raid on a moonshine distilling operation being carried out in the jungle in 2003. However, as he and his colleagues approached the stills, they discovered that they had been booby-trapped with a wasp nest, releasing a swarm that stung Sarath to death and hospitalized eight other officers.

CATCHING A BUZZ

If there is such a thing as bad luck, Janette Duncan, 74, certainly had it. As she and her husband walked in the Essex village of Galleywood in 2011, a neighbour prodded a nest of wasps in his garden, causing them to swarm and attack the innocent couple walking past. The multiple stings suffered by Mrs. Duncan brought on a fatal heart attack. The person who stirred up the nest was unstung.

MOONSHINE MORTALITY

Just because you are illegally making vodka using potatoes and isopropyl alcohol – a solvent and cleaning fluid unsafe for human consumption – it does not mean you should neglect health and safety. Five Lithuanian men died at a blast at an illegal vodka factory in Boston, England in 2011, when they forgot that most basic of rules of chemistry – an open flame and alcohol have a somewhat fiery relationship. Blast survivor Rytas Gecas told an inquest that the dead men all regularly smoked whilst working, despite the room being filled with alcohol fumes, and that just before the blast he had seen a colleague light a cigarette.

GAMBLING WITH DEATH

There are probably worse places to run an illegal gambling den than a funeral parlour. However, death came a-knocking when police from Weliweriya in Sri Lanka busted a gaming session held at an undertaker's in 2003. One of the gamblers was so shocked at the raid that he suffered a fatal heart attack. Well, at least dropping dead there made it convenient for funeral arrangements.

KILLER KITE

Marcus Garwood, 27, was flying a kite with a 6m wingspan on Dunstable Downs, Bedfordshire in July 2011 when a gust of wind lifted him 15m into the air. Unfortunately for Garwood, what goes up must come down, and the wind and gravity then dashed him at high speed into the ground. A friend of Garwood said: 'It was a freak way to go, but at least he went out doing what he loved.'

TO HELL IN A HOVERCRAFT

New Zealander Dr Alastair Kenneth Senior died whilst demonstrating his home-made hovercraft on Muriwai Beach in August 2011. Dr Senior had made the machine from a kit and was attempting to drive it for the first time when one of its propellers sheared off and decapitated him. A local policeman said: 'It is sad to think he spent so much time making the thing that killed him.'

A RUBBISH WAY TO GO III

Doing your bit for the environment should not be deadly, but for poor Sheila Decoster of Ohio, a simple trip to the recycling bin in her garden ended rather badly one night in 2011. Realizing she had accidentally put something into the 65-gallon bin, Sheila tried to fish it out, but ended up falling into it. She was later discovered upside down in the bin, her legs sticking out, by her husband. An inquest learned she had died from positional asphyxia in which the placement of her body amongst the recycling prevented her lungs from filling with air.

TAKING METHOD ACTING TOO FAR

Brazilian actor Tiago Klimeck took playing the role of Judas in an Easter 2012 *Passion* play just a bit too far when he accidentally hanged himself during the scene of Judas Iscariot's suicide. A badly tied knot meant that Klimeck played out the death for real, as it took more than four minutes before any of his fellow actors realized something was wrong.

CUT!

Some actors are perfectionists –and perfection always comes at a price. Former stunt performer turned Bollywood superstar Jayan always insisted on doing his own stunts. This backfired during the filming of his 1980 action movie *Kolilakkam* (*Shockwave*). Even though the director was happy with the first take of Jayan climbing aboard a flying helicopter from a speeding motorbike, the star insisted on three retakes. On the last one, the helicopter dipped, crushing Jayan, who was hanging onto its landing skids.

MAGICAL MORT IX

Sri Lankan sorcerer Kurulu Kumara died whilst performing a ritual to harness spirits into an amulet for a client. The patron deity of sorcery that Kurulu was calling upon required sacrifices of both alcohol and coconuts. This proved unfortunate, as the somewhat tipsy sorcerer tripped whilst stamping on a coconut and fell onto a trident he had been wielding as part of the ceremony. It never went that way for Harry Potter.

JUST NOT CRICKET

Cricket is a game that gets even an Englishman's blood boiling, but for poor Mohamed Abusali Pasreen who was umpiring at a cricket match in Kahapathwala, Sri Lanka in 2004, things got well and truly out of hand. Pasreen got into an argument with one of the players and was beaten around the head with a cricket stump. The blows proved fatal, proving once again that the referee's job is never a happy one.

HOWZAT!

If murder does not show how seriously Sri Lankans take their cricket, the following deaths surely do. D.W. Sirisensa, 60, and his son, 27, were watching the 2003 World Cup semi-final between Sri Lanka and Australia when the loss of Sanath Jayasuriya's wicket caused both to suffer fatal heart attacks simultaneously. The Matara City coroner recorded that the intense excitement and disappointment of the match had played a significant role in triggering the family tragedy.

THE DANGERS OF BAGGING A BARGAIN

Borko Novak was a Croatian pensioner with an eye for value. Having spent more than 15 minutes haggling a prostitute down to just $6.50 for oral sex, he was so excited at the prospect of getting his bargain that he suffered a heart attack on his way back to her place of business. A neighbour of Mr Novak told a local newspaper that the manner of his death was not unexpected, saying: 'He was the sort who would look for sex with his last breath.'

SUGAR RUSH

Two stowaways from the Dominican Republic made a fatal error when they hid aboard the freighter *Santiago* in 1982. They chose to hide amongst 2,000 tonnes of sugar that shifted in high seas, coating them in a crushing and suffocating amount of the sweet stuff.

BELOW PAR V

Lieutenant George M. Prior played a round of golf at the Army-Navy Country Club in Arlington, Virginia in 1982 and began to feel ill before he got to the 18th hole. Four days later he was dead after having a severe allergic reaction to Daconcil – a fungicide used on the golf course. Medical authorities determined that Prior's habit of carrying a tee in the mouth whilst playing had introduced the Daconcil into his system.

UNLUCKY HORSESHOE

There is a long-established folklore tradition that horseshoes are meant to bring luck. That certainly was not the case for one veterinarian. Erica Marshall was operating a hyperbaric chamber at the Kesmarc Equine Rehabilitation centre in Florida in 2012 when a horse kicked the side of the chamber with its metal shoes. The resulting spark in an oxygen-rich, enclosed space led to a massive explosion that killed Marshall.

IT'S IN THE BAG

People will go to ridiculous lengths to get high. Especially dumb teenagers. Jennifer Jones, 15, used a plastic bag to collect Freon™ gas from the air conditioning unit of her mother's Palm Beach house and then inhaled it. Unsurprisingly, death ensued.

YOUR SIGNATURE OR YOUR BRAINS, SIR

The conversation with your boss when he refuses to sign your leave form might make you angry, but would you shoot him over it? Sri Lankan police constable Sitendra Senaratne did, killing Sub Inspector R.S.M. Rodrigo at the Pamunugama police station when he was refused leave in September 2004. Note to any bosses: make sure your employee is unarmed before kyboshing their holiday plans.

BOOZE BATH BAD FOR HEALTH

Panicking about the prospect of dying is often an action that makes it more likely you will die sooner rather than later. During the SARS outbreak in 2004, a rumour spread in Taiwan that bathing in ethanol could prevent the infection. This led a 45-year-old woman to take a 12-hour soak in ethanol, during which time she absorbed so much alcohol through her skin that her blood alcohol content was 1.35 per cent. A blood alcohol content of 0.5 per cent is enough to poison and often kill. She may not have caught SARS, but that was only because she was already dead.

CELL HELL I

To be honest, I am surprised this book is not full of ridiculous deaths related to mobile phones. Given how much I have wanted to kill people for talking loudly on them or having irritating ringtones, they should be the cause of a lot more blood. However, poor Xiao Jinpeng, 22, from Gansu in China, is one of the few who can truly be said to have been killed by their cell phone. Whilst working as a welder in August 2012, the battery in his phone exploded whilst it was in his shirt pocket, breaking his ribs and sending shrapnel straight into his heart. He had been using a battery not licensed by the phone's manufacturer, which was unable to withstand the heat of his workplace, leading to the lithium in the battery becoming a volatile explosive.

MAGICAL MORT X

When it comes to the death of some witchdoctors, you cannot help but think they got what was coming to them for exploiting vulnerable people's belief in their alleged magical powers. A ridiculous case in point is the death of self-styled sorcerer Marotrao Kolhe. The 65-year-old fraud from India was murdered by Sushila Madavai and her husband when his claims to be able to heal did not help resolve Sushila's mental health problems. Funny, that. Roping in another disappointed client of Kolhe as their driver, they kidnapped him from his home and beat him to death in October 2011.

MAGICAL MORT XI

There can be no smugness nor thinking that death due to a perceived failing of magical powers is not a first world problem. In 2010, Tanya Nelson from North Carolina was sentenced to death for the murder of a fortune teller and her daughter when the alleged psychic's love spell failed to bring Nelson's ex-lover back to her. When Ha 'Jade' Smith then told Nelson to get over it, Nelson took it very badly, and stabbed Smith and her 19-year-old daughter to death before covering them both in a gallon of white paint.

DEATH SUCKS

Veteran airline mechanic Donald Gene Buchanan, 64, was sucked into the engines of a Boeing 737 as passengers boarded it ahead of a flight at El Paso airport in 2006. Though he had years of experience of safety around planes, investigating authorities ruled that Buchanan got plain careless and walked too close to the engine.

DEATH DOGGY STYLE

Human sexuality is insanely diverse. There are people into everything and people who are into having everything in them. Just how diverse and deadly sexual preferences can be was brought into the public spotlight in Ireland in 2011, when Seán McDonnell found himself in court after he arranged for a 43-year-old woman to have sex with his Alsatian. Unluckily for the mother of four, her first bestiality experience turned out to be her last experience of anything as she had an extreme allergic reaction to the dog's semen and died from a heart attack brought on by anaphylactic shock.

DO YOU FEEL LUCKY, PUG?

As any newspaper editor will tell you, dog bites man is not a story. However, stray dog bites cop and three people die because of police overreaction is a story. The incident happened in Haputale, Sri Lanka in 2004. When a policeman was bitten by a stray dog in the street, he and a colleague opened fire on the animal. Their attempt at self-defence and summary canine justice went awry, just like their shooting. Letting off a storm of automatic gunfire, they managed to kill a passing woman and critically injured three other bystanders. The dog ran off and lived to bite another day.

UNEXPECTED COCK SHOCK PROVES DEADLY

Shock kills, but some people bring it on themselves by either being too thick to see the obvious or a little too ridiculous about what they find shocking. Mr. H. Reiner, a 55-year-old truck driver from Germany, died in a brothel in Halle in August 2010 when he discovered that the prostitute he was about to have sex with, called Priya, was a transsexual. According to the investigating medical authorities, Reiner's death was due to a combination of 'excessive use of Viagra combined with extreme surprise'.

CELL HELL II

Indian man Gopal Gujjar, 23, was found dead in a forest near the village of Bandha in Rajasthan in August 2010. His body had burns on his left ear, neck and shoulders. The shattered remains of his mobile phone were found scattered around his electrocuted corpse. Indian medical authorities believe that Gopal's cell phone was hit by lightning whilst he was talking on it, causing it to explode and kill him.

AN ANSWER TO PAUL McCARTNEY

A Namibian couple seem to have taken The Beatles' song "Why Don't We Do It In The Road?" a little too literally. In 2003, the pair from Brakwater were hit by a truck as they had sex in the middle of the highway. Subsequent post-mortems showed, somewhat unsurprisingly, that both of them had exceptionally high levels of alcohol in their blood at the time of death. There you go, Mr McCartney, that's exactly why you shouldn't do it in the road.

CHOCOLATE BOMB

The Chocolate Mountain Bombing Range in Arizona sounds non-threatening and probably quite inviting to chocolate addicts. Maybe this explains why a motorcyclist decided to ride into what was clearly a restricted Marine Corps bombing range in May 1990. Whilst the fact that pilots were not using it for practice at the time was a plus on the staying alive side, running over an undetonated bomb and the subsequent blast was not.

ELECTRIC WEED I

It is easy to understand why farming can often be deadly – all those cows and industrial machines – but Doug Sother and Tina McGarvey probably thought a bit of indoor marijuana farming was fairly safe to undertake in their Florida home in 2009. However, whilst the pair tried to hook up growing lights in their basement, Sother slipped, brought down wires and managed to electrocute both of them. There is a lesson somewhere, possibly: Do not smoke pot and do DIY.

ELECTRIC WEED II

The high cost of electricity needed to power Adelbert Joncker's marijuana
nursery in September 2012, led him to dig a tunnel under the foundations
of his home and under a neighbour's house in an attempt to steal some
juice. Joncker may have had weed farming and tunnelling skills, but
he was woeful when it came to DIY electrical engineering and ended
up electrocuting himself in the crawlspace he had created under his
neighbour's living room.

DEATH CHARGE I

The original charge of the Light Brigade during the Crimean War in 1854
killed 118 British cavalrymen due to stupidity. When Hollywood recreated
it with Errol Flynn in 1936 for the film *Charge of the Light Brigade*, it killed
only one stuntman. Some people would see this as an improvement, but
the point was probably lost on the poor fellow who fell from his trip-
wired horse and onto the discarded prop of a broken sword unluckily
wedged upright.

DEATH CHARGE II

It seems as if there is nothing Hollywood likes more than a sequel. Jack
Budlong was a polo player who was appearing as a stunt extra in the
1941 Errol Flynn western *They Died With Their Boots On* just for the fun of
it. However, it was nothing like fun when he purposefully fell from his
horse during a charge and landed on the blade of a sword that had got
wedged between two rocks during earlier filming. The sabre went into his
abdomen and whilst Budlong was rushed from the location at Calabasas to
a Los Angeles hospital, he died within hours.

REPTILIAN BOOK WORM

Sri Lanka is clearly not a place for bibliophiles. While the most that libraries
might throw at you is dust, spiders and a passive-aggressive librarian, events
at the National Library in Colombo led to the death of one of its browsers in
1990. When picking a book off a shelf, she was bitten by a snake and suffered
heart failure brought on by the shock of her surprise encounter.

SWIFT JUSTICE

In 1991, 3,000 paratroopers mutinied in the Zairian city of Kinshasa, going on a vile orgy of rape and pillage. One of the looting soldiers, Julius Kongo, got his just deserts very quickly when he broke into a car showroom, intent on stealing a top of the range Mercedes. Having obtained the keys at gunpoint, Kongo got behind the wheel and sped away via the showroom's window and straight into the wall of a building opposite, totalling both the Mercedes and himself.

SEX PEST-LE

According to the defence at her trial, the last straw for Chandni de Silva was when her husband announced he wanted to have sex with her sister. Jurors at her 1992 trial in Colombo, Sri Lanka, heard this was the provocation for throwing a pestle at him across the kitchen, which struck him in the forehead, bringing instant death. However, de Silva also admitted her husband had infuriated her by banning her from watching her favourite soap opera.

WHAT A DOPE

Being caught by the cops with a large amount of cocaine on you is enough to make all but the coolest of crooks a bit jumpy. When police flashed their lights to pull over Grover Baker in London in 1992, he panicked and swallowed a 5cm plastic-wrapped ball of cocaine. Having survived being stopped and searched without arrest, Grover tempted fate by boasting to his friends about the fast one he had pulled. It was at this moment the plastic burst and Grover died from an overdose of 20 times the amount of cocaine usually needed to kill someone.

NO ESCAPE

Despite what you have seen in dozens of Hollywood films, escaping from a castle by tying bed sheets together is not a good idea. Gruffydd ap Llywelyn was a Welsh prince held prisoner in the Tower of London by King Henry III. Whilst imprisoned in the White Tower in 1244, Gruffydd attempted to escape on a rope made from clothes and bed linen. Being a large bloke, his weight was too much for his improvised escape route. It broke, plunging Gruffydd more than 27m to his death.

WAR AGAINST TWO WHEELS

Vietnamese farmer Tran Van Vuon from Ben Tre Province was charged for murder in 1988. He had dug huge holes in the road and then camouflaged them in the hope that passing motorcyclists and cyclists would ride across and fall into them. The war veteran, who had previous experience of making deadly traps, managed to snare two cyclists and one motorcyclist before being caught by the police. When asked to explain why, he claimed it was revenge for being hit by a cyclist two years before and because he did not like the motorbikes' noisiness.

BOOZING THE STAIRWAY TO HEAVEN

Stair lifts are designed to make life easier for the elderly and disabled, but they are not the speediest of contraptions, which is possibly why Shirley Perkins, 55, decided to try climbing the stairs even after having one fitted. Despite suffering from breathing problems, she occasionally had the strength to make her way up the stairs without relying on the lift. However, on June 27, 2012, relying on her own two legs proved a fatal error for Mrs. Perkins, as did getting drunk before going upstairs to bed. Inebriated and more than four times over the drink drive limit, Mrs. Perkins toppled at the top of the stairs, fell backwards and jammed her head between the metal rung of the lift's seat and the wall.

THE SHORT FUSE OF THE LAW

It is never a good idea to offer a cocky reply when a policeman asks you a question. They always have a ready answer – jail. In Sri Lanka there are even better reasons for not provoking a cop. Sunil Gratien was walking home in 2002, slightly the worse for several drinks. Stopped by a motorcycle cop who asked him why he was swaying, Sunil replied: 'I've got the money to drink, you are just jealous because you cannot afford to get drunk on a policeman's wages.' The reply so infuriated the policeman he threw his helmet at Sunil, incurably cracking his head open.

TOP 10 RIDICULOUS SPORT-RELATED DEATHS

10. Possibly the worst sportsman in history was Cleomedes of Astypalaea. He killed Iccus of Epidaurus during a boxing match at the 492 BCE Olympic Games by punching him in an area below the belt. Cleomedes was so angry at being disqualified and fined for his foul play, he pulled down a school containing dozens of children, killing them. Not surprisingly, he was then stoned by the locals.

9. Young Russian champion diver Sergo Shalibashvili, 21, died whilst competing in the World University Games held in Edmonton, Alberta in 1983. Whilst attempting a tricky reverse three-and-a-half somersault in the tuck position, he struck his head on the board and plunged into the pool. He went into a coma and died seven days later. The total score he received for the dive was 0.0.

8. Blackpool FC centre-forward Frank Wilson dropped dead on the day he was to be transferred to Aston Villa. The coroner recorded his death as being due to: 'Maniacal exhaustion and football.' Personally, I would blame the prospect of playing for Villa.

7. Barcelona defender Julio César Benítez was so popular that a few days before a grudge match against Real Madrid in 1968, he was being treated like royalty and eating for free in a popular local restaurant. This was his undoing. He was served spoiled shellfish and died two days later of food poisoning. More than 150,000 fans attended his funeral. His last words were: 'Come on, friends, let's beat Madrid 2–0!' The game was a 1–1 draw.

6. There is a horrible rumour that most footballers are stupid. Trying to prove this true was Lazio midfielder Luciano Re Cecconi AKA 'the blond angel'. The 23-year-old idiot was shot dead in 1977 whilst donning a mask and pretending to rob a friend's jewellery shop as a practical joke.

5. Jim Creighton was a baseball player from the game's golden amateur era. In 1862, Creighton died when he swung the bat a bit too hard and ruptured his bladder. That sure is some swing!

4. One baseball player who died through swinging his fists instead of a bat was Len Koenecke. Sent home from a Buffalo Bisons road trip in 1934 due to drinking, he chartered a flight home, but became drunk, argued with the pilot and tried to fly the plane. This led to the pilot and a fellow passenger having to beat him into unconsciousness with fire extinguishers. After an emergency landing on a racetrack, it was discovered Koenecke was dead.

3. Belgian racing car driver Camille Jenatzy was the first man to break the 100kp/h barrier in his electric car La Jamais Contente (The Never Satisfied). He was known as the 'Red Devil' due to his ginger beard and daredevil ways, and you might expect Jenatzy to have gone out in a speeding rush of glory. Oh no. He died in 1913 from the absurdly idiotic practice of crouching behind a bush whilst friends are out hunting and making duck noises. He died from multiple gunshot wounds en route to the hospital.

2. Italian football coach Franco Scoglio was known as 'The Professor' for his comments such as: 'There are 21 ways to take a corner kick'. In 2005 he was on live TV, arguing with his former club's president Enrico Preziosi when the curt exchanges became too much and Scoglio slumped in his chair, having succumbed to a fatal heart attack. Journalist Domenico Ravenna, who was sitting next to Scoglio said: 'I thought he was messing around, pretending to go to sleep while Preziosi was talking. But he was dying.'

1. Dick Wertheim was an American tennis linesman at a match during the 1983 US Open officiating at the centre line when Stefan Edberg accidentally sent his serve straight to his groin. Ouch! The ball in the balls knocked him backwards, causing Wertheim to fall out of his chair and hit his head on the hardcourt surface. Despite being rushed to hospital, Wertheim never recovered consciousness, permanently out of the game of life.

LA PETITE MORT

A 30-year-old British nanny was discovered dead in October 2009, naked from the waist down, a sex toy beside her and pornographic material playing on her laptop. Her employer and a neighbour found her when she did not turn up for work. The pathologist investigating her death told an inquest that she died from sudden heart arrhythmia, probably brought on by a state of arousal. The coroner agreed, saying: 'It is not always possible to determine an exact cause of death, but it is likely that her activity before death contributed towards it.'

IT IS ROCKET SCIENCE

An awful lot of the absurd deaths in this book have come to pass due to stupendous levels of stupidity, but just sometimes, death is rocket science. It certainly was for David Bagley, an unemployed rocket scientist who was so unhappy at being out of work and spending his daylight hours volunteering at a charity shop in Hartlepool, that he used the skills honed during decades of work in aerospace to rig a sophisticated homemade bomb. He then paid for his own funeral, wrote a note apologizing to the police for any trouble caused, drove to an abandoned industrial site in Old Cemetery Road and blew himself up in his Nissan Micra.

BUDDHIST BICYCLE BUTCHERY

When I think of Buddhist monks, the first words that come to mind are not dangerous drunks and violent, unstable killers – but that is a weakness in my understanding of the world. Sri Lankan monk Haggale Vajira Thera downed two bottles of arrack (a drink made from fermented coconut sap) and began to attack his fellow monks in 2002 because they wouldn't let him have any more money to buy liquor. As he was throttling the chief monk and could not be prised away, one of the other monks began to beat him with a bicycle. Haggale released his grip only after receiving a fatal crack on the head with the bike.

TERMINAL TICKLING

A friendly tickling game led to tragedy for aspiring model LaShawna
Threatt. Celebrating her 30th birthday in May 2011, one of her friends,
Cierra Williams, was tickling Threatt when both women then leant on the
glass window of a ninth floor hotel room. The window shattered and a
pressure difference pulled both women outside. Williams survived the fall,
but regrettably Threatt did not.

TROLLEY DASHED

A freak gust of wind caught the shopping trolley of Emily Jordan, 43,
whilst she was unloading bags from her supermarket shop in Hull in
1995. The trolley, complete with her young son in it, shot across the car
park before smashing into the disability scooter of 82-year-old Margaret
Horrigan. Although both Mrs. Horrigan and Jordan Jr were uninjured,
Emily Jordan became so panicked that she began to hyperventilate and
suffered a heart attack.

CANNON BALLS-UP

Want to avoid death? Avoid being fired out of cannons. Matt Cranch had
been working as a human cannonball for only five weeks in April 2011,
when his fifth attempt at the daredevil stunt proved his last. After he was
fired 12m in the air during the show in Kent, the safety net meant to catch
him collapsed. A friend of Cranch said he had been hugely excited at his
new career and had bought 'his own safety helmet and cape.' Shame he did
not also buy his own safety net, too.

ROCKETS TO THE CRYPT

Carnival is a big deal in Brazil; so are fireworks. In February 2011, a crowd dancing behind a sound system truck in Bandeira do Sul, north of Rio de Janeiro thought the party atmosphere called for fireworks, and decided to shoot off dozens of rockets. Lacking the type of foresight someone not partying their heads away might have possessed, they fired them directly below the town's overhead electrical supply cable, bringing it down and electrocuting 17 of them.

GUTTED

John Gale, 29, stole $350 worth of hunting knives from a store in Atlanta in 1996. Fleeing the scene pursued by security guards, he shinned up a fence, only to become unbalanced. He fell forwards and down, landing on the knives he had concealed in his pockets, slashing open his femoral artery and stomach. He died from loss of blood before he reached the hospital.

O, CANADA

Downing beers in a pub's garden whilst looking out across the river to Canadian parliament – what could be more patriotic on Canada Day? When Martin Jensen had enjoyed a few beers and could not face queuing for the toilet, he decided to relieve himself into the Ottawa River whilst singing the Canadian national anthem – despite the howls of protest from other drinkers. He had just reached the line: 'The True North strong and free!' when he fell off the bluff he was standing on, tumbling first onto a concrete post and then into a watery grave. That's patriotism for you.

THE TORCH SHALL SET YOU FREE

Irina Polzin, 65, used the rail tracks in Khabarovsk, Siberia as a less snow-bound shortcut between her home and the local shop. However, she slipped and fell against a fence. Despite having six decades of experience in -30°C, she was not wearing gloves and so her flesh fused to the metal and she could not pull herself free. She remained stuck for almost an hour till her screams finally attracted help. When she saw the oxyacetylene torch rescuers were intending to use to cut the fence, she became convinced they were going to use it to amputate her hands and suffered a heart attack.

THE LION EATS TONIGHT

I do not know why countries spend billions of wasted dollars on border patrols and high-tech surveillance of known crossing points, because the solution is obvious – lions! Lions and a side helping of leopards. In 1996, rangers in South Africa's Kruger National Park found Wilson Nhamussua in a tree. The illegal immigrant from Mozambique had crossed over the border during the night through the game reserve with three other friends. However, he was the only survivor as his companions had been attacked and eaten by lions, the only remaining trace of them being their trainers.

It is a common problem in the park, but when I spoke to one of the rangers he was not too worried about the dozens of deaths of illegal immigrants each year caused by lions and leopards. 'They are bloody fools. I'm not bothered by what happens to them. I am just annoyed because they have caused the big cats to get a taste for human flesh. The cats are lazy animals and know it is much easier to catch a person than an impala.' Oh well, it is a change from the usual line about immigrants coming over here and taking our jobs, I suppose.

WELL, WELL, WELL ...

Riding any vehicle whilst drunk can be deadly, even the humble bike. In 2002, W. Somachandra, 44, rode home to Minuwangoda, Sri Lanka on his bike after a heavy drinking session. In his alcohol haze, he decided to take a shortcut down an unlit lane and tumbled straight down a 18m well, where his body was discovered the next morning.

THE COSMIC JOKER STRIKES AGAIN I

Lena Guilbert Brown Ford was the lyricist for the hit World War I song "Keep The Home Fires Burning". It seems the Cosmic Joker may have been having a laugh given that Ford died in a fire when her London home was bombed in 1918.

DEATH GETS A TICKET

Most suicides would like to think people would notice if they died. Unfortunately for Rochelle Cremona-Simmons, 47, when she took her life in the parking lot of the University of New Mexico in 2010, no one did for a week. Her corpse was clearly visible in the SUV, but life went on regardless around it, even for the parking attendants who ticketed the vehicle three times.

ANGEL OF DEATH

A cast-iron statue that fell off a truck on an Australian highway, turned from a smiling cherub to the angel of death for one motorist in December 2012. Helena Curzon was a passenger in a car that could not avoid the angelic hazard, struck it and then veered across the highway and into the path of two cars coming in the opposite direction. Sometimes gods and angels have no mercy.

MAMMARY MORT

German reality TV star Carolin 'Sexy Cora' Berger died at the age of 23, after her sixth breast enlargement operation in just 18 months. Berger kept having her breasts boosted to try to keep herself in the publicity spotlight. Her last operation was planned to take her from 34F to 34G and the weight of each of her silicone boobs from 510g to 794g. Unfortunately, Berger suffered two cardiac arrests during the ridiculously unnecessary operation and died in a coma in January 2011.

THROUGH A GLASS DEATHLY
It is not just scissors you should not run with. Northern Illinois University student John Frenzel, 21, bled to death in 1987 after he fell whilst running across his lawn. He tripped and fell onto the beer glasses he had in his trouser pockets. Unsurprisingly, they shattered and the resulting shards of glass severed his femoral artery.

FAKE DEATH LEADS TO REAL TRAGEDY
Udayakantha Jayathilake and his wife took out a large life policy with an English company and then staged his death in a fake robbery that left a burnt-out car and unrecognizable corpse in Habarana, Sri Lanka in 2002. They may well have got away with their crime if they had not used a female body in the wreck – a small fact that took four months to emerge. When it did, the police swooped in and arrested a very much alive Mr. Jayathilake and his wife. However, when he appeared in court, the shock of seeing her son whom she had believed dead for months, caused his mother to die from a heart attack.

DISINFECTANT – KILLS ALL KNOWN POETS, DEAD
American poet Vachel Lindsay grew up with a fear of germs thanks to his father, who was a doctor. As his longstanding depression worsened during the last few months of his life in 1931, he became convinced that germs were the root of all his problems – from his writer's block to the non-existent venereal disease he thought his wife was trying to give him. On the final night of his life, he took all the newspaper clippings and accolades his career had produced, piled them up and sat on them, before drinking a mug of Lysol disinfectant. He then spent his last moments running around his home screaming: 'The germs. I got them before they got me! Let them try to explain this, if they can!'

DEMON CORE I

The Manhattan Project was codename for the development of the atomic bombs dropped on Hiroshima and Nagasaki, which claimed the lives of 150,000 in two instances of godlike fire and then several hundred thousand more from radiation-induced disease. The pioneering work on the project was undertaken at the Los Alamos laboratory, where scientists had access to a 6.3kg sphere of plutonium for testing. At Los Alamos on August 21, 1945, scientist Harry K. Daghlian Jr made a mistake whilst stacking tungsten carbide bricks around the core. He dropped one onto the plutonium death ball and caused it to go critical. Daghlian quickly removed the brick, but he had already set off a self-sustaining chain reaction and he died 25 days later from receiving the fatal dose of radiation that went it. After this, his colleagues began to call the plutonium ball 'the demon core'.

DEMON CORE II

On May 21, 1946, Canadian physicist Louis Slotin was performing a test on the demon core known as 'tickling the dragon's tail'. However, he tickled too much when he dropped one part of a beryllium sphere onto another, the result of which was certainly critical for him. Witnesses observed 'a blue glow' and felt a 'wave of heat' as Slotin collapsed. He was rushed to hospital, but died nine days later of massive organ failure. After Slotin's accident, hands-on criticality experiments with the demon core were stopped and remote-control machines were designed by Dr Schreiber – one of the witnesses to the blast Slotin created – to perform such experiments with all personnel at least a quarter of a mile away.

WHAT'S THE USE OF WORRYING?

In a touch of irony that is impossible to overlook, Felix Lloyd Powell, writer of the music to the most optimistic song of all time – "Pack Up Your Troubles In Your Old Kit Bag" – shot himself in 1942. Clearly he could not manage to take the advice offered in the lyrics written by his brother George. They go: 'What's the use of worrying?/It never was worth while, so/Pack up your troubles in your old kit-bag/And smile, smile, smile.'

LAST OF THE NAPOLEONS

The last direct living male descendant of Napoleon Bonaparte was Jérôme Napoleon Charles Bonaparte. An American citizen, Mr. Bonaparte died in New York in 1945. The mighty Bonaparte line ended with something of a whimper as he died whilst walking his wife's dog in Central Park, tripping over its leash and breaking his neck.

A RIGHT ROYAL NIL BY MOUTH

King Charles VII of France died in 1461 from a combination of a mouth abscess and extreme paranoia. The physical pain of the abscess convinced him that everyone around him was trying to poison him on behalf of his eldest son and heir Louis, so he began to refuse all food and drink. He was already in ill health, and the self-imposed starvation killed him within a week.

SICK TO THE DEATH

Margaret, known as the Maid of Norway, became rightful heir to the Scottish throne in 1286 when her grandfather King Alexander III died (check out his own entry on page 38). However, it was not until 1290 that disputes over her authority were settled and she left Norway to travel to Scotland. She never made it to her kingdom, becoming so exhausted from severe sea sickness during the voyage that her boat stopped at Orkney, where she was carried ashore to die.

WHAT A PEACH

History tells many lies about King John of England and he was certainly not the 'bad king' portrayed in numerous Robin Hood myths. Whilst ascertaining his exact cause of death in 1216 still provides work for historians, it is clear that he became ill after a stay at an abbey near King's Lynn, Norfolk (I'm not surprised; King's Lynn is a festering hell-hole to this day). Many popular contemporary accounts suggest the reason for his illness and death nine days later was 'a surfeit of peaches and new beer', bringing a royal attack of dysentery.

HISTORIANS SLUG IT OUT

History is not static. In fact, it succumbs to fashion. When we wrote the first 1001 *Ridiculous Ways To Die*, many historians seemed to believe the Babylonian Talmud account of the death of Roman Emperor Titus. The history books we consulted all repeated that he died from an insect which climbed into his nose and began a several-year feast on his brain before eventually killing him in 81 CE. Today, the historical position has changed. Most historians now claim Titus died from being fed a poisonous sea slug by his brother Domitian – whose first act on becoming Emperor himself after his brother's death was to announce that Titus was now to be considered a god. Either way, not a good way to go.

THE SWORD IS MIGHTIER THAN THE POISON

King Mithridates VI ruled Persia from 113 BCE till his violent but absurd death in 63 BCE. Defeated in battle and facing capture from Rome, the king tried to take his own life with poison. However, he had built such a strong resistance to it across his reign by ingesting small amounts as an aid to preventing his assassination, it had no effect on him, despite the fact that the same poison had just killed two of his daughters. Unfazed by being able to commit suicide the standard royal way, Mithridates then ordered his Gaul bodyguard Bituitus to run him through with a sword.

COCONUT SHY TURNS DEADLY

When police moved in to help officials of the central Kandy market in Sri Lanka throw out illegal vendors who did not have market licences in 1992, one drunken street hawker took great offence and began to throw the fruit he was selling at those evicting him. Alas, his aim with a coconut proved a little too true and forceful, striking cop Jothiratna Dharmadasa in the head, killing him.

SMART, BUT NO COMMON SENSE

Like many pioneering scientists of her time, Marie Curie did not pay too much attention to safety when exploring new frontiers. To put it frankly, she was a genius but lacked the common sense to be cautious when dealing with the unknown. After a lifetime of carrying test tubes with radioactive isotopes in her pockets, and storing radioactive substances in her desk drawer, she died from cancer caused by radiation exposure in 1934. Her papers, including her cookbook, are so radioactive they have to be stored in lead containers and can be handled only by those wearing heavy-duty protective clothing.

FATAL FEATHER

There are several differing accounts of the death of Roman Emperor Claudius in 54 CE, but one thing many of them agree on is that he died as a result of a feather. Whilst some contemporary accounts claim his doctor poisoned him with a feather, others – which have the ring of truth – suggest that Claudius accidentally choked to death when his physician used a feather in his throat to try to make him vomit out a poisoned mushroom that had been fed to him by his wife Agrippina.

IN THE BAG

Downton Abbey has become a huge international hit, but it is hardly historically accurate. For a start, it suggests that many English aristocrats led productive lives. Poppycock. Most English aristocrats led lives and ridiculous deaths like Frederick Robinson, the 2nd Marquess of Ripon. He dropped dead in 1923 at the age of 71 after over-exertion from shooting 52 grouse in one morning on Dallowgill Moor, Yorkshire. His death was entirely fitting, as the only remarkable thing about the Marquess was that he held the greatest recorded lifetime bag of birds shot – 556,000, including 241,000 pheasants.

A RIGHT ROYAL LATHER

Think it is only ancient kings that die ridiculous deaths? Oh no, royalty has been carrying on the tradition of shuffling off the mortal coil with grand ridiculousness into more modern times. King Haakon VII of Norway slipped on the soap in his marble bath, fell and broke his thigh. Physicians claim that it was this fall which led directly to the decline in the king's health and eventual death in 1957.

HOLY SHIT I

The Rev. Bobby Parker met his maker sooner than expected in 2005 whilst performing a baptism at his church in Texas. Standing waist-high in water, Parker pulled on his corded microphone and managed to fill the pool with enough volts to end his life. Ironically, the last prayer he had said with his congregation ended with the line: 'Surprise me, God.' The woman he was baptizing in the pool at the time was miraculously unharmed.

HOLY SHIT II

Whilst lightning might not like striking twice, the Grim Reaper does not care if he is seen pulling the same move for a second time. In 2009 at another Texas church, the Rev. Abel Jordan was standing waist-high in a baptismal pool when he reached out to adjust a microphone sat on the edge of the pool, thereby giving himself a fatal shock. According to one of the congregation: 'It was a real tragedy. Just an hour before he died he was telling me that we all have to be ready for the Lord, that we can get the call home anytime.'

THE FINAL WHISTLE

The Army Cup football final replay held at Aldershot in 1948 was the scene of tragedy when lightning hit the pitch. The fatal flash killed two players and left two spectators, the referee and three other players with severe burns. At the subsequent inquest, it was determined that the cause of the lightning strike was the referee taking out his whistle, thereby proving what many football fans know – overuse of the whistle can ruin any match.

PUTTING THE BOOT IN

Boot sales are harmless enough, aren't they? The public gets to pick up a bargain and/or clear their house of junk and a farmer gets a bit of extra income from turning his field into a temporary flea market. In the case of one boot sale in Essex, however, events took a tragic turn. One rainy Sunday morning in 2009, things went ahead as usual, but when scores of vehicles came to leave the sodden field, they deposited a layer of mud on the road. This then caused a passing motorcyclist, Paul Ferry, to lose control and to skid into a tree with terminal consequences.

NO MORE CLOWNING AROUND

When the driver of a train fell asleep in June 1918, he ploughed his locomotive into the rear of another train and made Hammond, Indiana the site of one of America's worst train wrecks. The 86 people killed all working for Hagenbeck-Wallace Circus. Regrettably, as so many of them had just recently joined the troupe, their real names were unknown. Dozens were laid to rest in graves marked with descriptions of their job or nature, such as 'Clown', 'Smiley', 'Baldy' or '4-Horse Driver'.

IT'S FOR YOU

Adele Newman of Illinois suffered from telephonophobia – the fear of answering telephone calls. In 1992, after two years of therapy, she agreed to have a phone line installed and was waiting for her therapist to ring at a prearranged time when the phone rang unexpectedly, causing her to suffer first a panic attack and then cardiac arrest.

STOPPED FOR GOOD

This book provides ample evidence that drunks have very poor judgement when it comes to sleeping off the booze. Premaratna Kaluarachichi had spent the whole night of April 22, 2001, drinking arrack (a drink made from fermented coconut sap) and then crawled under a bus parked in a garage in Colombo, Sri Lanka at around 3am. When the bus started its working day at 6.30am, the driver was convinced something was caught under his vehicle and got out to look at his first stop, some 450m from the garage, where he discovered what remained of Premaratna.

BALLOONS BURST WOMAN

Mandy Gorman of Manchester strained so hard whilst blowing up balloons for her husband's 50th birthday party in 1988 that she suffered a fatal brain haemorrhage. Her sister Kerry originally thought her collapse was a joke and left her on the floor for several minutes whilst she continued to put up paper chains.

ALL BECAUSE THE LADY LOVES

Amanda Helston had clearly watched too many Milk Tray adverts as an impressionable teenager because her idea of sexual role play was to get boyfriend Martin Hunter to wear a black polo neck and climb into her bedroom via the balcony of her Dalston flat whilst holding a red rose and a box of chocolates. One night in 1993, after a bit too much booze, the climbing proved difficult for Mr Hunter. He slipped and discovered that even a mere 3m fall is enough to break your neck.

PROVIDENT LIVING FAILS

A 75-year-old Mormon woman from Florida died in 1988 carrying out her faith's belief in 'Provident Living' – which meant storing seven years' worth of food. Rose Evans was checking her supplies when a shelf holding 50 cans of tuna, 50 tins of beans, 80 tins of sweet corn and more than 200 tins of corned beef collapsed and crushed her to death.

WAIT FOR IT ...

If you command an army – even a small one – it is best to wait until it's arrived before you give battle. Robert of Rhuddlan was a Norman baron who held lands on the north coast of Wales. One day in 1093 he was enjoying an afternoon nap when word reached him of an attack by Welsh raiders. He sent out messengers to gather his men, and hurried to the spot. When he got there, he saw that the Welsh had loaded their ships with plunder and were about to sail away. Without waiting for his men, Robert charged into battle, accompanied by only one retainer. Unsurprisingly, the battle was short; and the Welsh ships were soon sailing away, one of them with Robert's head dangling from its masthead.

WHEN YOUR NUMBER'S UP

Sometimes the Grim Reaper seems to behave as if he has been watching the horror film franchise *Final Destination*. Head teacher at a school in Sri Lanka, Doreen Kulandaivelu, rode a motorcycle to and from work. Returning home one afternoon in 2001, she got her sari caught in the wheel and fell from her bike.

Kulandaivelu was rushed to hospital in a three-wheeled taxi, which was then involved in a collision with a car. Further injured, she was then transferred to another taxi – which broke down several miles from the hospital. With her condition worsening, she was picked up by an ambulance, which then experienced engine failure. When she eventually reached a local hospital, Kulandaivelu was immediately sent to a specialist unit several miles away. Unfortunately, the ambulance transferring her collided with a van travelling in the opposite direction, causing further trauma for the now gravely ill woman. By the time Kulandaivelu finally made it to hospital, she was dead. When your number is up ...

UNDRESSED TO KILL

I am not knocking nudism, but possibly some devotees of the lifestyle take it too far. Carlu Morelli died at a nudist village in southern France when he was struck on the head by a branch he was felling from a tree. He was not wearing a safety helmet. In fact, Morelli was not wearing anything – which, according to the medical examiner on the case, was a deadly error.

OFF HIS NUT

John Benton, a plumber called to a San Francisco school to deal with a sewerage problem in 2002, loosened a nut on a valve, only for a stream of high-pressure water to fire the nut straight into his neck with the force of a shotgun. Benton died from blood loss on the way to hospital.

SLAPSTICK

Some tragic accidents seem to unravel in the style of an old Keystone Cops film. As a concrete pipe was being lifted by crane on a New Jersey construction site in 1995, the pipe swung unexpectedly and hit a lever on a five-tonne excavator, causing it to start up and move forward. The excavator hit another concrete pipe, knocking it down an embankment and crushing worker Bill Rand, who could not hear the commotion above as he was wearing ear protectors whilst operating a pneumatic drill. Mack Sennett could not have thought up a better routine.

IN THE CAN

Marcia Stamford, an auditor, died whilst using the toilet at her workplace in Oklahoma City in 1982 when high air pressure caused the ceramic stool to shatter. Whilst Stamford received shrapnel wounds in the buttocks and thighs, the medical examiner determined she died from cardiac arrest brought on by the shock of the exploding toilet.

THE FINAL STRAW

The dismal state of the economy and the rising price of hay in England led to something of an epidemic of 'hay rustling' in 2012 when the price of a bale leapt from £2.50 to £8.50 in the space of a few months. However, hay thief Rick Osborne came unstuck as he attempted to steal some bales from a farm in Wiltshire. The dumb criminal removed bales from the bottom of a haystack, causing it to collapse down onto him, first crushing his body, then suffocating him.

IN HIS FATHER'S FALL-STEPS

Trying to follow in the footsteps of a renowned father can warp any life. It certainly had a strong and finally fatal impact on the life William 'Red' Hill Jr. His father had been a celebrated daredevil and rapids barrel rider, who had saved dozens of accident victims from the Niagara River just below the Falls.

Poor old Jr inherited his father's obsession with Niagara and in an attempt to raise funds to put up a statue of his dad at the Falls, he attempted something his pa never dared to do – going over the Horseshoe Falls. Jr was convinced that his self-invented design of a barrel called 'The Thing' – made from 13 inflated inner tubes held together by canvas and fish netting – would make the fall totally survivable.

Despite the stunt having no permission, many thousands gathered to see Jr's attempt in August 1951, and police were powerless to hold back the crowds or stop Hill. Onlookers quickly worked out that the 51m fall had all gone horribly wrong when they saw pieces of The Thing float to the surface. The body of Hill Jr was recovered the next day. At the time a close friend of Hill said: 'He wanted to go one better than his pa. Escape with everyone knowing his name, but thinking only of his old man. In the end you could say he was killed by the ghost of his father's fame.'

WHAT A NUT

Nutmeg will kill you if you inject it intravenously. How do we know this? Geoff Latchmere, 17, from Gravesend, Kent, having heard that raw nutmeg has psychoactive effects, pulverized the spice and injected it in 2001. Whilst it might cause psychedelic delusions, nutmeg can also cause nausea, pain, convulsions and, as Latchmere showed, death.

ON THE NUT

Sangeetha Mawatha from Galigomuwa in Sri Lanka saw a coconut fall from a neighbour's tree and went out to collect it in 2001. This act of petty larceny proved fatal when, as she bent down to pick it up, another coconut fell from the tree and smashed her head open.

HAVING A REAL BALL AT WORK

Playing around at work is usually not a good idea. For Phil Humphrey, playing around with colleagues in an Arizona parking lot whilst they waited for construction materials to be delivered proved deadly. After growing tired of throwing a bowling ball like a shot put, a colleague challenged Humphrey to see if he could smash the ball with a sledgehammer. He could. It shattered, one shard entering his eye, one severing the carotid artery in his neck.

KILLED BY DEATH VII – ASHES TO ASHES

Following the last wishes of a loved one can be dangerous, as Frenchwoman Anais Bordelon found in 1994, when she went to the rocky but staggeringly beautiful Côte de Granit Rose in Brittany, to throw her sister's ashes into the sea. Unfortunately for Anais, as she scattered the ashes a freak wave hit the rocks and swept her out into the Atlantic and a watery grave.

WORK IS SUCH A GRIND

Anton Abramovic was cleaning a meat-grinding machine in a New Jersey sausage factory in 1992 when he slipped and fell into the machine, one of his flailing limbs hitting its start button with horrific results. Possibly Anton could have avoided his grisly fate if he taken the hint and quit working at the plant the year before when both his uncle and his cousin lost limbs in two separate accidents.

POULTRY JUSTICE

It is a good rule of thumb never to give a deadly weapon to someone or something with a good reason to hate you. If the vile Singrai Soren had spent more time contemplating such obvious maxims instead of torturing animals, he might have lived. Even in the unpleasant world of cock fighting, it is customary to allow the birds an hour of rest before bouts in the ring, where they have to fight with razor blades attached to their legs. Soren ignored even this rule, forcing his cock to fight battle after battle in the Bengal village of Mohanpur in 2011. His battling bird revolted and when Soren tried to force it into a fourth consecutive bout, it turned round, ran up to its owner and slashed at his neck, killing him instantly.

TRAIL OF DEATH

Some tragic deaths are rendered ridiculous by their banal causes. Poor Janie Moran, 19, was killed in 2010 when a set of traffic lights failed, sending her car straight into the path of oncoming traffic. An inquest in Ireland heard that the traffic light fault was caused by the slime trail left by a slug or snail causing a short-circuit. A friend of the dead girl said: 'I've never heard of a worse bit of bad luck.'

HIS FANS HAD A CRUSH ON HIM

A wannabe Sri Lankan strongman, who had been training for an attempt on the world record for pulling a 40-tonne train carriage with his teeth, bit off more than he could chew when pulling a 35-tonne fishing boat on a trailer with his gnashers in 1994. When he stopped and clutched his chest just a few feet from the finishing line, over-enthusiastic supporters of Sirisunanda Padeniya gave the boat a shove to help it on its way, sending it sailing over the prone strongman, crushing him to death.

TOP 10 RIDICULOUS SEX-RELATED DEATHS – GOING OUT WITH A SMILE?

10. Former exotic dancer Nicole Lynn Faller agreed to be videotaped having sex with a middle-aged man at his house. Unfortunately, Nicole was a little too exotic for her partner and he died from a heart attack during intercourse. Faller forgot to turn off the camera and was caught by it stealing the dead man's valuables and drugs as she waited for paramedics.

9. Deborah Yvette Parker, 38, of Houston faced manslaughter charges for accidentally shooting her boyfriend Broderick Craig Crachian in July 2009 during a sex game they called 'Dirty Cowboy'. Parker admitted using the gun as a toy during foreplay when it went off, killing her partner.

8. In July 2010, a couple pulled their trailer over from the busy Via Dutra highway near Sao Paolo in the hope that the early morning fog would obscure anybody seeing them from having sex. The fog hid them a little too well and whilst enjoying the act, their vehicle was hit by a truck, killing them both instantly.

7. A 74-year-old Taiwanese man died in New Taipei City when he accidentally swallowed his dentures whilst having sex with a prostitute in February 2012. The 30-minute sex session had loosened his teeth, leading to the fatal choking.

6. Sergey Tuganov, a 28-year-old mechanic from Russia bet two women friends £3,000 that he could continuously have sex with them for 12 hours. He was so determined to win the bet that he swallowed dozens of Viagra tablets. Within minutes of getting the love action on, Tuganov died from a heart attack brought about not by the two ladies but the overdose of the erectile dysfunction-resolving drug.

5. Former silent film star Ramon Novarro paid two young male prostitutes for rough sex. It was not just the sex that was rough, as they beat the star and left him tied and gagged with an art deco lead dildo stuffed into his mouth. The dildo had originally been given to him by Rudolph Valentino. The unfortunate gag caused him to choke to death on his own blood.

4. Security guard Ralph Santiago used the computers at the office he guarded to Google for new types of sexual suffocation play. He obviously found them, as in 2009 his body was recovered from the office's toilets dressed in a latex bodysuit and diving mask after he had suffocated from taking poppers.

3. The body of 53-year-old Lu Wei was discovered partially clothed in his chicken coop. Lu had spent an evening watching pornography on his computer and gone outside to the coop to relieve his excitement. According to the authorities, the shock of the cold temperature and elevated heart rate from masturbation caused a fatal myocardial infarction.

2. There are better and safer places to enjoy some al fresco sex than railway tracks in South Africa's Mpumalanga Province. However, that did not stop one amorous couple from making love on the line with fatal consequences when they were run over by a freight train. According to the police, the driver had shouted a warning to them, but they 'continued with their business and ignored him.'

1. Nigerian businessman Uroko Onoja returned home from a bar in Ogbadibo in July 2012 when he was attacked by five of his six wives. Brandishing sticks and knives, they complained he gave too much sexual attention to his youngest wife, Odachi. The five wives forced Uroko to have sex with four of them in succession, but as the fifth climbed onto the bed, Uroko stopped breathing. According to Odachi, 'I tried to resuscitate him, but it was no good. The other wives all ran off into the forest laughing.' Police later arrested two of the wives.

RED MIST + WHITE GOODS = DEATH

A row between an Argentinean couple from San Isidro, Leo and Laura Ruiz, proved fatal for an innocent passer-by in 1989. Laura was so angry about Leo's recent weight gain that she began to beat him with a candlestick. Leo fled their fourth-floor apartment into the street below when Laura decided to throw the fridge down at him whilst shouting: 'Eat all of this, you fat bastard!' Unfortunately, the fridge hit not Leo but Ramon Romero, 54, who just happened to be walking to work.

WHAT A TWEET II

If you have the prescience to tweet: 'Gusts of wind up to 60mph today will be fun at work ... guess I've lived long enough', it might be worth following your own logic and not climbing a tower to film your college's football practice. However, Declan Sullivan, 20, of Notre Dame University ignored his own Nostradamus prediction, climbed the tower and was killed when it was blown over by huge gust in October 2010.

GALLIC GUST ENDS WITH A SPLAT

Many people have a daredevil streak, but Frenchman Thierry Charron combined his with a dash of overconfident dickhead. Despite other kite-surfers on the beach at Saint-Jean-de-Luz packing up for the day when winds began to reach 96km/h, Charron kept on going. Regrettably, the high-speed flurries were more than he could handle and when one gust hit close to 160km/h, he was blown not across the waves but inland and straight into the chimney of a hotel.

EXTRA VIRGIN, EXTRA DEADLY

The West Bank is dangerous enough at the best of times, but for olive farmers it is not always being on the faultline of the Arab-Israeli conflict that proves deadly. Emad al Khofash fell into a giant vat of fermenting olive mulch left-over from the olive oil-manufacture process. When two of his friends tried to pull him out, they were overcome with the fumes and fell in with him, all three eventually drowning in the goo.

DOCTOR DEATH

You would hope a doctor would have some common sense, but this was not the case for Ranjith Ranasinghe. The idiot doctor began to joke around with the security guard at his hospital in Colombo, Sri Lanka in 2009, asking the guard if he would take some phone photos of the doctor posing with the guard's revolver. Ranjith adopted a number of classic Clint Eastwood stances, before adopting the iconic blowing smoke from gun pose, at which point he accidentally fired the weapon into his mouth. Fool.

MORTAL MERRY-GO-ROUND

I have no sympathy for the idiots who die after being inspired to do dumb stuff when watching appalling stunt TV programmes. If you really think being a 'jackass' is worthy of your aspiration, humanity may be better off without you. In 2012, Otto Bieber from Bavaria got his friends to film him being taped to a child's merry-go-round that was attached by rope to a BMW, which then pulled away at high speed. The playground amusement certainly spun faster than ever before. In fact, it turned so quickly that the tape broke and Otto was flung into the air, travelling a grand 6m before hitting the ground and breaking his neck.

FATAL THREESOME

The family of an Arizonian man were awarded a $3 million pay-out against a doctor who had failed to tell Dale Marr, 31, to stop all physical activity until cardiac tests had been carried out a week before he died. Marr had consulted the physician about chest pains, but despite having them, carried on doing everything he wanted as normal – including having a threesome with his best male friend and another woman who was not his wife. A medical examiner determined that the vigorous sex session had brought on the cardiac arrest that claimed Marr's life.

THE AMERICAN FLAG – LOVE IT OR DIE

In a story that will be so pleasing to some American patriots it ought to be apocryphal, Pakistani Abdullah Ismail died from inhaling the smoke of burning stars and stripes flags at a rally protesting against the anti-Islamic film The Innocence of Muslims in September 2012. However, having spoken to some staff at the Mayo Hospital in Pakistan, I can confirm that they believe it actually happened. Abdullah was taken to the hospital from the 10,000-strong rally after complaining of feeling unwell from inhaling the smoke. He apparently died not directly from poisoning and pulmonary irritation, but from cardiac arrest due to the strain on his body.

KILLED BY DEATH VIII – DIG YOUR OWN GRAVE

Gravedigger Zailan Hamid, 40, died on the job when the grave he was digging collapsed in on him at a cemetery in Kampung Penak, Malaysia in August 2012. Fellow gravediggers immediately tried to rescue him, but the weight of earth had already broken his neck.

DEATH MEME

If the Internet memes of planking and Batmanning were not already doing enough to increase teenage idiot deaths, 2012 saw a raft of hyperventilating videos spreading around the Net in which young idiots were filmed deliberately hyperventilating to the point of passing out. That sounds like such fun, does it not? How I ever passed my teenage years just listening to music and chasing after girls, I will never know. Young fool Bertrand Ozon, 16, from Toulouse, got a friend to film him hyperventilating. Sadly for Bertrand, he passed out straight onto a table containing a glass tumbler, which smashed as he fell on it, sending shards into his neck, severing his carotid artery.

UNPLEASANT PHEASANT

Being a motorcyclist can be a dangerous business. You may be exceptionally skilled on two wheels, but the roads are so populated by four-wheel drivers with camel dung for brains that you are in a constant gamble with the Grim Reaper. However, adding to the dangers in England is a non-car menace – the pheasant. In 2011, Don Lock was speeding down a road in Suffolk when a pheasant ploughed into his helmet. A witness described the biker being engulfed in an 'exploding cloud of feathers' before his bike cartwheeled and landed on top of him. Authorities at the inquest called it 'death by sheer bad luck.'

FINAL DESTINATION: DEATH

If you are looking for proof that the Grim Reaper is either a stalker or he has been watching the *Final Destination* series of films, take the case of 24-year-old Jessica Ghawi. After narrowly escaping being shot at a mass shooting in Toronto, she was fatally shot one month later during the mass shooting at the midnight showing of *The Dark Knight Rises* movie in Aurora, Colorado. It really does seem when your number is called, death will get you. After the shooting in Toronto, Jessica had written: 'I was shown how fragile life was on Saturday. I saw the victims of a senseless crime. I saw lives change. I was reminded that we don't know when or where our time on Earth will end. When or where we will breathe our last breath.'

FOUR WHEELS OF FATE

Running yourself over is a hard trick to pull off, but a 65-year-old from Clearwater, Florida managed it with aplomb in June 2012. Police officers discovered the woman trapped under her Pontiac Vibe and had to call firefighters to lift the vehicle off of the body. An investigating cop told me: 'For some reason she had put it in drive before getting out to put a grocery cart in the back and then walking in front of the car to get to the driver's side. I've seen some dumb stuff on the force, but this is way out in the lead of dumb as a way to go.'

HUG GOES WITH A BANG

A friendly hug ended up killing Melissa Van King when she grabbed an off-duty police officer at a Chicago party in July 2012. Van King embraced the officer from behind and accidentally caused his holstered gun to discharge into her chest.

CLOWNING ALL THE WAY TO A GRAVE

French Clown Antoinne Archambault died when the door of his clown-mobile did what it was meant to and fell off. However, one night in 1973, it fell on Archambault's foot, puncturing his oversized shoes and cutting him. Archambault had a fear of doctors and delayed seeing one about the wound, which is a shame because it turned septic and he died from blood poisoning. On his death bed, Archambault blamed elephant shit on the car door for causing the infection and told fellow clown Bobo: 'At least I'm dying on a laugh. That car door always gets a laughs.'

ASHES TO ASHES, SAWDUST TO SAWDUST

It is a mystery why worker Bobby Patterson had got a rope around his neck that was attached to a pile of wood being fed into an industrial wood chipper as he and co-workers trimmed trees in California in January 2012. However, as the chipper digested the wood, it chewed in the rope, dragging him towards its maw. Despite his screams, colleagues could not free him from the entanglement and could only watch in horror as he was beheaded. A sergeant from the local sheriff's office described it as 'the purest type of freak accident I've seen and the worst way to go.'

IT WILL ALL COME OUT IN THE WASH

Workers at a laundry in California regularly climbed onto conveyor belts to dislodge stuck piles of clothing going into the industrial dryers. They stopped in 1996 after Fred Sinha did not jump off the conveyor belt quick enough once he dealt with the jam and was carried by it into the dryers' fatal 200°C heat.

DID THEY SEE PINK PEOPLE?

Sri Lankan man Chandimal Kumura ran an illegal distillery in the jungle making the spirit kasippu. One night in August 1998, the smell of fermenting pineapple and sugar cane attracted a herd of elephants that first drank the brew and then began to trash the moonshine operation. Seeing his equipment trampled, Kumura tried to scare off the elephants by firing a revolver into the air. Unfortunately, this just brought the now drunk elephants charging in his direction, crushing him to death before they went on to destroy legitimate farming crops worth thousands of dollars.

AIN'T THAT A KICK IN THE HEAD?

Blair O'Hara was employed to supervise the life-size mechanical bronco horse ride at a party in California in 2009, when instead of enforcing safety regulations, he ignored them all and got behind the ride as it was bucking. He got a metal horse hoof in the head, killing him instantly.

EXTREME RESEARCH

I am all in favour of writers doing a lot of research, but Greg Blomfield took it too far in 1988 when he illegally pulled up a manhole cover and began to explore the sewer system of Tulsa as background for a planned novel. He was quickly overcome by fumes, fainted and drowned in a few inches of really quite disgusting water.

TILIKUM, THE ULTIMATE KILLER WHALE

You would think the fact that the other name for an Orca is 'Killer Whale' would give authorities a big clue it was not a safe and suitable animal to keep in captivity. However, if that was not enough of a neon danger sign, how about the fact that one particular Orca has already killed twice? Do you not think that might make those holding the whale think that possibly he ought not to be anywhere around humans?

If you have read the original 1001 Ridiculous Ways To Die, you might remember a Killer Whale called Tilikum, who had already killed one trainer and one Hare Krishna. After his last human kill, Tilikum had a brief period off from shows at SeaWorld, Florida, but he was soon back entertaining the crowds. He was also soon back indulging his hobby of killing people.

In August 2010, Tilikum grabbed trainer Dawn Brancheau by her ponytail and pulled her into the water, where he refused to let her go, killing her through a combination of blunt force trauma and drowning. SeaWorld was fined $75,000 for this latest incident, but that did not stop Tilikum from reappearing in the crowd-pleasing shows in March 2011. Whether he continues his human-slaughtering hobby is yet to be seen.

GODS' GIFT?

Whilst being held captive by the Tamil Tigers in 2001, Malavi Gunasekara promised assorted gods that if he survived and was freed the first thing he would do is make them an offering of kiribath (rice made with coconut milk). On his release 15 months later, he was determined to carry out his promise. Realizing he had no coconut milk, he climbed a tree to harvest some and promptly fell to his death. Maybe the gods would have preferred a cash offering.

PLAYING CHICKEN ON THE HIGH SEAS

It is a good idea for small ships to stay out of the path of big ones. This principle was fatally overlooked by the American destroyer Frank E Evans in 1969 when she took part in an exercise with, amongst others, the Australian aircraft-carrier Melbourne. Before the exercise, it was emphasized that great care was needed during close escort operations, that it was the responsibility of the smaller and more manoeuvrable ship to take evasive action if necessary, and that HMAS Melbourne had a track record of ramming and sinking errant destroyers.

When in the small hours of June 3 USS Evans was ordered to take close station with the Melbourne, she promptly put herself on a head-on collision course. The Melbourne signalled this to the Evans, which acknowledged, but continued on the same course. At the last moment, the Melbourne veered to port; but at more or less the same time the Evans veered to starboard. The Melbourne sliced the Evans in two, resulting in the deaths of 74 of the crew.

It later transpired that the Evans' Captain was asleep in his bunk, and that of the two officers on the bridge, one had failed his watch-keeping exam, and the other was at sea for the first time.

Oddly, the stern section of the Evans remained afloat, and was used for target practice.

KEEP TAKING THE TABLETS

Generally, doctors prescribe medicines for a reason. When a 38-year-old roofer from Derbyshire, Jimmy Purvis, found that he suffered from vertigo-induced blackouts, he was given pills to combat the problem. They worked perfectly. However, Purvis thought he knew better than someone with medical training and decided to wean himself off them. Unfortunately, when asked to trim a tree for a neighbour, he suffered another blackout and fell to his death. Oops.

MORTAL AND PESTLE I

It seems the preferred way of some women dealing with appalling men in Sri Lanka is the humble pestle. When the husband of Padmna Ranasinghe was branded 'the most drunken man in the village' at a local meeting in 1997, she was so embarrassed that she went home and struck him in the testicles and groin with an ebony pestle whilst he was passed out drunk. He eventually awoke to internal injuries, which resulted in his death four days later. It is not known if the village later awarded Padmna Ranasinghe the title 'scariest woman when annoyed'.

CHAIN REACTION

Sometimes death comes knocking thanks to a ridiculously unlucky chain of events. It is as if a trap is being sprung by the Grim Reaper, set up like a carefully planned fall of dominoes. Take the case of George Blackford. He was working on a boom, using a cutting torch to take down a sign from the side of a building in California in 1989 when one of the hot bolts from the sign fell to earth. It fell in exactly the worst place, straight onto the hydraulic hose of the boom, sending a spray of pressurized hydraulic fluid right into the path of Blackford's cutting torch. This set Blackford, the boom and sign on fire, causing him to fall 9m to the ground. As a passer-by rushed to see if Blackford was OK, the boom came tumbling down, crushing both Blackford and his would-be rescuer to death.

DUNKED IN THE DOO-DOO

You would not think working in a doughnut shop carried much of a death risk, but Bogdan Berisha took some garbage out back at a Chicago store and fell down an uncovered manhole. Rescuers talked with the poor fellow as he struggled to stay afloat in 3m of sewerage, but it was no good and by the time they pulled him out of the cesspool it was all over for Berisha.

ONCE BITTEN, TWICE DEAD

More proof that the Grim Reaper is a relentless stalker comes from the death of Sri Lankan woman Asuntha Tanagshiwar in 2001. Just six hours after being bitten in the foot by a potentially deadly viper and surviving thanks to being rushed to receive a life-saving anti-venom injection, she was on the veranda of a local hospital. It was at this point she was struck by lighting attracted by the aluminium crutches she was using.

NOT SO BRIGHT SPARKS

A Texas gas station employee, Abdul Ismail, died in 2001 when he climbed onto a metal cage used to store propane tanks to change a lightbulb. Ismail was electrocuted and fell to the floor dead, causing his manager Ashraf Farouk to suffer a fatal cardiac arrest triggered by the shock and grief caused by witnessing the death.

DEADLY DUMBO

Poor old circus elephant Dumbo of the James Hamid Circus was only trying to protect his handler Andrew Anderton in 2010. Anderton was fixing some wires in the ceiling that were sparking above Dumbo when the elephant grabbed Anderton and tried to move him out of harm's way. Unfortunately, Dumbo was a little clumsy and in trying to help his handler, ended up crushing him. Life sure is not like the movies.

DYING FOR A PEE III

Garbage man Mike Malloy's need for a pee was so great it ended up costing him his life. In 1994, the New Yorker stood on a platform on his garbage truck as it was backing up and prepared to urinate into the vehicle. However, before Malloy could answer the call of nature, he fell and the truck backed straight over him. Possibly the safety sticker on the vehicle should have been amended from: 'Do not use riding step when vehicle is reversing' to: 'Do not use riding step to pee from, you idiot'.

NOT SO GREAT FALL

Andy Riley, a 74-year-old greeter for a giant retail chain's store in Alabama, died in 2010 after falling from the second step of a ladder. He had been reaching up to take a toy from a storage rack. As stunned colleagues said: 'He hit his head, but I had no idea you could die from falling from such a little height.'

CANDY BAR BITES BACK

Felicity Poulton suffered a panic attack when she caught her hand in a vending machine whilst trying to retrieve a candy bar that would not fall. She had been doing some late night overtime at her New Jersey workplace in 1982, when she felt like she needed a sugar rush. One of her office colleagues alerted by her cries went to find help, leaving a panicking Poulton screaming: 'Get me out of here! I can't breathe!' When her colleague and a security guard returned, Poulton had already suffered a fatal heart attack brought on by her agitation at being stuck.

CHOPPER COMES A CROPPER

Two forest service employees had just finished loading a helicopter sling with the marijuana from an illegal grow they had discovered in a Washington forest in 2010 when the Reaper came calling. The wind generated by the copter's rotors caused a dead tree to topple, crushing worker Hector Kaas.

SIREN SAYONARA

We are so used to thinking of the fire truck rushing to save lives, we rarely think about them being dangerous. Poor Meryl Ledbury, 82, died when a hose dangling from a speeding fire engine hit her in the head. She was standing on the traffic island, waiting to cross the road, when the truck turned the corner. The hose swung around like a slingshot and the metal nozzle found its tragic target.

DELAYING THE INEVITABLE

When the Grim Reaper is stalking you, he is more relentless than any Mountie. Jimmy Shepherd, 32, fell from the back of a friend's boat in Florida in 2012, but managed to haul himself spluttering out of the water. Jimmy had a beer to celebrate a close shave with a watery grave and then was driven home, but suddenly began to complain of feeling unwell, passed out and died. The medical examiner determined that Shepherd had died from secondary drowning more than three hours after getting out the water. According to experts, 'dry drowning' can happen up to 48 hours after water has initially entered the lungs. I knew there was a reason why I do not swim!

NO SLEEP LEADS TO ETERNAL REST

Men, if you are not already bummed out by learning that excessive video game playing is a killer, prepare to go through life knowing that marathon sport-watching sessions can also do more than ruin your marriage. Jiang Xiashan, 26, from Changasha, China died after going 11 nights without sleep to watch every match in the Euro 2012 football tournament. The time difference for committed soccer fan Jiang meant he watched the games in the middle of the night and then went to work the next day.

Whilst doctors believed his immune system may have been weakened by smoking and drinking, they attributed the primary cause of death as exhaustion through watching football. What makes it worse was, Jiang was supporting England. Any old-time England fan could have told him that they did not stand a snowball's chance in hell of getting to the final.

LETHAL LAPTOP

For those of you with cyberphobia – a fear of computers – the death of Angela Barton, 25, from Surrey in 2009 may confirm your worst fears in a very new way. Barton had put her laptop on the back seat of her car, a common enough event, but one that had fatal consequences for her when the car collided with a stationary truck. The unsecured computer flew forward and hit her on the back of the head and neck, killing her instantly.

LIKE FATHER, LIKE SON

If your father was a Christian preacher who had died through handling a rattlesnake at a service, you might think twice about taking up his mantle. However, Mack Randall Wolford had no such qualms despite, at the age of 15 in 1982, seeing his father die from a snake bite. In a tragic, if somewhat predictable, case of history repeating, 30 years later Randall Jr died when the rattlesnake he used during services bit him on the thigh. He initially refused to seek medical help, believing the bite to be a test of faith. By the time he had realized that his faith was not going to save him and he went to the hospital, it was too late.

FAMILY DOUBLE I

This book provides ample evidence that the Grim Reaper does irony and cruelty in great measure. He is also often wont to combine them, such as in the tragedy that afflicted one Romanian family in June 2012. Emanuel Davidescu, 27, died when he lost control of his car and spun out into the path of a truck coming in the opposite lane of the E70 motorway. Just four hours later, his sister Maria Patrascu, 22, died at exactly the same spot on the road as her brother as she rushed home after hearing about his death.

FAMILY DOUBLE II

On an ordinary day in 2002 Sheila Wentworth, 45, from Alabama drove along Route 25 to visit her sister, Doris Hall. At the same time Doris, 52, was driving in the other direction to visit Sheila. The sisters, both driving Jeep Cherokees, collided head-on, fatally for both. The accident happened at almost the exact spot where their father had died some years before.

DON'T FORGET THE LYRICS

Charles Davies, 67, from Cheltenham was a keen chorister. In 1995, at a gathering of the Cotswold Male Voice Choir, he gave a solo performance of the song "Goodbye". He had just sung the words 'I wish you all a last goodbye' when he collapsed and died on the spot.

WRAPPED IN PLASTIC

Adam Stone, 50, from West Sussex, made some money by impersonating mutant superhero Wolverine, but his death in 2012 was merely ridiculously odd, not heroic. After friends and colleagues became worried about him, police broke into his home to discover his dead body on a weight-lifting bench wrapped in three rolls of cling film and a nylon sheet. The subsequent inquest determined that Stone died from autoerotic asphyxiation after wrapping himself a little too tightly at the ankles and neck.

INSTANT KARMA

Is there such a thing as instant karma? John Lennon thought so, but then again he had a good imagination. We can imagine it, however, by considering the death of Paul Porter in 2012. Directly after Porter had fatally stabbed a family friend he had dated 15 years previously, he got into his truck to return home. At this point, instant karma struck. Porter suffered a heart attack and crashed his vehicle into a rock wall, ending his life.

BELOW PAR VI

Drinking and driving kills, even on the golf course and in a vehicle that has a top speed of 29km/h. Canadian Roger Jackson had a few drinks at the clubhouse after a round of golf in June 2012, then went out to play in a foursome. Taking the wheel of the golf cart after the ninth hole, he hit a rock, drove across a grassy mound and then over a 7m high embankment, plunging onto the road below and fracturing his skull. The coroner decided that 'alcohol impairment was a contributory factor' to the smash.

TERMINAL TANTRUM

I was an arsehole as a teenager. Most teenagers are. Their tantrums at the unfairness of life would shame most toddlers. Pakistani 13-year-old Kamran Khan took things way too far even by teenage standards when his parents could not afford to buy him a new school uniform. In the ultimate misplaced protest, Kamran set himself alight and died from self-inflicted 65 per cent burns.

SMOKING KILLS VI – BOOZE LOSER

Alcohol is a dumb multiplier. It acts like idiot growth hormone. You want proof? Barry Wayne Jordan had enjoyed a few drinks at his friend's home in New Orleans when, in a boozy haze, he mistook a jar of gasoline for another alcoholic beverage. He quickly spat out the gasoline all over himself and announced he was going outside to have a smoke to get the taste out of his mouth. Unsurprisingly, Jordan set himself alight and died in hospital from his burns.

BIG STOMACH, SMALL THROAT

Russian Boris Isayev, 48, met his end at a pancake-eating contest in Chernyakovsk. He gobbled down 43 – stuffed with cream and banana – before foaming at the mouth and collapsing. The cause of death was a piece of pancake lodged in his windpipe, which choked him to death. A witness said: 'He was the most active participant in the contest. He ate all the types of pancake on offer and won fairly.' Hopefully, this would have been a comfort to him.

THE LAST DANCE

A lap dance at an Alabama strip club was just too much for 67-year-old Arthur Herek. After his fourth lap dance of the night, Herek's heart gave out, but it was not until the dancer tried to obtain payment that she realized that he was dead. One of the ladies at the club said: 'I guess that last dance was just a little too much for him, but I'm sure he enjoyed it.'

KILLED BY DEATH IX – BACK FROM THE DEAD

In 2011, 49-year-old Russian woman Fagilyu Mukhametzyanov was declared dead. As mourners at her funeral filed by her open casket, she suddenly woke up. Realizing she was at her own funeral, Fagilyu started screaming before clutching her chest and actually dying. A subsequent investigation blamed doctors for misdiagnosing a deep coma as death and the shock of being in a coffin and hearing prayers for her soul for causing the fatal cardiac arrest.

MUM DOES NOT ALWAYS KNOW BEST

Nervous Angela Havering from Bedfordshire was the sort of woman who, even aged 34, asked permission from her mother before getting her tongue-pierced. Unfortunately for Angela, her mother said yes, because just two days after having a 2cm steel bar inserted, she died from septicaemia and acute tonsillitis. The last thing she wrote on her Facebook page was: 'I feel like crap'.

DROWNING IN DRAMS

A master-blender at one of Scotland's most treasured distilleries drowned in an 50,000-litre vat of water and yeast – known as a washback – which is used in the early stages of distilling whisky. The 46-year-old who had worked at the distillery for 23 years threw himself into the vat in a successful suicide bid.

CRACKERED AND KNACKERED

Reading reports of old inquests should not make you laugh, but sometimes you cannot help yourself. In September 1933, another ridiculous death happened in Rockhampton, Australia. Pensioner Michael Rooney got out of bed during the night, slipped on a corn cracker and managed to get his head jammed between two bed posts. Unable to free himself, he died from asphyxiation.

TOP 10 RIDICULOUS DEATHS OF INVENTORS BY THEIR OWN INVENTIONS – TOO CLEVER BY HALF

10. Li Shi was Prime Minister under the Qin Dynasty. Before his death in 208 BCE, he had made changes to the Five Pains system of torture and punishment, introducing execution by tearing off an offender's head and four limbs by attaching them to chariots. Guess how Li Shi ended up dying upon being convicted of treason?

9. Whilst working for General Electric in 1903, William Nelson created a prototype motorized bicycle. During a test run, he got the machine up to impressive speeds, but inventing a motorbike does not mean you know how to ride one and Nelson fell off his creation and died from his injuries. He should also have invented a crash helmet.

8. Swedish scientist Carl Wilhelm Scheele was one of the pioneers of modern chemistry. Scheele was the first to isolate and identify an astonishing number of elements and compounds. Unfortunately, he developed the habit of investigating the properties of any new chemical by smelling it and tasting it. He managed to taste hydrogen cyanide and live to tell the tale, but in 1786, at the age of 44, his habit caught up with him and he died from symptoms resembling mercury poisoning.

7. Ismail ibn Hammad al-Jawhari was a Turkic scholar renowned for creating the Arabic dictionary *Taj al-Lugha wa Sihah al-Arabiya (The Crown of Language and the Correct Arabic)* in 998 CE. Inspired by reading about an early glider flight, he constructed his own craft out of planks of wood and rope. On its test flight, he jumped from the roof Nishapur mosque, sailed a few feet and then plummeted straight down to the street below.

6. Horace Lawson Hunley was a marine engineer and inventor of the first combat submarine the CSS *Hunley*. Hunley was aboard the craft for a routine test of the vessel which had sunk two times previously, when it went down for the third time in 1863, killing its inventor and seven other crew members. The CSS *Hunley* was recovered and made naval history by becoming the first submarine to sink a ship in 1864.

151

5. Jean Francois Pilatre de Rozier was one of the early pioneers of balloon flight. In those days there were two schools of thought in ballooning. One school favoured the lighter-than-air hydrogen; the other leant towards ordinary air heated by what was effectively an on-board flame-thrower. De Rozier rather optimistically experimented with a combined balloon, obtaining lift from both sources. Unfortunately, he ignored a significant formula: naked flame + hydrogen = Bang. On June 15, 1785, de Rozier fell to his death from 5,180m.

4. People laughed at Henry Smolinksi in 1971 when he founded Advanced Vehicle Engineers and announced he was going to build a flying car based around the Ford Pinto called the Mizar. Though he actually got the Mizar off the ground during a test flight, they were still laughing up to the moment in 1973 when the craft's right wing folded and Smolinski's dreams and life came down to earth in a fireball crash,

3. Charles Richard Drew was a pioneering African-American surgeon and medical researcher who was at the forefront of improving blood transfusion, including creating the blood banks used during World War II and fighting against the racial segregation of blood. However, with tragic irony, after a car crash in 1950, Drew died from complications from a botched transfusion.

2. Russian engineer Valerian Abakovsky created the Aerowagon, a highly experimental high-speed train fitted with an aircraft engine to utilize propeller traction. A test run carrying several top Soviet officials and Abakovsky safely made it to Tulla from Moscow in record time, but on the return journey, the Aerowagon derailed and killed everyone on board, including its inventor.

1. Even inventions designed to increase safety can kill. Colonel Pierrepoint was so worried about being hit by a horse-drawn carriage whilst crossing the road to his club in Piccadilly every day that he came up with the idea of the traffic island, paying for one to be built in St. James Street outside his club in 1864. He was so excited to test it out that when finished he ran over to it, tripped and was then fatally hit by a carriage.

A SENSE OF PROPORTION

I am a cat lover, but as any pet lover or Buddhist will tell you, attachment always leads to sorrow when your beloved animal dies. However, for 44-year-old Michael McAleese, the death of his 13-year-old tortoiseshell cat Sophie was beyond devastating. He was so distraught he slept with her dead body for three days, and when someone eventually came to collect the corpse, McAleese told them he planned to kill himself now his Sophie was gone. He was as good as his word and took his own life. His sister told an inquest: 'I tried to persuade him life was more than a cat, but in his case it was not.'

DOWNHILL DEATH BALL I

Zorbing – rolling down a hill inside a giant plastic ball – has a lot of fans amongst the adrenaline-junkie fraternity whose palates are jaded by jumping off of bridges whilst attached to elastic. Those of us who think zorbing is not so much cool as an accident waiting to happen, will cite the death in 2013 of 27-year-old Russian Denis Burakov. The orb he was in was meant to come to a gentle stop after rolling down a slope in Dombay, but it veered off course and kept rolling till it plunged over a cliff, dropping 305m. The orb eventually came to a stop more than 800m away, but Burakov himself had stopped breathing after the initial fall.

JUST A NIP TURNS DEADLY

Even minor injuries can kill if not treated correctly. In 2009, Kevin Roche was bitten in the ankle by his half-blind pet dog Buster during a game of fetch the stick. He did not treat the tiny wound with antiseptic and six days later was rushed to hospital when he began to lose feeling in his fingers. Despite emergency treatment, he died the next day from inflammation of the brain caused by blood poisoning.

DOWNHILL DEATH BALL II

Just in case you think I am unfairly highlighting a lone zorbing death, there is also the 2009 case from the Czech Republic when a two-person orb went hurtling down a hill near Trinec at speeds of 56km/h. It was meant to be safely caught in a net at the bottom, but the net burst and the zorb carried on downhill, killing one of its occupants before coming to rest on a road. A local policeman said: 'It is a sad death, but there will always be risk when throwing yourself down a hill.' Quite.

CLAPTRAP KILLS I

The spiritual bollocks spouted by some self-appointed New Age gurus is offensive to the ears of anyone familiar with concepts such as logic and fact. Unfortunately, some of it is also bloody dangerous to the body. Misguided Canadian Emma Sue Bolton, 35, died in 2011 when she attended a personal development seminar called Dying In Consciousness. This involved her being covered in mud, wrapped in plastic, put under blankets and with a box over her head into which she was instructed to hyperventilate. The coroner investigating her death determined she died from hyperthermia, with a body temperature of 40.5°C instead of the normal 37°C, the process, according to him, effectively 'cooking her'. Whether she reached the consciousness she was after is unknown, but the course certainly lived up to its promise of dying.

DIY SURGERY DISASTER

Englishman Bob Porter, 65, lost the use of his legs after he was shot three times by a neighbour at his holiday home in France during an argument about a dog. Porter was depressed about having to use a wheelchair and the difficulty he had in getting in and out of his luxury Jaguar XJ car. One afternoon in 2011, frustrated by what he called his 'useless legs', he decided to try his hand at self-amputation. Using a plastic bag as tourniquet and a hacksaw, he had almost severed his right leg when he called the emergency services suffering from heaving bleeding. By the time the ambulance arrived, Porter was already dead from blood loss.

THE KISS OF DEATH

Shy British teenager Sarah Bell, 18, died when she was kissed for the first time by her boyfriend. An inquest in 2011 heard that Sarah had the rare cardiac condition SADS – Sudden Arrhythmic Death Syndrome – and died just moments after she embraced her boyfriend of three months.

WHAT A BIG BOOB!

Adult entertainment actress Echo Valley had picked up a number of titles during her life, including Miss Exotic Big Bust 2000. Appearing in such films as *Double Air Bags* and *Mega Tits*, her 65NN breasts might have been the basis of her career, but they were also her undoing. In 2011, she died when her car was rear-ended and she was sent through the windscreen. Friends told investigating police officers that she never wore a seatbelt because her breasts were too large for it to go round.

SHAFTED

Argentinean repairman Diego Otero was at the bottom of a lift shaft in an office block in Salta when he called up to colleague Marcos Paz. Poor Paz, being hard of hearing, lent down in the shaft to try and make out what Otero was saying, overbalanced and fell down, killing both himself and his pal at the bottom.

BLAME CANADA

American Felix Morelle was not used to the Canadian winter where temperatures drop to -34°C. Finding the engine of his truck frozen after he had recently moved to Winnipeg, he decided to try and thaw it out by heating around it with a propane torch. Bad move. The torch went out and gas leaked and when Morelle lit it up again, the resulting explosion turned him and his truck into fireballs.

MONSTER MASH

Monster truck show promoter George Eisenheart publicly defended his industry's safety record in a TV interview in January 2009. However, just a week later at a monster truck rally in Wisconsin, Eisenheart accidentally stepped out in front of one of the oversized vehicles, its massive tyres crushing him to death before its driver had a chance to react.

TIL DEATH DO US JOIN

The lengths some people go to, to end their lives, is a testament to both their deep sadness and absurd ingenuity. Whilst most people meet others on the Internet for fun things, 34-year-old Elaine Bishop wanted to find someone to join her in death. She posted an ad on a suicide forum in 2010 which read: 'I'm desperately seeking a pact in the UK. I'm 34, female and live in the Manchester area'. Strangely and sadly enough, she got a reply from 35-year-old Derek Rose. Between them they obtained a combination of chemicals to make a deadly gas and placed tape on the windows of Ms. Bishop's car, turning it into a driveable gas chamber. When police found the car, the pair had left suicide notes on the windscreen as well as a warning that they would need to get firemen with breathing apparatus to open the doors if they wanted to get their bodies due to the toxic vapours inside. Thoughtful.

LEAVING FOR GOOD

Massachusetts landscape gardener George Craven fell into a pile of leaves and plastic bags he was using for composting in 2008. In most cases this sort of trip would have just been an inconvenience, but as Craven fell he broke a wrist and an ankle, meaning he could not get up and suffocated under the leaves.

CLAPTRAP KILLS II

You do not have to be an atheist to see that sometimes misplaced faith can be harmful. In 2011, medical authorities in London blamed the death of three women who stopped taking their HIV medication on the advice of evangelical Christian preachers as a form of 'terribly misguided hope'. One of them had been buying 'Anointing Holy Water' from her church. She had been promised it could not only cure cancer but would also make the need for her antiretroviral drugs redundant. It did not. Preying on the illness and fear of others is beyond vile. If there is a hell, we can only hope these poxy preachers face it.

TEMPER TANTRUM TUMBLE

Korean Chung Lee, 40, was a wheelchair user with some temper issues. When he missed the elevator in a shopping centre in August 2010 because a woman did not hold the doors for him, he repeatedly rammed the lift with his electric scooter in a whopping fit of anger. Unfortunately for Lee, as he reversed into the lift's doors one last time, they gave way and he tumbled 6m down the shaft to his death.

VOLCANO NO-GO

Live volcanoes are known to be dangerous. In fact, you would be hard pressed to find a seven-year-old who was not conscious of the fact that walking around one might not be the safest way to spend a day. However, that did not stop a 25-year-old Swedish tourist from hiking up and then tumbling 152m down into the crater of Mount Batur in Bali in 2010. Local officials say that whilst hiking up the volcano is safe, great care needs to be taken when taking photos with your iPhone close to the edge.

HIGH FORCE TO NO LIFE FORCE

It is not just volcanoes you have to be careful around whilst taking photos. Brian Crighton, tripped and slipped into a river after taking photographs at the top of the High Force waterfall in County Durham. Once in the water, the currents were too strong and he was carried over the 21m waterfall to his death. It was not the first time someone had lost their life at High Force. In 2007, Phil Ripton died when he was swept away after he lost his footing whilst attempting to collect rocks for his tropical fish tank.

RIVER OF DEATH I

In classical myth the river of death was Styx. However, every nation, has a river with a reputation for helping the Grim Reaper make his target figures. In England, one of those rivers is the Wharfe in Yorkshire. There is even a local rhyme, which goes: 'The Aire is still, the Wharfe is lithe, where the Aire kills one, the Wharfe kills five'. The River Wharfe certainly has played host to its fair share of ridiculous deaths.

In September 2010, Jimi Heselden, the owner of Segway Inc., the makers of the iconic Segway two-wheeled electric gyrobike, fell off a 65m cliff into the Wharfe whilst riding an off-road version of the Segway. Heselden was one of Britain's richest men, having built a huge business empire after wisely investing his redundancy payment when he lost his job as a coal miner. It is thought that his Segway reversed off the cliff through driver error. Ironically, Segway once had to recall vehicles because a software glitch caused the wheels to suddenly reverse direction.

RIVER OF DEATH II

Heselden was far from the first famous man to have died in the River Wharfe in ridiculous circumstances. In 1934, acclaimed painter Reginald Arthur Smith, who had built much of his reputation on landscapes featuring the Wharfe, died whilst attempting another masterpiece. He was trying to paint Bolton Abbey where the Wharfe narrows and topples over waterfalls into an area known as The Strid. This spot was the sight of another celebrated and ridiculous drowning that he hoped to reflect in his picture. However, he slipped whilst trying to get the perfect view and drowned in the foaming Wharfe.

RIVER OF DEATH III

The spot at which Reginald Arthur Smith fell into the Wharfe was close to that where another celebrated victim met a ridiculous end. William of Egremont, a cousin of King David of Scotland and known as 'Young Romily', was out hunting one day in 1157 on the moors surrounding the river. With him was his faithful greyhound. Young Romily attempted to leap over the river, but he was holding his dog's leash and the beast held back as he jumped, causing the nobleman to plunge into the water and drown. Even William Wordsworth found this death ridiculous and celebrated it in his poem *The Force of Prayer*, which includes the verse:

'He sprang in glee – for what cared he That the river was strong, and the rocks were steep! But the greyhound in the leash hung back, And checked him in his leap.'

NOT SO HAPPY LANDINGS

Zaheer Ahmad was so enraged when a helicopter landed near to his house in Keti, Pakistan, in 1999, that he got into a major row with the pilot. When the helicopter tried to take off, Zaheer grabbed hold of one of the landing struts in an effort to prevent it leaving until he was given the compensation he believed he was due. As the pilot struggled to correct the lurching of his craft and return to the ground, he accidentally crushed and killed the argumentative fool. There is a lesson here, boys and girls: never pick a fight with a helicopter.

SITTING IN JUDGMENT – TERMINALLY

Car thief Barry Ward was suffocated to death in 2010 when 108kg John McClaren sat on him when Ward tried to steal his Mitsubishi Shogun. McClaren caught Ward mid-theft and restrained him by sitting on him until the police arrived. McClaren thought the thief had stopped struggling after he said, 'Give it up, son, you aren't going anywhere', but Ward had in fact stopped trying to escape because he was dead.

KILLDOZER

Businessman Marvin Heemeyer lost a planning dispute with his local town council in Colorado in 2004. His response? Turn a bulldozer into an armour-plated tank and destroy the town of Granby. After two hours he had almost obliterated nine buildings – including the town hall – whilst evading the bullets of the SWAT team thanks to the 1.25cm thick plating he had welded onto his D-5 Caterpillar. However, one of the shots fired by the police damaged the vehicle's hydraulics and it ground to a halt within the wreckage of a warehouse Heemeyer had destroyed. Although no bullets could penetrate his armour, Heemeyer shot himself when faced with capture. A State Patrol officer said: 'He was like a one-man A-Team, but bad.'

INTO THE LIONS' DEN

Next time you think you have a bad boss, be thankful that they are not as bad as Mark Scott-Crossley. The South African farm manager was sentenced to life imprisonment for a 2004 murder in which he threw a former employee into an enclosure used for breeding lions. Nelson Chisale had been returning to the farm where he used to be employed to pick up his personal belongs when Scott Crossley had him tied up and fed to the lions. The crime was uncovered when police discovered Mr. Chisale's skull, body parts and the remains of his clothes in the enclosure.

TURN THE OTHER CHEEK BUT NOT THE CHANNEL

It is well-known that TV causes a large proportion of family arguments, but things got a little out of hand in 2010 when South African father David Makoeya wanted to watch the Germany vs. Australia game in the football World Cup. This led to a row with his wife and two grown-up children, who wanted to watch a religious show because it was Sunday night. A struggle for the remote control turned most un-Christianly violent and Mr Makoeya's wife and children ended up beating him to death.

THE WEDDING THAT WENT OFF WITH A BANG II

A bridegroom accidentally killed three of his new relatives when he fired into the air at his wedding feast in the Turkish village of Akacagoze in 2010. The groom was firing a volley of shots with an AK-47 to celebrate his marriage when he lost control and raked his guests.

A POTTY WAY TO GO

Californian Claire Foken, 26, died after a portable toilet seat smashed through her car's windscreen in 2010. While she was driving on a highway at 11am, two portable toilets fell from the trailer of a pickup truck, breaking apart and sending shrapnel in every direction – including a seat right into the path of Foken's car. This caused her to veer off the road and hit a tree, killing her.

OH, THE IRONY IX – RA RA RASPUTIN

Boney M were disco legends across the globe in the 1970s. One of their most remembered number one hits was *Rasputin* – a song celebrating the infamous life and strange death of Russian mystic Grigori Rasputin. The frontman of Boney M was dancer Bobby Farrell (the group mimed to their hits). Farrell died in a St Petersburg Hotel on December 29, 2010 at the age of 61 from a heart attack. Nothing ridiculous there, except by strange coincidence Farrell died in the same city and on the same day as Rasputin. However, Rasputin's death was somewhat more violent, allegedly resisting death from being fed cakes laced with cyanide, beaten, stabbed and having his penis severed his assassins only finished him with four shots in the back and then throwing him into the icy River Neva.

FIRE AND ICE

The strange desire to see something new and something dangerous drew a party of three tourists to see what in 2010 was the world's newest volcano – Fimmvoruhal. Driving out completely unprepared for Iceland's frozen highlands, their SUV became stuck near Fimmvoruhal's molten ring. Instead of dying from intense heat, the sightseers froze to death when the vehicle's petrol eventually ran out and temperatures dropped to below -30°C during the night.

AN OPEN AND SHUT CASE?

Poor pensioner Max Verhoeven plunged to his death after being caught walking on a drawbridge in Georgia as the bridge opened in 2009. Verhoeven hung onto the side of the bridge as it swung into the air, but eventually his strength failed him and he toppled 9m onto the concrete below. He often used the bridge and it is unclear why the flashing lights and bell used to warn people of the bridge opening did not alert him to the danger.

HOG ROAST TURNS INTO LONG PIG TRAGEDY

Californian Terry Rivera died when he fell into the backyard fire pit he had created to roast a pig. Rivera and friends had spent the afternoon drinking beer and making the 90cm deep pit, but an inebriated Rivera stumbled into the flames when it came to cooking the whole hog later in the evening. His friends could not drag him out and he died before emergency services could arrive.

A RUBBISH WAY TO GO IV

As we have already seen, bins and booze do not make a good mix. More proof comes from the absurd death of 35 year-old schoolteacher Adam Rowland in 2010. After a night of heavy drinking and unsuccessfully trying to chat up women in Blackpool, he began the walk home alone when it started to rain. Police believe that in a drunken state, Rowland climbed into a commercial waste bin to avoid the downpour. Regrettably, he fell asleep in the bin and was crushed to death when the bin was being transferred to a waste handling plant.

A RUBBISH WAY TO GO V

Being crushed is not the only ridiculous way to die when you crawl into a rubbish bin. In 2007, banker James Morton had a few drinks and instead of walking home, climbed into a commercial waste bin behind some shops in London's East End. His dead body was found early the next morning by garbage collectors, and an inquest ruled that Morton had died from a lack of oxygen caused by a combination of his own CO_2 breathed out whilst he was in the bin and a build up of the gas caused by fermenting rubbish. If he had not been a banker, I would have felt sorry for him.

DOWN THE RABBIT HOLE

Zimbabwean Energy Kamuruko was out hunting with his dogs near the village of Mandipaka in 2010 when he shouted out to his friends that he had seen a rabbit. What happened next is a matter of speculation, but given that the next day, a neighbour found Kamuruko's body sticking out of a rabbit hole and his head stuck firmly inside, whilst an autopsy showed death by asphyxiation, we can place big bets that he peered down the rabbit hole, got stuck like Pooh Bear, and died as a rabbit looked on.

SHOOTING PAINS LEAD TO SHOOTING

Someone who takes the easy way out when they're terminally ill deserves nothing but sympathy. Someone who kills themselves when they only think they're ill, however ... Arthur Shrewsbury was one of the foremost cricketers of the 1890s – at one stage being the first man W.G. Grace said he'd pick for his team. In 1903, he experienced abdominal pains. A doctor was unable to pinpoint an exact cause but assured Shrewsbury that he was not suffering from any serious disease. Nevertheless, Shrewsbury purchased a gun and shot himself.

BELOW PAR VII

A teenager accidentally killed his 16-year-old brother on an Irish golf driving range in 2010 when his swing sent a golf ball straight into the left side of his brother's head. Medical experts at the subsequent inquest said the teenager should have no guilt, as it was a 'completely exceptional case which had no direct comparison in medical literature anywhere in the world.' The ball had managed to hit the temporal region – the softest part of the skull – causing a blood vessel to rupture whilst doing very little visible damage.

X-RAY THAT DID NOT MARK THE SPOT

You have to feel sorry for anyone who has a job where getting it wrong is a matter of life and death. However, you have to feel even sorrier for the family of Eric Davenport of Lancashire. When his doctor got it wrong in 2010 by reading an x-ray back to front, it meant curtains for the 85-year-old grandfather because the medical moron then tried to drain fluid from the wrong lung, killing him.

A REAL PAIN IN THE NECK

Dr Rachel Ferguson died in 2010 when her leather cord necklace became twisted into the rotating part of an electric neck massager. With the necklace wrapped around the control knobs of the machine, she could not turn it off and it strangled her to death.

GIVEN OUT

Lifelong cricket fan Gareth Jones, 72, was umpiring a village match in Herefordshire in 2010 when a cricket ball hit him on the side of the head. One of Jones' friends commented: 'He always said he would like to go whilst watching a match, so I think he wouldn't be too upset he was given out by the great umpire in the sky like this.'

HE'S NOT GOD, HE'S A VERY NAUGHTY MAN

Iranian Abdolzera Gharabat declared himself to be God manifest upon Earth in 2009 and began to attract a handful of followers from his province of Khuzestan. As you can imagine, claiming to be God does not sit well with Sharia law, so in January 2011, the Iranian religious authorities had Gharabat beheaded for apostasy. Not unreasonably, his followers deserted him at this point, because if you were God, your omnipotent powers really ought to be able to stop something as simple as a blade across the neck.

MAGICAL MORT XII

Rubina Maroof paid Gambian witchdoctor Alfusaine Jabbi thousands of pounds to sacrifice several camels in an attempt to ward off bad luck caused by evil spirits. When this did not work to Rubina's satisfaction, she lured Jabbi to her home in England. When he refused a refund on his magical services, she beat him with a giant roll of tinfoil, stabbed him multiple times, rubbed salt into his wounds and then dumped his body in a car park. Although she tried to flee to Pakistan, she was caught and jailed in 2010.

TV SHOW TERROR

Bulgarian TV executives had to publicly declare in 2011 they were considering cancelling TV show *Otechestven Front* after people claimed it was cursed. The show featured people who had done extraordinary things, but when six of its guests all died within days or hours of appearing, rumours of a curse began to spread. Former gangster Marin Ivankov died of a heart attack two days after being on the show, as did three other guests. Ivanka Arsova who appeared to talk about her statue of the Virgin Mary which she claimed wept tears, died within two weeks of appearing from previously undiagnosed cancer, whilst herbalist Halil Baev died when he returned from filming to find his home ablaze and rushed into it to save his cat. As one TV exec said: 'Naturally, this ridiculous talk of a death curse does not make interviewees less willing to appear on the show.' Clearly, the 15 minutes of fame is a price worth paying for some.

DEAD HEAT

Shoot-outs between rival drug gangs are not uncommon, nor are the deaths resulting from them. However, a shoot-out that left 17 criminals dead in the Guatemalan town of Santa Ana in 2008 qualifies as ridiculous thanks to the issue causing the dispute. It was not territory, nor control of the local drug trade, oh no. It was not even some imagined insult or violation of the criminal code. The reason for the mass slaughter was that the two gangs disagreed over the winner of a horse race that was declared a dead heat.

PERMANENT RETIREMENT

A 60-year-old Japanese man from Kyoto died in 2008 from injuries received at his retirement party when his colleagues threw him into the air to celebrate his leaving, but failed to catch him as he returned to earth with a bump that left him paralyzed. The poor man eventually died through ongoing complications to the spine and neck injuries he received. Perhaps next time the company will stick to just getting retiring staff a gold watch.

SPARE TYRE DEFEATS FOUR TYRES

Mobility scooters are life-savers for many of the morbidly obese who use them to get out and about. However, for Annie Maines, 36 – who was more than three times her ideal weight – the scooter turned into a killer when she took it off-road and attempted to take a short-cut that involved going up a grass embankment in Sussex. The scooter, unable to cope with Annie's weight and the incline, rolled back down the slope and into the path of a reversing SUV.

SUPERMARKET SWEEP

Two teenage crooks, Daryl Barton and Leroy Philips, stole a supermarket trolley loaded with groceries from the car park of a major supermarket in West London in 1994. Drunk and tired from the hard work of stealing, they rode the trolley down the slope of a hill in a somewhat miscalculated getaway attempt. The trolley overturned, throwing both thieves into the path of a passing bus, which rolled over Barton.

SKEWERED! UNWILLING DON-OR KEBAB

Don Jennings died whilst walking along a Manchester street in high winds in March 2002. A gust pulled loose a sign advertising a kebab shop and was carried along at speed until it fatally impaled Jennings in the chest with the end designed to resemble a kebab skewer.

WHAT A COCK-UP III

Afghanistan has been a dangerous place for invading and occupying troops since 330 BCE, when Alexander the Great invaded the region. Given the hostile conditions of being under siege from resisting tribesmen who wish to kill you to free themselves from your rule, you would think any occupying soldier would have enough on his hands to keep him out of trouble. Regrettably this was not the case for some Soviet soldiers stationed outside Kabul in 1986. After one soldier was teased and humiliated over his small penis by drunken comrades, he stormed out of a mess tent, went to the armoury and returned to confront his abusers armed with a rocket-launcher. Although the deaths of 14 men who died at the time was initially covered-up during the Soviet era, the embarrassing truth about the ridiculous cause of their demise was eventually uncovered by researchers going through Kremlin military archives.

TRUNK TRAP

Ken Malik had enjoyed several beers during a night spent at a bar in Denver in February 1996. Wisely he decided not to attempt to drive home. However, instead of calling a cab, he climbed into the boot of his car to sleep it off. Bad move. In getting into the trunk of his vehicle, he dropped the keys to it on the sidewalk, trapping him inside. His wife called the police when Malik did not come home and they eventually found his body two days later. An autopsy showed he had died of asphyxiation and had severely injured his hands whilst attempting to escape from his self-sprung trap.

DEAD ON CUE

New Zealander Mike Swanson, 26, drank himself to death in an attempt to win a pool table in a bet in 2012. The Kiwi was drinking with family members when he bet the owner of the coveted table that if he drank a bottle of vodka, he wanted to take the table home as his prize. The bet was accepted and Mike downed enough vodka to win. A bit worse for wear, he fell asleep on his new possession and the others thought it best to let him sleep it off. However, in the morning they found he was dead. A subsequent autopsy showed he was five times over the legal drink drive limit.

A BIG BRAIN IS NOT A GOOD IDEA

It is impossible to know what goes through some people's brains in the run-up to their ridiculous deaths, but thanks to medical science it is at least possible to know what happened to their brains. In 1997, Brighton-based rubber fetishist Anne Marsh, 36, took copious amounts of cocaine whilst dressed head-to-toe in a rubber suit accessorized with a gasmask. When her body was found on her bed by friends after they had not seen her for a few days, an autopsy was carried out. It determined that the combination of coke and overheating caused by the rubber wear led Anne's brain to swell fatally.

MOURNING AFTER THE NIGHT BEFORE

Student James Mayberry from Oxfordshire, tried to climb up his college's 8m tall flagpole in 1992 to display the underwear of his best friend's girlfriend the morning after he had slept with her. Possibly the Grim Reaper hates sleazeballs as much as the rest of us, because before he got to the top, the pole snapped. Mayberry fell to earth and was impaled in the neck by a piece of the broken pole.

KILLED BY DEATH X – MOUNTAIN MISERY

Italian Federico Dean, 41, was carrying out his dead brother's request to have his ashes scattered at the Jof di Montasio peak in the Alps in July 2008 when a new tragedy hit the family. A sudden thunderstorm engulfed the mountain and Federico was hit by a lightning bolt that blasted him off the peak, throwing his burnt body 100m down the mountain.

THE GREAT ESCAPE – NOT!

A clever criminal can cheat the system, but they can never cheat death. Anastasio Figueroa must have felt pretty clever to have escaped from the Hendry Correctional Institution in Florida via a garbage truck in 1994. However, his great escape did not last long and authorities were soon using fingerprints to establish his identity when, instead of delivering him to freedom, the garbage truck compacted him and dumped out his crushed remains at a landfill site.

DO NOT PASS GO ...

Student Roddy McGowan, 21, attempted to complete the London Monopoly pub crawl drinking game, where you drink in a pub on each of the locations that feature on the Monopoly board, in 1996. By the time McGowan had got to Pall Mall, he had drunk four pints of lager, four double whiskies, four rum and cokes and a Red Bull with vodka. As his friends staggered into their 13th pub of the day – The Lord Moon of the Mall – McGowan collapsed on Whitehall and was rushed to hospital, where he died from alcohol poisoning.

MORTAL AND PESTLE II

Indian deliveryman Rohit Kumar died on the job when a couple in a fourth-storey apartment of the building he was delivering to began to row violently. Nisha Dhyani threw a pestle at her husband, but it missed him and went through a window before crashing down and smashing the skull of Mr Kumar as he was getting into his truck.

MIDSUMMER MADNESS I

Every year, Midsummer's Eve in Finland is ground zero for ridiculous, alcohol-influenced deaths. The Finnish authorities record dozens of booze-related ones on the Juhannus (John the Baptist) holiday weekend. One of the many way Finns celebrate is by lighting bonfires and then attempting to leap over them. This proved fatal for Erkii Ollila in 2009. He set himself alight whilst leaping over a fire beside Lake Joneri. Ollila rushed into the lake in an attempt to douse himself. Unfortunately, the beer and vodka he had been drinking for 12 hours straight meant that whilst he put out the flames, he soon drowned.

MIDSUMMER MADNESS II

Kuisma Tolppanen also died in a Finnish Midsummer's Eve bonfire incident in 2009. However, Tolppanen had drunk so much he did not catch light by leaping over the fire, but rather in his extreme drunken state, he thought that building and lighting a bonfire in the kitchen of his apartment in Espoo was a good idea. It was not. The resulting blaze from Tolppanen's internal bonfire claimed his life and burnt his housing block to the ground.

SATELLITE OF DEATH

When his London council refused Kabhir Ahmed permission to place a satellite dish on the top of the 15-storey tower block in which he lived in 1996, he took matters into his own hands, sawing off the lock that prevented access to the roof. However, Kabhir's attempts at DIY satellite installation went awry. A passer-by below saw him hanging off the building, desperately clinging to a swaying cable. By the time emergency services had arrived on the scene, Ahmed had already toppled to his death.

WAY OUT

You cannot accuse suicide John York of not having a sense of irony. The 54-year-old plumber with money problems hung himself from the 'Way Out' sign of an industrial estate in Kent in 1995.

TOP 10 RIDICULOUS ALCOHOL-RELATED DEATHS – BOOZE LOSERS!

10. Kenyan Olympic gold medal-winning marathon runner Samuel Wanjiru turned to drink to cope with the pressures of success. One day in May 2011, he got drunk at a local pub and took a prostitute back to his marital home. When Wanjiru's wife discovered them in bed, she locked them in the bedroom and stormed out of the house. Wanjiru rushed to the bedroom's balcony to shout to her and took a drunken tumble from the second storey to his death.

9. Drinking and driving is never good, but when brothers Ken and Bobby Berger got into a row over directions to a cousin's house in Nevada in 1994, Ken began to beat Bobby with a bottle of beer he was drinking, causing Bobby to lose control of their car and smash into a parked trucked. Both brothers were killed, but their mother Eileen who was in the back, survived the crash.

8. Yorkshireman Adam Arnott drank 13 pints on a rugby club coach outing in 1986. Inebriated and with a desperate need to relieve his bladder, Arnott opened the emergency door on the vehicle and attempted to urinate out onto the M1 motorway whilst travelling at speeds of 80km/h. Unsurprisingly, he fell to his death.

7. Filipino Enrique Calixto had threatened to kill his wife's dog several times. One night after drinking in a bar in Makati, he returned home and tried to shoot the pooch with a revolver. He managed only to shoot himself in the leg twice and was too drunk to raise help, leading him to bleed to death.

6. Don't make a bet whilst drunk. Cambodian Neth Sary was bet by drunk pals that he would not stand under a hornet's nest whilst they threw stones at it. Drunk as them, he agreed. Unsurprisingly, the stone throwing brought out a swarm of angry insects that stung Neth and one of his friends, recorded only as Bo, to death.

5. Ihor Doroshenko died at Moscow's Sheremetyevo International Airport in September 2009. After being told he could not bring two 1.5-litre bottles of vodka onto a plane in his hand luggage and that he either had to surrender the bottles or have his hand luggage go as cargo, Doroshenko staged a sit-down protest and began to drink the vodka. He emptied the bottles into himself, and when airport security tried to remove him, he fled and ran directly into the path of a taxi and was killed instantly.

4. In 1987, boozed-up rugby supporter Andrew Dinsmore was so annoyed when a vending machine at a London train station swallowed his money but did not give him a chocolate bar, that he climbed on top of the machine to try to rock the whole thing to the ground. Unfortunately his plan worked too well and the machine came crashing down, but with him underneath it.

3. There are good places to be drunk and bad places to be drunk. A battlefield is a bad place. Drunken Romanian soldiers awaiting an advancing Ottoman army at Caransebeş in 1788, shouted 'Turcii! Turcii!', causing their Austrian, Balkan and Italian comrades to think the Turks were coming. The allied troops then began to fire on each other. When the Ottoman army arrived two days later, they found 10,000 already dead or wounded soldiers and easily won the day.

2. When Andy Chapel's wife left him for another woman in 1988, his mates in a Bristol pub bought him drinks to help cheer him up. In fact they bought him eight pints of lager, six double whiskies, four brandies and a pint of bitter in just under two hours. Whether it cheered Chapel up or not, it certainly gave him the acute alcohol poisoning which killed him that night.

1. When the iron sailing ship the *Royal Adelaide* ran aground on Chesil Beach in Dorset in November 1872, a huge crowd gathered not to help save the 60 passengers and crew, but to pillage its cargo – the bulk of which was gin and brandy. Whilst six passengers and one looter died in the waves, four of the wreckers died on the beach from exposure after having become so drunk on retrieved barrels of booze they could not make their way home.

DIVINE JUSTICE? IV

Metal theft has become endemic across the globe with even 22-tonne bridges being stolen in Ukraine and Turkey. Hundreds of churches in England have had the lead stolen from their roofs, but one in Essex seemed to have more than its fair share of divine protection. Jaakob Lepp was struck by lightning at a church near Epping forest, his partners in crime leaving his burnt corpse on the roof after the vengeance of the Lord persuaded them to knock the thieving on the head for that night.

IS TONY BLAIR THE ANTICHRIST?

To be fair to August Odinga, he was not the only person in the world to think Tony Blair is the antichrist. However, as far as I know, he is the only one who has committed suicide because of his belief. Odinga stepped in front of an express train at a station in London in 2009. In his pockets at the time of his death was a 14-page suicide note explaining he wanted to die before the former PM brought about the apocalypse. The note also urged others to read the 'proof' Odinga had left in his home. The 'proof' turned out to be several notebooks full of his theory, including strange numerological interpretations of Blair's name and a code unlocking a speech made by Cherie Blair which proved she was the whore of Babylon.

LIGHT SABRE DUEL

Alan Holt and his pal Jamie Barnes went out for a night of heavy drinking in the English town of Bolton in 1999. On their way home from the pub they came across a skip filled with old fittings from a shop which was being refurbished, and pulled out two 1.8m long fluorescent light bulbs and began, according to Barnes, 'to have a light sabre fight with them, like those Jedi in Star Wars.' Predictably, the bulbs soon smashed, but Holt was too inebriated to realize that when they shattered, a shard of glass had embedded itself in his neck. Although he appeared fine when he went to bed, Holt was dead when Barnes tried to wake him the next morning.

OUTFOXED

If you are going to go shooting with a shotgun, always unload it before carrying it home. If farmer George Ives had followed this basic rule, he might still be alive today. Unfortunately, Ives returned from destroying foxes on his Norfolk farm in 1996 and snagged the hammer of the gun as he was taking off his coat, managing to blast himself in the head from a range of a few inches.

WHAT A GAS

Belgian lorry driver Fabian Neyrinck suffocated after overdosing on nitrous oxide in 2002. His wife found his body, naked aside from an army surplus gasmask, beside three empty canisters of the 'laughing gas'. You can bet she was not amused.

TILL DEATH DO US PART

Brazilian Fabio Maciel, 33, died at the reception of his own wedding in November 2012 when he was fooling around with the bridesmaids and fell onto his front. The beer glass which for some unknown reason he had put into his left-trouser pocket, shattered and a shard of glass severed his femoral artery. Maciel died from blood loss as attempts were made to rush him to hospital.

OFF HIS HEAD

Englishman David Phyall, 58, was the last resident on an estate that was to be demolished and then rebuilt. Phyall was so upset about being forced out of his housing association flat that he mounted a terrible protest when he received his final eviction notice in 2008 – he cut off his own head with a chainsaw.

BASE-IC MISTAKE I

BASE (Building Antenna Span Earth) Jumping is a 'sport' where idiots of a certain ilk jump off tall objects using a parachute or wingsuit. I trust, dear reader, you can see why BASE jumping off skyscrapers, radio antennae, bridges and rock formations and ridiculous death go together. The fact that so many adherents to the sport cannot see this is more than something of a basic mistake.

In BASE jumping circles, the name of Carl Boenish is a legend. Considered one of the founding fathers of the sport, Boenish did a huge amount to spread its popularity by expertly filming his freefalls. In something of an oxymoron-ish move, he also published BASE *Magazine* to promote safety in the world of BASE jumping. In 1984, he was killed leaping off Norway's Troll Wall – the highest vertical rock face in Europe at 1,100m – whilst filming himself for a segment of the TV show *That's Incredible!* Whilst most of us might learn something from such an incredibly stupid stunt, BASE fans have not, with the Troll Wall having taken another seven BASE jumpers' lives since 1984.

THE DEATH OF WOLVERINE

What the police thought when they got a call that Superman was fighting with Green Lantern, Batman, Captain America and the Hulk in Liverpool in 2001 is not recorded, but they still turned up to a stag night brawl that had broken out over which one of Darren Alsop's friends had the right to wear the cape of Superman. As a squad car approached with its sirens blaring, the wannabe superheroes scattered into the night to avoid arrest. Unfortunately, Robert Bovis – who was dressed as Wolverine – ran straight into the path of a car and was sent hurtling into the air. Without any innate mutant healing powers, the collision proved fatal.

CHRISTMAS SPIRITS

It was an unhappy Christmas for the families of four men from the Brazilian city of Aracaju in 2008. They were working to erect a 120m aluminium Christmas Tree when it fell on them, crushing them to death.

DEATH BY THE BOOK

Petite Bibliophile Kate Collins, 36, had books stacked in shelves all the way up to the ceiling of her London flat, but she did not have the common sense to buy a stepladder. Instead, when she wanted to reach a book on the top shelf she improvised by piling books onto a chair until she could get the intended tome. According to her partner Sue Evans, this arrangement worked well until one day in March 2008, when Kate overbalanced, fell backwards and smashed her head on a coffee table. Speaking at her inquest, Sue said: 'It's a tragedy that Katie was killed by something she got so much pleasure from. With hindsight, we should have got a ladder, but we both thought they were just so ugly to have around the place.'

BATMAN, THE JOKE'S ON YOU

The Cosmic Joker seems to like to have the last laugh on those dressing up as superheroes. Will Buxton donned a Batman costume for a friend's stag night in Newcastle. After several pints he began to get into character and started leaping off benches and bins shouting: 'Kap-pow!' and 'Whammo!' When one car owner objected to the caped idiot using his bonnet as a platform, Buxton attempted to jump onto another parked car, misjudged his leap and smashed his head onto the concrete below. He died on the way to hospital.

THE COSMIC JOKER STRIKES AGAIN II

At first glance there is nothing ridiculous in the story of James Karl Bach, who was arrested by Alberta police for manslaughter after a body was discovered with multiple stab wounds. Nothing at all ridiculous until you discover that the victim's name was Brent Stabbed Last.

DEAD AS A DOG

Bill Dalton went outside his Colorado home to pour his dog a beer in July 1995. He tripped and fell into his pooch's drink bowl, managing to drown himself in less than 7.5cm of water. An autopsy subsequently showed Dalton to be almost four times over the drink drive limit at the time of his death.

KILLED BY KINDNESS

This sad story of death will warm the cockles of all those conservatives who do not believe in the idea of welfare or helping others. Wu Shan, a 36-year-old homeless man from the Chinese city of Nanjing, died in 2008 thanks to the charity of those around him. When people heard that Wu had not eaten for several days, he was given so much food that he was able to gorge himself. According to one benefactor: 'When he collapsed, we all thought it was just tiredness. Now we know he ate himself to death. I do not feel bad about giving him food, but I will be more careful when helping the homeless in the future.'

SLEEPWALKING TO SUICIDE

Poor Claire Brent, 18, hung herself with a silk scarf from her shower rail, probably whilst sleepwalking. A 2008 inquest in England heard that Claire had become increasingly disturbed by rumours that a previous occupant of her flat had hanged herself – rumours which had no basis in fact. Her sister told the coroner that Claire was frightened by the supernatural and constantly talked about feeling a presence in her home. The inquest recorded an open verdict on the basis of the strong possibility that the vivid nature of Claire's dreams about the non-factual hanging may have influenced her pattern of sleepwalking.

DOG EAT DOG

Cambodian hunter Ra Bophal saw his friend and fellow hunter Noun Sen's dog killed by a monkey in 2008, incensing Noun by doing nothing to stop the simian killing canine. Ra crossed any remaining line of friendship when instead of burying the dog for his friend as promised, he took it home and ate it. When Noun discovered what Ra had been feasting on, he took a crossbow and shot his former friend in the head.

SLEEPWALKING (AND SWIMMING) TO MURDER

Sleepwalkers killing themselves or others is not a new phenomenon. Tragic and ridiculous cases have been recorded across history. One of the most notable was recorded by seventeenth century Polish physician Jan Jonston in his book *Thaumatographia Naturalis*. The case happened in Paris in 1630 when a citizen of the city whilst asleep, took his sword, swam across the Seine, killed a man and returned home to his bed without waking. Unlike judges today who are more likely to entertain a somnambulist defence, the Parisian sleepwalker was executed for his night-time crime.

THE COSMIC JOKER STRIKES AGAIN III

Spanish truck driver Alfredo Rios was making a 32km pilgrimage on foot in August 2011 to give thanks at the Virgin of Miracles shrine in Calon for his miraculous recovery from what should have been a fatal traffic accident. Less than 1.6km into his sacred walk, Rios and his two aunts who were with him, were hit and killed by a car driven by a man who had fallen asleep at the wheel.

MATERIALISM KILLS

Compulsive shopper Babs Piper had stuffed her home in Birmingham, England with so many things – including more than a hundred unused umbrellas and 200 teddy bears – that when a stack of suitcases fell on her, she became trapped in the piles of her possessions and died of dehydration. The police began to search for Babs when she was reported missing in 2008, but it took them three days to find her body amongst her hoard of consumer items.

STRIKE, NO SPARE

Idaho resident Nathan Pointer, 62, got his first perfect score of 300 in more than a decade of playing on a tenpin bowling team in October 2008. However, as he was high-fiving his team-mates, the excitement brought on a heart attack that led to him dying in hospital the next day.

BASE-IC MISTAKE II

The world of BASE jumping is thick with ridiculous death. One of the many that stands out is that of Jean-Marc Boivin. An extreme sport pioneer, the French mountaineer had achieved fame through making films of his daredevil hang gliding, paragliding and skiing stunts. In February 1990, he successfully BASE jumped off Angel Falls in Venezuela, the highest waterfall in the world. Repeating the stunt the following day, he hit the cliff and landed in some trees. The helicopter team following him thought his waving meant he was uninjured rather than that he was attempting to summon help, and so proceeded to another rescue. This left Boivin to die in the trees from internal injuries and blood loss he had sustained in the fall.

OVER THE LIMIT, OVER THE EDGE

Doing anything with a hint of danger is always a dumb idea when you have had too much to drink. University student Shannon Gill, 20, used fake ID to go out and raise the level of alcohol in her bloodstream to more than twice the drink drive limit. Whilst that is not dangerous in itself, she then attempted to break into her boyfriend's fraternity room via an adjoining window ledge nearly 9m off the ground. Just before she took a tumble to her death she called out: 'I'm not sure I can make this.' Sometimes it is a bitch to be right.

CURSE OF THE MUMMY?

Ten would-be grave robbers were buried alive while illegally digging for ancient Egyptian relics under a house in the village of Arab al-Manasra near Luxor in March 2013. Local residents said one of the men was cursed from performing a previous grave-robbing in the city of Ismaïlia.

SMOKING KILLS VII – STICK TO MATCHES

Yorkshireman Len Hatton, 72, died when he tried to refill his Zippo lighter with fluid. The pensioner, who suffered from tremors, used a pair of scissors to widen the hole at the top of his can of lighter fluid, causing a spark that led to it exploding in a fireball that claimed Hatton's life.

MAKING MORTALITY OUT OF A MOLEHILL

Polish gardener Zbyszek Ziola was so outraged by the molehills on the lawns of his home in Zbaszyneck that he persuaded his son to steal 15 sticks of explosive from the military base where he was stationed. At just after midnight on March 12, 2012, Ziola Sr proceeded to place the illegal explosive in the network of mole-made tunnels in his garden. However, the would-be mole murderer misjudged his timing and the force of the explosion, and his poor wife awoke to a massive blast and the discovery of several pieces of her husband's body scattered around the garden.

IT SHOULDN'T HAPPEN TO A VET

You would think that a vet would have the common sense not to get too close to a wild pygmy elephant. Oh no, not in the case of Claire Powell. The 25-year-old English vet was a tourist on a wildlife reserve in Borneo when she spotted the elephant trampling in a mud volcano and moved to within 6m of it to take pictures. The elephant then charged at Powell, who fell in the mud and was gored by the pygmy pachyderm.

THE SHOCKING PRICE OF PETROL

The price of petrol is truly alarming these days. In fact, it is so astronomical that when German driver Manfred Wehner, 73, saw the amount he had to pay when he filled up the tank of his BMW in February 2012, he suffered a fatal heart attack due to the discrepancy between the price per litre advertised outside the gas station and the electronic price at the pump.

A TERRIBLE BRUSH WITH DEATH

Englishwoman Claire Tobin got a 15cm toilet brush handle embedded in her buttock after a drunken fall in a friend's bathroom in 2005. Despite showing doctors her wound, she could not convince them there was anything inside it and it was only after two years of pain that she was able to prove the plastic was still inside her. Unfortunately, during the two-year interval, the handle had moved from her buttock to her pelvis and two operations failed to retrieve it. She underwent further surgery to try to get it cut out in 2009, but died on the operating table.

BASE-IC MISTAKE III

In the idiotic annals of the ridiculous sport of BASE jumping, few names are as celebrated as Thor Alex Kappfjell. The Norwegian twat made a name for himself by jumping off the 61st floor of the Chrysler Building in 1998 and the observation deck of the World Trade Center in 1999. With more than 200 BASE jumps accomplished, Kappfjell was somewhat arrogant, telling one journalist: 'I am only worried by getting arrested by the cops, not death.' We all know what that sort of pride goes before ...

In July 1999, Kappfjell died leaping off Norway's Kjerag Mountain. Ignoring advice, he made his jump in thick fog. He quickly lost his bearings and hit the face of the cliff, sliding down it for several hundred feet. Cocky idiot.

ONE MORE FOR THE ROAD TO HELL

You never get thanks or sensible actions from a drunk. Tasmanian labourer Pat McGuinness was dragged in an insensible drunken condition from his burning cottage by his wife in April 1901. Instead of thanking her, the boozed-up ingrate threw her to the ground and then staggered back into the building to retrieve a bottle of grog. He was burned to death as the cottage disintegrated around him.

KNOWING WHEN TO STOP

Getting so drunk you do not care or do not know what is in your next drink is a definite sign not to take another drop. It is a shame Susie Poulton, 20, from Vancouver, was already too drunk for such rational thought. Whilst at a party in 1994, she mistook a bottle of anti-freeze being stored in a soda bottle for more booze and ended up pouring herself a life-ending shot of ethylene glycol.

BOSS HOG

According to his friends, German hunter Gottlob Huber, 72, had enjoyed a good day of sport shooting animals in the woods around Linthe. The prize of the day was a wild boar he had shot and brought to ground. When he went to inspect his 'kill', to his surprise, the beast reared up and attacked him. A bite in his leg severed Huber's femoral artery, leading to massive blood loss and death.

PLANE DAFT COMEDOWN

Drug smuggler Graham Marples, 44, was so desperate to get off the small plane he had hired to transport 20 kilos of cannabis from Holland to England in 1996, that as soon as it landed he ripped open the canopy, jumped out and ran straight into the propellers. Pilot Graham Jones said: 'I've never had a more nervous passenger.'

BASE-IC MISTAKE IV

Canadian Shane McConkey was a professional skier who combined skiing with BASE jumping. He made his name starring in extreme sport films, performing such stunts as skiing off the Eiger and going into a BASE jump. In March 2009, McConkey was filmed in Italy's Dolomite Mountains. The planned stunt was for him to ski off a mountain, go into a double back flip and then glide away in a wingsuit. However, McConkey could not release his skis and by the time he had got them off he had been free-falling for 12 seconds and was too close to the ground for his wingsuit or emergency parachute to do him any good.

HOARDING HELL

Englishman Colin Broad, 74, died of thirst after becoming lost in the complex network of tunnels he had built through the rubbish that he accumulated in his home in Bolton across more than two decades. When he was not seen for several days, firemen had to don breathing apparatus to deal with the fetid smell of years of rotting rubbish. After a day, they discovered Broad's body amid a confusing system of passageways and tunnels built from rubbish bags, boxes and car parts.

MAGICAL MORT XIII

Zimbabwean football player Justice Nhengu was told by his team's witchdoctor to bathe in a river near Victoria Falls to cleanse himself of bad spirits ahead of an important match in September 2008. The witchdoctor was insistent that Justice go into the river despite it being prohibited due to the triple whammy of strong currents, crocodiles and hippos. Unsurprisingly, Justice did not get to play in the big game due to drowning.

WATER OF DEATH

Some Christians talk about the water of life, but drinking good old H_2O proved to be the death of Englishman Daniel Lewis. The unfortunate man had developed an addiction to water, but the mania for drinking multiple pints of water per day did not do him any harm until one day in 2008 he decided to drink directly from a hosepipe. This led to him overdosing and developing water intoxication – a fatal disturbance of brain functions that occurs when the balance of electrolytes in the body is thrown out of whack by overhydration.

MORTAL MOCHI

Seven Japanese pensioners died in New Year celebrations in 2012 through choking on mochi rice cake. Mochi are traditionally added to ozouni soup in meals to celebrate New Year. However, they have a track record of causing death, with the highest previous mochi pensioner wipe-out record occurring in 2010, when six people over the age of 70 choked on the glutinous balls of death.

SMOKING KILLS VIII – WORST WAY TO QUIT

Malaysian man Mohamed Ibrahim Kader Mydin, 47, was visiting relatives in Kuala Lumpur during Ramadan in 2008 when they suggested an unusual method to help him stop smoking – a religious ritual in which he would be beaten. Mohamed agreed to the very alternative treatment and they proceeded to hit him with broomsticks and a motorcycle helmet until he passed out. The beating proved so severe that an ambulance had to be called, but Mohamed died en route to the hospital. Personally I would have stuck with the nicotine gum.

POLICE CONFIRM MUTANT KILLER PIG

This book led to one of the strangest phone calls I have ever made as a journalist. To verify a story, I rang the police in Prey Veng, Cambodia. The conversation went as follows:

Me: Can you tell me, did a man called Sean Sok die from being eaten by a five-legged pig?

Police: Yes, this is a famous story.

Me: Did it really happen?

Police: You insult us if you think it did not. Why would we lie?

Me: A five-legged pig, it just sounds ridiculous.

Police: These things happen here from time to time. It was a bad business.

Me: What happened?

Police: The gardener (63-year-old Sean Sok) found the pig eating his vegetables. He tried to beat the pig away, but the pig knocked him down and began to eat him. People came and found the big pig eating and chased it away. The son then killed the pig.

Me: And the pig had five legs?

Police: Yes. Very big pig.

Me: This really happened?

Police: Yes! You make me angry saying it did not.

There you go, according to police in Cambodia, a man was eaten by a five-legged pig and that sort of thing happens from time to time on their patch. Frankly, that is one of the most ridiculous things I have ever heard said about one of the most ridiculous and singular ways to die I have come across.

THE WEDDING THAT WENT OFF WITH A BANG III

Weddings and guns should never go together like love and marriage. In 2010, Pakistani groom Pankaj Kishore was accidentally shot by his uncle when he fired his handgun into the air at the wedding to celebrate his nephew's nuptials.

BOLTS FROM THE BLUE

Barry Hawkins told his girlfriend Cindy Edwards they were going on a scenic hike when he led her to the top of Max Patch Bald in North Carolina in 2010. When they were at the peak, he surprised her by taking out a ring and proposing. Cindy said yes, but within moments of accepting, the pair were hit by three bolts of lightning, killing poor Cindy and giving Barry third-degree burns.

SAFARI, SO BAD

South Africa's Kruger National Park is a dangerous place to go poaching. In 2010, rangers caught two poachers fleeing from hippos. When they investigated further, they found part of the head and clothing of a third poacher who had run from the hippos straight into a pride of lions, which had promptly eaten him.

TRUCKING HELL, IT'S WINDY

A 35-year-old engineer was crushed to death when high winds blew a lorry off all of its four wheels at a notoriously windy area near a Leeds skyscraper in 2011. The driver of the truck survived the accident and told the subsequent coroner's court: 'I was doing 32km/h when suddenly I was floating through the air. The wind just carried me like a hot air balloon.'

SUED IN THE AFTERLIFE

Poor 18-year-old Hiroyuki Joho died as he hurried across the track of the Edgebrook Metra station in Chicago. He was using an umbrella to shield himself from heavy rain and did not see the southbound Amtrak train approaching at more than 112km/h. What makes his death ridiculous was that his family was subsequently sued by Gasyane Zokhrabov, 58, who had her leg and wrist broken when the train sent a large part of Joho's body smashing into her. Zokhrabov won her case and her lawyer said: 'If you do something stupid, as this guy did, you have to be responsible for what comes from it, even if you are dead.'

WHAT AN OFFAL WAY TO GO

Austrian recycling plant worker Martin Hueber died when the offal and out of date food which had been left to rot in a steel container generated so much natural gas that it exploded, showering him in lethal shrapnel.

LAST BREATH

I had hoped when we did the first 1001 *Ridiculous Ways To Die* that deaths through the insane religious belief in breatharianism would die out after the deaths of Timo Degen and Verity Linn. No such luck, the idiot faith keeps on killing. Believers in breatharianism think you can live without food and water, holding to the idea humans can be sustained solely by mystic prana energy or sunlight. This belief is not harmless hokum, as some of those who swallow breatharianism give up swallowing food.

In 2011, Swiss woman Anna Gut, 53, died from starvation. She had been following ideas on breatharianism she had seen in the 2010 Swiss film *In The Beginning There Was Light*, which features claims from anthropologist Michael Werner to have lived without food for nine years and yogi Prahlad Joni, who said he had not eaten in 70 years. Misguided Gut is not the only Swiss person in history to believe in the bollocks of breatharianism; the country's patron saint – Nicholas of Flüe – is meant to have lived for 19 years without eating or drinking.

IN THE SOUP

A worker at the Erasco Soup Factory in Lübeck, Germany climbed a giant cauldron used in the manufacturing process to clean it out in 2009. Unfortunately, the lid closed on the cauldron whilst he was in it, triggering an automatic steaming process, cooking him alive.

TOP 10 RIDICULOUS DIY-RELATED DEATHS – PLANKS AND NAILS IN COFFINS

10. I am of the view DIY is so dangerous, one day it will be banned. It certainly proved deadly for 80-year-old Edgar Broughton. The stepladder he was using to clean out his gutters collapsed under him, sending him headfirst into a water butt. He was found some time later by a neighbour with his legs poking out of the 1.2m deep container.

9. Former Major League Baseball catcher Bo Díaz tried his hand at DIY satellite dish repair in 1990 when high winds knocked his receiver off line at his home in Venezuela. The elite sportsman should have left the job to a professional because the dish collapsed as he adjusted it, crushing his skull and neck against its base.

8. If you are going to do DIY, at least use the right tools. Guy Cassidy, 23, was fixing some metal panels to a pal's fast food kiosk in 2010, when he slipped from the tub of mayonnaise he was standing on instead of a ladder. As he fell, he pressed the power drill he was holding into his chest, making one hole not fixable with a bit of plaster.

7. James Scott from Arizona could not figure out how to get an old couch out of his living room in November 2010. Becoming frustrated by trying to push it through the door and window, he decided to cut it up with a chainsaw. His plan turned fatal: whilst swinging the chainsaw, he connected with the light fitting above, electrocuting himself.

6. Welshman Ben Parks was using a cordless nail gun whilst building a walk-in wardrobe in his girlfriend's bedroom in 2004. When the front doorbell rang, he came down the stairs to answer it, tripped and managed to shoot several nails into his chest, hitting his heart and lungs.

5. Donald Fraser Baker of Georgia was so frustrated his botched attempt to construct a flatpack display cabinet in 1999, that he began to smash his horrible handiwork. Unluckily for Baker, shattering one of the panes of glass sent a razor sharp fragment into his neck, severing his carotid artery, leading to his death from blood loss.

4. Bungling DIYer Barry Holden wanted to create an open-plan kitchen and dining room in his Manchester home in 1996. A barrier to his grand design was the load-bearing wall separating them, which Holden was knocking out with a sledgehammer when the bedroom from the flat above toppled in on him, leaving him crushed to death by a wardrobe and a bed.

3. Al Spencer from Everett, Washington, thought that the best and quickest way to demolish an unstable chimney on his house was to attach chains to it and try pulling it down with his truck. After several minutes of seemingly getting nowhere, Spencer got out of his truck, angrily slamming the vehicle's door, and died from the subsequent shower of loosened bricks.

2. Ronald Long from Deepwater, Missouri was attempting to install a satellite TV dish on his house in 2008. Failing to punch a hole in a wall with conventional work tools, Long fired his .22 handgun into the wall, but ended up not with a convenient space to pull wires through, but a dead wife and a lot of explaining to do when the police arrived.

1. How would you expect the second-in-command of the Montreal Mafia family to die? A hail of bullets? A garrotte twisted around the neck? Try an absurd DIY disaster. Second-in-command of the Canadian Mob, Underboss Luigi Greco was trying to save some money by doing some DIY to renovate a family pizzeria in December 1972. Greco used a mop-dipped in gasoline and then a metal scraper to try and remove a build up of grease on the floor. A spark from the metal interacted with the gasoline resulting in a terrible explosion and flash fire, leading to Greco dying in hospital from burn and blast injuries.

PIGEON ANNOUNCED DEATH

Frenchman Gerard Gagne died in his sleep aged 78 in 2008. What makes his death ridiculous is that his mummified body was discovered only after more than three years because a pigeon flew into his Strasbourg apartment and sat on the radio, turning it on so loud that neighbours complained and the police investigated.

THE COSMIC JOKER STRIKES AGAIN IV

English road safety campaigner John White, 66, was killed by a speeding van in 2012 on the very stretch of road in North Yorkshire where he had protested to have the speed limit reduced from 96km/h to 48km/h.

NO PYJAMA PARTY

An inmate at the infamous Paris prison of La Santé weaved a pair of allegedly 'suicide proof' paper pyjamas into a lethal noose and rope and hung himself in February 2012. Authorities pledged they would look more closely at the contents of the anti-suicide kit issued to prisoners thought to be at risk of topping themselves.

BANG GOES THE ALIBI

Italian Salvatore Scandale, 51, shot his wife Mariella with a Beretta handgun one August evening in 2011 and then rang the police to confess. When they arrived to find her dead in bed, Salvatore told them he had killed her whilst sleeping because he had dreamed she was having 'sex like a prostitute with another man' and did not wake up until his gun went off. You probably will not be surprised to learn that the police did not buy his excuse and Scandale soon found himself up on a murder charge.

MOO-TAL BLOW TO A DINKY NINJA

How do you expect an expert Thai kickboxer and cage fighter with the nickname 'McCrazy' to die? In some bar room brawl? A bloody cage fight gone wrong? Oh no. Ally McCrae, 23, may have been a martial art specialist and champion fighter in the Dinky Ninja team, but he died when nearly one ton of cow carcass slipped from a hook as it moved along an abattoir conveyor belt and crushed him. A McCrazy way to go, really.

MAGICAL MORT XIV

There are some places in the world where whatever magical powers you think you have, being a magician is an appallingly bad idea. Top of those places would probably be Saudi Arabia. In October 2011, Sudanese magic man Abdul Hamid was publicly beheaded with a sword for sorcery. Hamid had been entrapped by an undercover officer of the Mutawa'een (religious) police into accepting 6,000 Saudi riyals to make a spell to cause the officer's father to leave his second wife.

BLOODY RIDICULOUS

Gardener Ken Kramer, 47, died just four hours after suffering a nosebleed whilst walking in his local town centre in Essex in 2011. He visited an emergency doctor, who advised him to go home and put ice on his nose, but he was later found dead in bed. An inquest heard he had died from blood obstructing his airways, but the pathologist was at a loss to explain it, saying: 'In 4,000 post-mortems I've never seen a case like it. We don't know how to explain it.' One of Ken's close friends said: 'It seems bloody ridiculous that something so minor as a nosebleed should have killed him.'

DEATH SNUGGLE

Every death, even if ridiculous, is also full of tragedy and heartbreak. Poor Iain MacDonald, 47, an 83kg ex-chef, rolled over onto his 51kg girlfriend Sandra Bromley for as little as 15 seconds as they snuggled whilst sleeping on the sofa in 2011. However, those few seconds were enough for him to accidentally smother her to death. A coroner recorded a verdict of accidental death after hearing from a pathologist that it was clear Bromley had died 'as a result of somebody sleeping on top of her.'

DOCTOR'S ORDERS BEST NOT FOLLOWED

Friday the 13th of April 2012 was definitely unlucky for Claire Somerton. Whilst a patient at an English hospital, she was ordered to go outside for a walk by one of her doctors. Out walking, she was attacked by a horse that had run away from a nearby gypsy encampment, and kicked to death.

A NUTTY WAY TO GO

Adam Wells had always adored peanut butter and had eaten peanuts safely for three decades, but on Christmas Eve 2012, he suddenly developed an extreme allergic reaction to them. He had a handful of the nuts and died when his body went into anaphylactic shock and his throat closed up.

THERE'S NO PLACE LIKE HOME

Swiss couple Daniela Weiss and Daniel Oelter had spent five years travelling around together, visiting some of the most dangerous spots in the Middle East – including Syria during the civil war. The pair died two days after returning home when they were hit by a train just yards from their flat in the town of Gränichen.

DIED STANDING UP

Guy Webster, 35, was found dead0 but standing up and with his right hand reaching into a cupboard in the kitchen of his Kent home in July 2012. An autopsy showed he was four times over the legal drink drive limit at the time of his death and an inquest decided he had hurt his head earlier, but had not realized how severe the injury was. He then blacked out, his body falling against the kitchen fittings and remaining standing up as he died from asphyxiation of the lungs.

POLICEMAN ON THE PISS

I grew up with the traditional saying of 'drunk as a lord' to describe high levels of intoxication. In Romania, a common saying is 'as drunk as a cop'. It might be a maxim based on fact if the death of Romanian policeman Vasile Kovesi is in any way typical of Romanian police behaviour. Kovesi, 26, was found dead, lying on his stomach outside of his mother's home in Botosani with his face in a puddle of rainwater and his own urine. Lamentably, his former colleagues were less than keen to discuss his demise with me. They did, however, share just how drunk that particular cop was when he drowned in his own pee, nearly four times over the legal drink drive limit.

DEATH SPOT

Bradley Bruce, 16, was a passenger in a car when he died in a head-on vehicle collision in September 2012 that occurred at exactly the same spot on a quiet Derbyshire road where his father had been knocked down and killed whilst out walking eight years earlier.

EGGED ON

Tunisian market stall-holder Dhaov Fatnassi died in December 2012 after he agreed to eat 30 raw eggs as part of a bet. He had managed to consume 28 eggs when he began to complain of acute stomach pains and died as he was being rushed to hospital by ambulance. An autopsy was unable to establish a clear cause of death, but the pathologist linked the sudden passing with the amount of eggs eaten.

HEAVY METAL DIET

Indian farmer Kamelshwar Singh died in 2011 after eating 6kg of metal across a nine-month period. Amongst the items in his metallic diet of death were 431 coins, 17 bolts, 196 iron pellets and three keys. Not unsurprisingly, the cause of Kamelshwar's death was determined by the Shreesti Medical Institute as chronic ulceration.

DOORWAY TO DEATH

Swede Fredrik Nylen, 28, was at the Danderyd Hospital in Stockholm in February 2012 for a routine outpatient appointment. However, he stood too close to a windowless automatic door and was sent flying when it opened, sending him smashing into a reception desk, which split his head open. Despite the accident happening where emergency care was on tap, Nylen never regained consciousness.

POST-DEATH SEX-CHANGE SHOCK

Canadian Elizabeth Rudavsky endured months of beatings from husband Angelo Heddington until it became too much for her and she snapped in 2003, stabbing him in the chest. It was only after Angelo's death that Rudavsky learnt her late husband was, in fact, a woman with a false penis. Born Angela, Heddington had claimed a previous girlfriend had burnt his penis so insisted on always making love with the lights out.

VENUS POOL IS NO LAZARUS LAKE

Stanley Stone, 55, wanted to investigate the health benefits of bathing in the Venus hot pool in the Waiotapu Reserve in New Zealand in October 1936. He had told a companion that he believed a dip in the geothermal spring would revive his body and take years off of him, even going as far to say: 'I believe this water could even revive Lazarus from the dead.' However, Stone was soon overcome by the heat and sulphurous fumes whilst swimming in the pool and the water refused to show any ability to raise him from the dead.

HOOK, LINE AND SINKER

Sydney-based amateur angler Oscar Philips croaked his last whilst fishing in February 1898. He lost his footing whilst casting his line into the Hawkesbury River, plunged into the water and as he fell, managed to get his line so tightly wrapped around his body he could not swim to the shore.

BANANA SKINS ARE NO JOKE

When the ridiculous deaths come up in conversation, one question I am often asked is: 'Has anyone ever died from slipping on a banana skin?' Yes, they have. The person being Mrs Olga Doreen Armstrong, 25, of Gouldburn, NSW who slipped on one left on a footpath whilst she was out shopping in December 1937. There you go, the banana skin – staple of global slapstick comedy and as deadly as arsenic on toast.

ARSENIC ON TOAST

Has anyone ever died from arsenic on toast, though? Oh ye of little faith. Of course they have. In 1926, groundsman James Hilton retired to his hut to make himself a pot of tea and enjoy a spot of cheese on toast after a long afternoon spraying insecticide on his employer's Berkshire estate. Lamentably, the insecticide contained lead arsenate and Hilton did not wash his hands before cooking, thereby managing to accidentally kill himself with a fatal dose of arsenic on toast.

STRUCK OUT

Fame is no protection against a ridiculous death, especially when you are a lousy drunk. Baseball Hall of Fame outfielder 'Big Ed' Delahanty was certainly a lousy drunk on the night of July 2, 1903 when he was thrown off a train in Buffalo for being drunk, raving about death and threatening fellow passengers with a razor. Delahanty then tried to make his way across the International Bridge near Niagara Falls when he slipped, fell from the bridge and into the raging waters feeding the Falls.

UP, UP AND DOWN

The history of ridiculous deaths has many stories of inventors killed by their own inventions. Among them is Michael Dacre, a British-born aviation pioneer who was testing out his Jetpod 'flying taxi' in Malaysia in 2009. Other aviation engineers had criticized his design for the five-seater craft as unworkable, unflyable and dangerous, but Dacre persevered. On his fatal flight, he refused a co-pilot's help and the warning signs as the Jetpod failed to take off three times. When it finally got airborne, it shot vertically up, before smashing down to the ground in a massive fireball. It is not always a good thing to have too much faith in your own cherished ideas. Sometimes when the world tells you you are wrong, you need to bloody listen.

HUMANE HUMAN KILLER

Clever men sometimes do very dumb things. A case in point is the death of Australian vet Harold Alderson in June 1940. He was showing two visitors around his Sydney laboratory when he displayed a 'humane killer' he had invented for destroying horses. Alderson, believing it empty, demonstrated how it worked by placing it against his head and firing. If he had checked, he would have found the humane killer was loaded and more than capable of killing a human.

THE GRIM REAPER STALKS AGAIN

Another ridiculous tale of the Grim Reaper's legendary ability to stalk those whose time he calls comes from the death of Johanna Ganthaler. The 74-year-old from Italy missed her flight to Paris from Rio de Janeiro on June 1, 2009. This was lucky because she was booked on Air France 447, which crashed into the Atlantic, killing all 228 passengers and crew. Ganthaler got another flight to Munich and she and her husband then hired a car to drive back to their home in the Tyrol. However, as they drove through Austria, their car spun out of control, ended up in the opposite lane of the motorway and was hit head-on by a truck, killing Johanna instantly.

NEVER PUT A GIFT GUN IN THE POCKET

Alfred Fuller was driving a lorry in Western Australia in March 1925 when he noticed a revolver lying on the road. He stopped his truck, picked it up and tested out that it was working by firing it successfully into the bush. Pleased with his lucky find, Fuller then put the gun into his jacket pocket, accidentally firing it and shooting himself fatally in the stomach.

TWO MEN, ONE HEART AND ONE WAY OUT

In 1996, Chicagoan Danny Robinson received a heart transplant from Maxwell Price, who had committed suicide by shooting himself. Although he never knew the donor, Robinson began writing letters to the dead man's family and went on to marry his widow. Twelve years later and still married to Price's former wife, Robinson himself committed suicide by shooting himself in the throat with a shotgun.

ONE STRIKE AND SHE IS OUT

Death by lightning is so far from uncommon that only a few bolts out of the blue qualify as ridiculous. One of them that does is the death of Mrs Bessie Fothergill from Cañiambo, Australia in January 1898. An inquest into her death by lightning strike determined she had been hit only because her corset contained so much steel that it had attracted the fatal bolt.

EXPERIMENTS IN LYNCHING

When 19-year-old typewriter mechanic Benjamin Stock hung himself in Southampton, in 1933, his father was stoic when offering an explanation for his son's behaviour at the inquest. Stock Sr. said his son had a 'curious mind and was often caught up in experimenting'. He also explained Benjamin had tried to hang himself before, but the string had broken whilst trying to test out a theory on lynching he had read in a book and that he believed his death was the result of a further 'experiment in lynching'.

STRIKER GETS STRUCK OUT

In 1994, workers at the San Francisco Newspaper Agency were in a fierce battle with management, so much so that striking truck driver Kent Wilson thought it would be a good idea to sabotage the power supply to one of the firm's distribution centres. In his attempt he touched a wire in a transformer box carrying 12,000 volts and was thrown 4.5m away in the subsequent explosion. He died en route to hospital without even the satisfaction of having stopped that night's papers from getting out.

BUS-TED OVER SAFETY WRANGLES

In another example of industrial action gone wrong, very wrong, the body of Kim Man Tseung was found crushed under a 12-tonne bus with a knife beside him in 1994. Kim was a mechanic for the New York Transit Authority and caught up in a bitter dispute with his bosses over safety issues. He had got under the bus to slash airbags in its suspension system in an attempt to get the TA to take safety more seriously, but had misjudged the time he needed to get clear once the suspension gave out.

MISER MORTALITY

The human capacity for dumb and deadly behaviour linked to money is remarkable. Two sisters, Charlotte Rubenstein, 83, and Marion Seelig, 84, died in Pittsfield, Massachusetts in 1982 from the effects of the cold. They had refused to buy heating oil for their home despite having access to assets worth hundreds of thousands of dollars and more than $20,000 in cash in their house as they slowly froze to death over the course of several days.

SMOKE 'EM IF YOU GOT 'EM

It is no surprise that a man who once wrestled jaguars live on TV died a ridiculous death. However, it is somehow apt that comic TV star Ernie Kovacs was killed by his smoking habit. In January 1962, Kovacs was driving home from a baby shower in Los Angeles when he tried to light up a cigar whilst turning fast and lost control of his Chevrolet Corvair, crashing into a power pole and being thrown halfway out of the passenger side. An unlit cigar rolled onto the pavement, just inches from his outstretched arm as he died from his injuries.

HAZING HELL I

Hazing – the hideous range of humiliating and abusive rituals used by everything from sports teams to military units to initiate a new person into their group – seems to reach its fatal nadir most often with the college fraternities of the United States. Having gone through the newspaper archive of the last 100 years, I can promise you there has not been a year since 1900 where there has not been at least one ridiculous and tragic death caused by a hazing gone wrong.

A typically ridiculous case happened in 1973. Phillip Bronner, 21, was abducted by his Chi Chi Chi fraternity brothers, had the glasses he relied on to see taken from him and was driven out to a desolate spot in the Los Angeles National Forest at 2am where he was dumped and left to find his own way home. Unsurprisingly, his body was eventually found at the bottom of a 152m cliff which he had stumbled over, half-blind and in the dark. Phillip's father said: 'My son had no chance of surviving. He was no athlete. He was fat. He was a momma's boy. He didn't walk, we drove him everywhere.'

DRUNKEN HIGHWAY TO HELL

Billy Renton was drunk-driving his buddy Pat Dolby home after a night drinking in Arkansas in 2005 when Dolby leaned out of the window to throw up. Renton was so drunk that he drove so close to a telegraph pole that its support wire decapitated Dolby. Renton then drove 19km home, so inebriated he was not even aware he had his friend's headless body beside him. A neighbour saw the corpse in Renton's car the next morning and called the police, who eventually found Dolby's head at the accident site.

DON'T FORGET TO DUCK!

Mike Stewart, the head of a hauling business, was being filmed on a moving flat bed truck in New Mexico for a 1983 TV news story about the dangers of low-level bridges. Stewart failed to duck when the truck went under a bridge and died from the resulting head injury.

KILLER COFFEE

Some random bad luck is horrifically ridiculous. Ben Crane, 46, from Minnesota walked into his drive holding a mug of coffee one morning in 1983 as a visitor pulled up in a car. A chip of stone thrown up by the wheels smashed into Crane's mug, shattering it and sending a ceramic shard in his carotid artery, severing it and killing him.

PLASTIC PERIL

Englishman Robert Coulson was kidding around at work in 1979, sliding along the factory floor in Manchester on a wheeled trolley, shouting: 'Whee!' However, during one glide, the trolley hit a bump and he was flung off and straight into a vat of melted plastic. Although pulled from it alive, he died en route to hospital.

FUR FINALE

Ram-raider Stan Weiss backed his car into the window of a Michigan furriers in 1979 and then proceeded to try to strip a fur coat from a mannequin. However, during the criminal disrobing, Weiss slipped and managed to sever his femoral artery on a piece of glass from the window he had broken. He fled with the fur, but died from blood loss before he could fence his ill-gotten gain.

OUT OF LINE OLD-TIMER

There seems to be no age limit on the lethal impact that jealousy and infidelity can have. Judith Elliot, a 78-year-old grandmother shot and killed Hal Harper, 84, her boyfriend of 18 months, after she discovered he was sleeping with someone else. The Atlanta grandmother was unrepentant when brought before the court for murder in 2008, saying: 'I shot him for cheating and I would do it again.'

BURGER BROUHAHA GOES BALLISTIC

Lethal pensioners with firearms are not restricted to cases involving infidelity. Atlanta resident George Richmond, 68, shot and killed his 24-year-old grandson Peter Richmond when the young man turned up at his apartment without bringing any hamburgers. Richmond Sr. had been drinking heavily before the argument.

HAZING HELL II

University students have masses of intellectual potential, yet some of them seem determined only to apply it to thinking up terrible ways of humiliating their fellows through hazing. William Flowers, 19, an honour student at Monmoth College, New Jersey died in 1974 when he was buried alive in a mock grave alongside four other pledges to the Zeta Beta Tau fraternity. As frat members placed flowers on top of the mock graves, the walls of Flowers' grave caved in, suffocating him and turning it into a very real grave.

A WOMAN SCORNED

Belgian skydiver Els Van leapt from a plane at 3,962m holding hands with the married man she was having an affair with in 2007. However, it was not a happy landing for the couple because the wife of the cheat – Els Clottemans – had sabotaged her love rival's parachutes by cutting the cords. Clottemans was prosecuted for the murder.

BACKTRACK THAT HACK

A genius schoolboy hacker aged 14 used a modified TV remote control to change the points of the tram system of the Polish town of Lodz in 2008, as if it was his own giant personal train. Unfortunately, his activities derailed four trams, injuring dozens of passengers, one of whom died in hospital three weeks later.

MEMBER IN EMBERS

According to Rajini Narayan of Adelaide, she did not intend to burn her husband to death when she doused his penis with flammable liquid whilst he slept in 2009, just to 'burn his penis so it belongs to me and no one else.' However, her plan went awry, resulting in Mr. Narayan's fiery death. Luckily for her, the courts agreed with her and she received only a suspended sentence for her crime.

LETHAL LEPRECHAUN LOOT

An armed robber dressed as a leprechaun robbed a First State Bank in Nashville in 2009. After snatching the money, he ran outside and leapt into a getaway car driven by an accomplice. However, being a leprechaun did not give the robber any luck as the pair were pursued by cops, finally ditching their vehicle in a field and engaging in a shoot-out which saw both of them killed. One of the cops involved said: 'I've never been shot at by a leprechaun before, but we had no choice but to return fire.' Dying with your boots on is one thing, dying with your Tam O'Shanter on is just plain ridiculous.

MORTAL BLUES AND MOOS

A 75-year-old English farmer died in 2009 after a firefighter tried to drive his engine through a herd of cows blocking his path to an emergency call-out. The flashing blue lights and sirens of the engine as he pushed through them caused the bovine herd to stampede and trample the farmer. The firefighter later received a suspended jail sentence for manslaughter.

LITTLE DEATH TIMES TWO

In 2009, two professional midget wrestlers Espectrito Jr. and La Parkita (Little Death) – who used to battle in the ring dressed as skeletons – were found dead in a Mexico City hotel room. The pair had been lured there by prostitutes who drugged the men's drinks. Unfortunately, the dosage they used was too large for the reduced stature of the wrestlers, knocking them out permanently. The prostitutes were caught and prosecuted for the deaths.

SMARTER THAN THE AVERAGE BEARS

When we wrote the first 1001 Ridiculous Ways To Die book, we assumed that some ongoing problems might have been resolved five years later. Unfortunately this has not been the case with the killer bears on the Adler-Krasnaya Polyana road, who seem to enjoy pushing rocks down mountains to smash into passing vehicles. In 2011, Matvey Vazov became another victim of the bears when a rock tumbled 91m down a mountain and smashed into his car. Passing motorists who stopped to help were forced to drive away when bears pushed further rocks down on them. A local police spokesman said: 'We still have the bear problem. It is said they used to roll rocks to kill cows, but it now seems they do it for fun.'

DOWN THE DRAIN

Gordon Webber became trapped in a storm drain in Lancashire whilst trying to retrieve his car keys. His dead body was discovered the next day by a passer-by who saw a leg sticking out of the 60cm-by-30cm drain. Neighbours had heard Webber screaming and shouting 'Please help me!' in the night, but no one had gone to investigate, as they thought it was a prank.

HEAVY DRINKER KILLED BY WATERING DOWN

Brian Jenkins was banned from buying extra-strong longer at his local pub in Doncaster in 2009 after his habit of downing five pints in an hour began to get out of hand. In protest, Jenkins spent a day in the pub drinking only water. After six pints, he had managed to give himself water intoxication, lowering his sodium levels to the point he suffered a fatal heart attack.

THE WORST PASSIVE SMOKING DEATH EVER

Even those who deny the existence of luck would have to feel the odds had dealt Iraq war veteran Barry King a low blow. He received a new pair of lungs in 2009 to save him from a breathing problem he developed during the war, but died six months later after it turned out the donor smoked 50 roll-up cigarettes a day and the lungs were, in fact, cancerous.

HAZING HELL III

Massachusetts Institute of Technology students have a reputation for being some of the brightest. However, in 1956, members of its Delta Kappa Epsilon fraternity were not clever enough to realize that blindfolding Thomas Clark and abandoning him near the edge of a frozen reservoir might lead to him walking unknowingly across it, the ice cracking and him drowning in the freezing water. Idiots.

LOONEY WAY TO GO

James Looney, 40, accidentally shot himself in the head in 2009 whilst demonstrating the safety mechanism on various guns to his girlfriend. The Montana man had been drinking before he started putting guns to his head and quizzing his partner on whether they would go off if he pulled the trigger.

JUST SAY NO TO DRUGS!

Brendan Cookson, 22, died in 2009 after being given an injection of an unlicensed drug by her sister. The drug had been invented by their mother in an attempt to reverse the ageing process. Poor Brenda died after suffering an extreme allergic reaction to the experimental substance her mother had spent a decade researching.

NOT MY PORSCHE!

When Gerhard Adolf Zeitler Plattner managed to get his Porsche Cayenne stuck on a railroad crossing in Italy in 2008, he had plenty of time to get out of the vehicle and run for his life. However, he so loved his car that instead of saving himself, he ran towards the oncoming train, waving his arms frantically, in an effort to try and get it to stop before it smashed into his vehicle. Unfortunately, his actions meant the train hit him as well as the Porsche.

DYING FOR A PEE IV

Urinating in public seems to be a big and sometimes lethal problem in India. In November 2012, a 17-year-old girl was shot dead when she asked a drunk neighbour not to urinate by the staircase to her house.

In 2009, Himanshu Sharma, 22, got into a fight with petrol station employees when he chose to pee close to their pumps. The row escalated to the point where the petrol station's armed guard shot and killed Himanshu when he started swinging punches and shouting: 'I'll piss where I want to! Even over you!'

In 2010, Prakash Kumar, 26, was shot by an irate homeowner in Gondia after he urinated on an idol of a god that had been placed outside a house to deter public urination.

THE REVENGE OF JAWS

In 1956, British navy ship HMS *Burleigh* was conducting diving operations when its divers attracted the unwanted attention of sharks. To scare the beasts away, the ship's commander ordered that a motor launch be dispatched to dynamite the sharks. Two blocks of fused-TNT were thrown at a shark and it became snared on it. However, it was far from mission accomplished because the shark then swam towards the launch and the TNT was so close when it exploded that it killed Lt Commander Brooks, who was in the boat at the time.

CROCODILE TEARS V

Hoping to gain a blessing, Bangladeshi Rubel Sheik travelled from his village to the shrine of Khan Jahan Ali in 2008 to make an offering of a goat to five crocodiles that lived in the shrine's pond. Part of the ritual involved him bathing in the crocodile's pond, and whilst normally the beasts are so well fed that they do not trouble pilgrims, Rubel proved too inviting a tasty treat and he was eaten. The attack did not stop 25 other pilgrims taking chances in the pond on the same day even when they had seen his grisly fate.

BAN BECOMES PERMANENT

Jimmy Hall was banned from a Sunderland pub in 1988 for attempting to assault both patrons and bar staff. As he was leaving the premises, he turned round and threw a beer bottle at the landlord. However, the bottle hit a column instead of its target, shattered and a shard of glass cut the carotid artery in Hall's neck. Although an ambulance was quickly called, he died from blood loss.

KILLER ROAD DOES WHAT IT SAYS IN THE NAME

If a stretch of road is known as Dead Man's Curve, you would think it the last place for a 2am drag race would you not? However, that did not stop Mike Palinetto from racing at 1060km/h on Dead Man's Curve at Staten Island. When Palinetto lost control of his car on the curve, it skidded 30m before crashing through a parking meter and slamming into a telegraph pole. His body was thrown from the car with such force that the pole's supporting wire sliced it in two.

BANGING THE DRUM FOR DEATH

Drum-maker Alonso Marrero, 35, died from inhaling deadly anthrax spores whilst working with the animal skins he used to make drums in his London workshop in 2008. It is far from the first anthrax drum death. In 2006, Scottish craftsman Jess MacDonald, who made and painted traditional bodhran drums, also died from contact with animal skins. A member of the UK Health Protection Agency said: 'The drum making community is not so big. You would think they would know the risks the way the deaths keep stacking up.'

GOODBYE COLD WORLD

All suicide is tragic, but some of those ending their lives take odd and frankly absurd ways out of this vale of tears. Poor Betty Williams was head cook at an English school. In 2008, worried about a £400 credit card debt, she climbed into a freezer. By the time her body was found 15 hours later, Williams had died from hypothermia.

DEATH DIVE

Another suicide from 2008 who eschewed the traditional route was Brad Klausner, 29, from New York. He persuaded a skydiving club that he was a photographer who wanted to observe a ride and so was on a plane when students and instructors were leaping out. Before the door could be closed, he rushed through it and began a 3,048m freefall without a parachute, taking photographs of his death dive as he went.

TOP 10 RIDICULOUS CRIME-RELATED DEATHS – CRIMINAL LIFE SENTENCES

10. Ernesto Garcia may have thought he was being smart when using a BB airgun to commit armed robbery on a Chicago store in 2009. If he had been caught alive, he would have faced a stiffer sentence if he had used an actual firearm. However, his plan backfired because his airgun looked so realistic that police fatally shot him when he refused to put his toy weapon down.

9. Kenneth Dean Hunt was obsessed with the shower scene in Psycho. Fitting, as he was a maniac killer who raped and murdered two women. His first victim was Myra Davis, who was the stand-in for the star of the film Janet Leigh. Hunt thought he was killing Leigh's body double for the shower scene, making the death of Davis both tragic and ridiculously unlucky, as the body double was actually actress Marli Renfro.

8. Being a member of a drug cartel is a dangerous occupation, but Ecuadorian criminal Rafael Ferreño died from something much more absurd than a hail of bullets. In 1996, undercover police saw him struck and instantly killed when a suitcase full of cocaine dropped from a plane and landed on his head.

7. Pony Malta is an unfermented beer soft drink from Columbia. Not only does it sound awful, it proved fatal for Maximo Rene Menendez in 1993 when he unwittingly drunk a bottle that contained more than 200 times the lethal dose of cocaine. Drug smugglers had used crates of Pony Malta to ship cocaine into America, but in a monumental criminal cock-up, some bottles mistakenly were sold to the public.

6. Any crime can turn deadly if you fall foul of trigger-happy police. In 2012, Kennedy Garcia was stopped and handcuffed for graffitiing in Los Angeles. Garcia fled, hiding under an SUV. Several policemen joined the hunt, but the cops who first stopped Garcia did not tell their colleagues he was wearing cuffs. When an officer saw a glint of metal under the SUV, he shot Garcia dead thinking he had a gun. Oops.

5. Polish crook Bartosz Skalka thought he was being a mastermind by attempting to tunnel into a diamond merchant's property through the Torun sewer system in 1992. Unfortunately for Skalka, his tunnelling brought him into contact with rat urine, leading him to contract the deadly Weil's syndrome, which finished him off within four days of the symptoms being recognized.

4. Vandalizing your ex-girlfriend's car may not be the biggest crime in the world, but when Bill Wilson of Arizona began to try to smash out the windscreen of his ex's Nissan Bluebird in 1996 with a shotgun, he should have checked to see whether the gun was loaded. It was, and whilst trying to break the glass, it discharged into his chest killing him.

3. Four grave-robbers intent on looting the El Faiyum burial complex in Egypt one night in 2002 may have got a touch of the curse of mummy when the wall they were attempting to make a hole in collapsed, causing several tonnes of sand and rubble above them to come crashing down. Their bodies, as well as those of several mummified dogs, were discovered by archaeologists the next morning.

2. Keshawn Santiago's attempted armed robbery of a Californian grocery store in 2002 was not going as well as he expected. Disappointed by how little cash was in the register, he fired shots up into the ceiling. Unfortunately, these ricocheted.

1. Calogero Lo Cocco was murdered by his ex-wife and her boyfriend in the Sicilian village of Campobello di Licat in 2010. Their weapon of choice was a slab of butter, which they used to suffocate Lo Cocco after restraining him. The murderous pair believed the butter would have melted by the time the police responded to an emergency call. They told the police he had arrived at his wife's home drunk and collapsed, but a pathologist spotted traces of butter in the dead man's airways and exposed their crime.

FRERE JACQUES, DORMEZ VOUS?

Gisborough Priory in what used to be North Yorkshire was enveloped in a terrible fire in 1289. Although the priory had a strong international reputation as a place of strict observance of the Augustinian rule, one recorded victim of the fire, William of Ugthorpe, did not escape the blaze due to his brother monks 'being not able to rouse him from the lure of sleep brought on by ale'.

WRAPPED UP IN HIS WORK

You have to worry about a zoo that lets a student zookeeper work a lone nightshift looking after anything more dangerous than guinea pigs. However, Erick Arrieta worked alone at the Caracas zoo in Venezuela on the weekend that a 3m Burmese Python killed him. When fellow workers turned up the next morning, they found the snake swallowing the keeper's head, but even after beating the serpent to make it release his victim, it was too late for Erick. According to the zoo's director: 'The young man underestimated the creature's instinct.'

ROAD RAGE TO HELL

Jasmine Parker-Holt died in a road incident in Surrey, England in 2008. Having rammed another vehicle for not getting out of her way, Parker-Holt then spun her wheels so fast that they began to smoke. As onlookers told her to get out the car, she told them to 'Fuck off out of it!' and kept her foot on the accelerator. Her wheels burst into flames, burning to the rims with Parker-Holt still in the car, then sparks were sent into the engine setting the whole car ablaze. Refusing opportunities to get out of the car, Parker-Holt stayed in it until she was overcome by smoke and flames.

CLOWNING AROUND II

Whilst we have already seen there can be good reasons to have coulrophobia – a fear of clowns – for one man in Columbia, having issues with clowns has got out of control. In 2007, an unidentified attacker leapt into a circus ring and shot dead a clown as he performed in Cucuta. The audience thought it was part of the act and the man slipped away. He had earlier shot and killed another clown standing next to a ticket booth. Police believe the killer was the same man that a year before had killed a clown called Pepe whilst he performed an evening show live on stage.

HAZING HELL IV

There are too many hazing deaths through alcohol poisoning for most of them to be anything other than tragic wastes of life. However, there is a touch of the ridiculous as well as the tragic in the 1998 drinking death of Walter Dean Jennings. Members of the Psi Epsilon Chi fraternity of State University of New York made Jennings down so much water across a 10-day initiation that his sodium levels dropped and his brain fatally swelled due to water intoxication.

HAZING HELL V

In September 1959 Kappa Sigma members of the University of Southern California made Richard T. Swanson eat a plate of oil-covered liver without chewing as part of his initiation. On his fourth piece of liver, Swanson began to choke and when slapping him on the back and putting their fingers down his throat did not help, most of Kappa Sigma went to pieces. Whilst most of them ran to their cars and prayed, one called an ambulance, but when paramedics arrived none would own up to the hazing prank and so neglected to mention the meat lodged in Swanson's throat, meaning the paramedics were not able to save him in time.

GOING DOWN

Possibly it was the novelty of using a lift in a two-storey home that led burglar Jimmy Gale, 28, to ride in the disability elevator of a property he broke into in Massachusetts in 1985. However, the lift became stuck between floors and when the family returned from a fortnight in Europe, they discovered Gale's body in the broken lift. An autopsy showed he died from dehydration.

SEWER EXPLORER ENDS UP IN THE SHIT

I have been down into London's amazing Victorian sewerage network for research purposes on another book. Even with the safety equipment, the dangers down there were evident. Given the stink and risk of death, you have to be deranged to want to illegally explore it for fun. However, that is what Andrew Baker, 28, did in 1979. The experience turned shitty when he was overcome by sewer gas after walking more than 5km underground, collapsing into the water and drowning. At his inquest, his mother said: 'Andrew always was too curious for his own good.'

FATAL FISHWIFE FIGHT

Workers in a Hull fish-processing plant Mandy Hayes and Rita O'Grady got in a spat over the married co-worker they were both having affairs with in 1979. The fight turned violent and Mandy began to throw fish at Rita, who responded by walloping her love rival with a cod, causing Mandy to lose her footing and fall fatally onto the edge of a conveyor belt, smashing her head.

UN-BEE-LIEVABLE!

What could make a fatal truck smash that killed the driver of both lorry and car it collided into even worse? How about if the truck was carrying dozens of beehives when it overturned, releasing a massive swarm of bees that stung a father to death? That is exactly happened what in 2008 just outside of Changchun in the Chinese province of Jilin.

YOU DIRTY RAT

There is a terrible phrase some people adhere to, that 'no good deed goes unpunished'. It was certainly the case for Vilma Mills of Eastbourne, England in 2008. Ignoring her husband's pleas for her to use gloves, Vilma freed a rat caught in a garden feeder and was scratched in the process. Although she treated the wound, the rat carried Weil's disease and within four days, Vilma was dead.

LET THEM EAT CAKE

A staff member of a cafe in South Wales died when he and his colleagues staged an after-hours cupcake-eating competition. Gareth Evans choked to death after stuffing a dozen fairy cakes into his mouth in an attempt to beat his co-workers to the title of champion cake chomper.

DEATH RAY

A day enjoying the pleasures of being out on a small boat in the Florida Keys ended fatally for Helen Burton in 2008 when a 34kg spotted eagle ray leapt from the water, hit her in the face and knocked her to the deck dead. A local wildlife expert said: 'Rays jump out of the water all the time to escape predators, but I've never known one to hit someone. It was a one-in-a-million freak accident.'

HEAD OVER HEELS! SOS!

Ola Brunkert, the former drummer for Swedish pop sensations ABBA, was found dead in his garden in Majorca in 2008 after he tripped and fell through a glass door. He had cut his carotid artery on a shard of glass and went outside, but died before he could raise any help. A safety expert said: 'This death was ridiculous. If he had used toughened glass in his door he would still be alive.'

OH, THE IRONY X – MISPLACED TRUST

Italian artist Giuseppina Pasqualino was hitch-hiking across the Near East dressed as a bride in an attempt to promote world peace, claiming that she wanted to show 'that it is entirely possible to put your trust in the kindness of people.' Her naked body was found on bushes near the Turkish city of Gebze. Speaking after her sister's murder, Maria Pasqualino said: 'She wanted to give a message of peace and trust, but not everyone deserves trust.' No shit.

DYING FOR THE SAKE OF ART

Texan-born artist Luis Jimenez spent 13 years working on a sculpture of a rearing horse. The 10m high fibreglass piece was nearing completion when its six-ton torso crushed him to death when it fell on him whilst he was moving it with a hoist. The sculpture was finished two years later by his son, and can be seen at Denver airport, a fitting tribute to a man who died for his art.

SHOULD HAVE KNOWN BETTER I

Lion taming is never going to be a safe job, but if a lion bit me twice in a week, I would not use it in my act. In 1872, Massarti the Lion Tamer gave a performance in Bolton, dressed as a Roman gladiator, and slipped whilst returning his sword to his sheath. It was at this point that Tyrant – the lion which had already attacked him twice – leapt on him, with the four other lions in the act joining in. At first the audience of 600 thought Massarti fighting the lions as a gladiator was part of the act and cheered as he fought a losing battle for his life.

SHOULD HAVE KNOWN BETTER II

In 1870, the band of the James Robinson & Co. Circus were told to perform in the parade through Middleton, Missouri whilst sitting on top of the lions' cage. The roof of the cage gave way after the trailer it was on hit a rock, and several band members fell into the cage to be attacked by irate lions. Ten of them died, newspapers at the time describing the scene as 'one of the most awful confusion and carnage'.

SHOULD HAVE KNOWN BETTER III

In 1876, a drunk Patrick Callaghan decided to release two tigers from their cage in a circus performing in Michigan. Quite why he thought this a good idea was never made clear, as in his attempt to release them, the tigers dragged him into the cage and mauled him to death. Two empty quart bottles of whisky were found in his coat.

GETTING THE HUMP

A Queensland woman who got a camel for her 60th birthday was killed by the beast in 2007 when it crushed her whilst according to the police 'Trying to play or do some sort of sexual thing'. Her body was discovered by relatives with her pet camel laid on top of her. Unfortunately for the woman, whatever the camel's intentions, its 152kg was more than enough to crush her to death.

SCRAP THAT IDEA

Andy Collings took his VW van to a scrapyard in Northampton in 2007, but as he was about leave, he suddenly remembered that he had left some personal possessions in the vehicle. He rushed back into his old van and began to look for them, when the scrapyard's crane came down and its hydraulic pincers crushed the van with Collings inside it. Ouch!

RUN IT DOWN THE FLAGPOLE

John Coulton, 63, was a flagpole repairman who was killed when the 4.5kg metal ball from the top of a flagpole he was meant to be repairing in Carmel, California fell more than 18m and hit him in the head. His wife said: 'It was just a freak accident. He had repaired hundreds of poles. It was a freak for the ball to come down right where he was standing.'

KICK THE BUCKET

A coroner in Essex decided that builder Darren King, 43, of Brentwood ended up drowning in a bucket of water through accident and not suicide. King was found by colleagues on a building site with his head submerged in a bucket in 1986. The coroner concluded King's underlying high blood pressure problems had led to him passing out and his head falling into the bucket.

HAZING HELL VI

It is not just male college fraternities that have a track record in causing ridiculous deaths through hazing. Female sororities get in on the act regularly as well. In 1970, members of the Alpha Gamma Delta sorority of Eastern Illinois University kidnapped Donna Bedinger and another pledge, drove them to remote countryside and dumped them. Donna panicked and attempted to throw herself on the back of the car as it left them behind, missing the vehicle and hitting her head on the ground with fatal consequences.

SHORTCUT TO THE GRAVE

Jamie Hurst thought he would take a shortcut to a friend's party by climbing over some railings and going through a graveyard in Manchester in 1989. This turned out to be a grave mistake, as he impaled himself on one of the railings' spikes, bleeding to death before he could get out of the graveyard and raise help.

HAZING HELL VII

It would be wrong of this book to create the impression that ridiculous hazing deaths are just an American issue. In 2006, Jan Angelo Dollete, a 21-year-old engineering student, died after being spanked in an Alpha Phi Omega initiation rite at Capiz State university in the Philippines. The beating on his buttocks and lower body was so severe it caused internal injuries that led to his death.

KILLER KITE

The 2007 spring festival in Lahore, Pakistan, celebrated by the flying of thousands of kites led to 11 deaths. Five were through celebratory gunshots which, after being fired into the air found unwitting targets on their return to earth. The other six were caused by sharp kite strings – often coated with ground glass to allow them to cut a rival kite's strings – cutting their flyers or spectators.

SLEEPING POLICEMAN

Manabu Tsukada was charged with a fatal hit-and-run after he ran over a policeman who had fallen asleep in the road in the Nagano Prefecture, Japan, in 2006. The police officer had gone to sleep after celebrating sitting a promotion exam with a night of heavy drinking.

AN UNLIKELY STORY

In December 1996, a writer of hard-boiled crime novels, Eugene Izzi, was found with a rope around his neck, hanging from a 14th-storey window. He was wearing a bulletproof vest and in his pockets were brass knuckles, a can of pepper spray and a computer disc containing his latest unfinished novel. Police described the manuscript as a 'suicide note' because the character of a mystery writer is attacked by white supremacists who loop a noose around his neck, tie the other end to a desk, then throw him out of a 14th-floor window.

GOING ALL OUT FOR A KILLER SHOT

Mike Baker was determined to get a killer shot of a gliding contest held in Gloucestershire in 2006, so he stood on the roof of his car to try to get the perfect position. Unfortunately, the perfect position was right in the path of a contender who took his glider too low in an attempt to get ahead in the race and ended up connecting the tip of his craft's wing with Baker's head.

DOING A DAMIEN

Some journalists will do anything for a story. In some English newsrooms, naughty behaviour in pursuit of a story is called 'doing a Damien' after a character in the classic British comedy Drop The Dead Donkey. TV journalists in the Indian state of Bihar were certainly doing a Damien in 2006 when they gave Manoj Mishra matches and diesel and encouraged him to burn himself in protest over unpaid wages. Manoj died after suffering 90 per cent burns to his body.

PAVEMENT PERIL

In a ridiculously avoidable death, Helen Washington died in 2007 after she stubbed her toe on a piece of uneven pavement near her Aberdeen home. Her doctor prescribed painkillers for the pain in her toe, but did not spot the infection in the wound. By the time it was recognized four days later, Washington had to be rushed to hospital to have her leg amputated, and died on the operating table.

PARKING PERIL

Parking rows often lead to fist fights, but in Rio de Janeiro in 2006, one dispute got out of hand when Edna Souza was sawn in half after she parked in front of an apartment block where parking was prohibited. Her murderer told police that he felt humiliated when she ignored his protests about her parking. Of all the bonkers reasons for killing someone in this book, that has to be close to the top spot.

PYTHON PERIL

Owning a pet that can easily kill you seems like a dumb idea to me, but even dumber is owning a python and then handling it whilst very drunk. This is exactly what Ontario man Chuck Branston did in 1992. The end result? His dead body was discovered with the snake still coiled around it, and an autopsy showed not only an alcohol blood level three times over the drive limit, but death by strangulation.

HAZARDOUS HIDE-AND-SEEK

University student Gary Chapel died during a drunken game of hide and seek in his London student accommodation block in 1986. His absurd idea of hiding in the trash chute went very wrong when he fatally fell down it and into a metal rubbish bin dozens of feet below.

HAZING HELL VIII

Ridiculous deaths through hazing are not new. Some have tried to lay the origins of hazing rites at the door of the English public school system and its fetishization of punishment – after all, it is not entirely coincidental that spanking is known globally as 'the English vice'. Some even suggest the true origin of hazing goes back as far as the Roman military. Whatever the truth, ridiculous, drunken hazing rituals have been claiming the lives of American students for more than a century.

In 1912, Isaac William Rand, a student at the University of North Carolina died whilst being initiated into a pledge. He was made to stand on a barrel guzzling booze, and ordered to maintain his balance as he became progressively drunker. When he eventually fell off, he landed on a broken bottle that slashed his jugular and led him to bleed to death.

ONE SUICIDE, ONE MANSLAUGHTER, ONE SHOT

When Charles B. Galston, 19, decided to shoot himself at a party in Atlanta in 2006, the bullet he used to claim his own life also took that of another. Poor Amelia Hyde did not know Galston, but she was struck by the bullet after it went through his head and into her chest. Authorities determined he only ever meant to take his own life.

ONE MAN WENT TO MOW

Dozens of people die each year in lawnmower accidents, but anyone who does it underwater is heading towards the ridiculous. Jed Garcia rode his mower too close to a pond whilst maintaining a golf course in Orange County in 1991. The mower turned over and pinned him in 1m of water, drowning him before help arrived.

OUT BY FRYING PAN

Being hit by a frying pan may be a slapstick comedy staple, but when it happens in real life it can be fatal. In 1976, John Murray, 49, from Leith, was killed when his wife Mary hit him with a cast-iron frying pan during a row about his drinking. He died from an epidural haematoma several hours after being cracked on the back of the head.

DYING FOR A PEE V

Like many men of his age, Eric Wendel, 68, felt an overwhelming urge to urinate. His need proved fatal when he pulled up along an Idaho highway in 2006, walked up an embankment to relieve himself and lost his footing, tumbling down and into the Payette River, where he drowned.

HAZING HELL IX

We can expect hazing to be a source of ridiculous deaths for years to come unless the great and good start to take the issue more seriously. In 1877, Mortimer N. Leggett was blindfolded and taken into the countryside by members of Cornell University's Kappa Alpha Society and left to stumble around in a panic. Eventually his blindfold was taken off him and two Kappa members helped walk him back to civilization, but not being familiar with the area, managed to walk him and themselves off a cliff to their deaths. Leggett's father, General Mortimer Leggett, decided that his son's death was just the result of some unfortunate 'hocus-pocus' and accepted honorary membership of the bloody fraternity!

JUST DESSERTS I?

A gang of teenage braggarts shook the ladder of 63-year-old window cleaner Jim Hamble whilst he was up it cleaning windows in Glasgow in 1986. As he clung to the ladder and begged them to stop, he lost his grip on his bucket, which fell onto the the the side of 16-year-old Bobby Dalston's head. The gang rang away and Dalston seemed relatively uninjured, until four hours later when he collapsed and died from an epidural haematoma caused by the bucket.

WURST WAY TO GO

In researching this book, I've come across people murdered with the most improbable objects – from ceramic gargoyles to stuffed animals – yet the most ridiculous murder weapon is probably the killer sausage. In 2006, German prosecutors in Zwickau charged a 50-year-old man with the murder of a 65-year-old woman by choking her with a bockwurst sausage he forced into her mouth during an argument about cooking.

PLATE PERIL

If being choked to death by a man shoving food into your mouth is not a bad enough way to go, how about being choked to death by having a plate shoved into your mouth? Erin Galverston was killed by her husband when he forced a decorative plate shaped like an Easter Bunny down her throat whilst arguing in 2006.

SLINKY STRANGLER

Luis Vela was moving out of his 14th floor apartment in Barcelona in 1993. The building's lift didn't work, so he was carrying everything out by exhausting trips up and down the stairs. On his final trip, he brought down only his vacuum cleaner. Unfortunately, he wrapped the hose around his neck as he carried it, so when the machine slipped from his grasp and crashed down a flight of stairs, it took him with it and broke his neck.

CUTTING THE CORDS INSTEAD OF HIS WRISTS

Some suicides put a ridiculous amount of thought and effort into their death. Englishman Mark Bellingham, 27, spent seven hours training to undertake his first parachute jump, but unknown to his trainers, it was all a plan to kill himself. On his first jump in 2006, when his parachute opened, he took off his helmet, cut through his cords and plunged to the ground.

WAKE UP! IT'S TIME TO DIE

Some wake-up calls hurry in the long sleep. Gordon J. Boone, 36, ordered a 5:45 alarm call when he checked into a hotel in Pasadena in 1992. Unfortunately for Boone, the shock of the call bringing him out of sleep brought about his sudden death due to an underlying heart disorder – Long QT Syndrome.

DIVINE JUSTICE? V

One of Britain's most infamous collectors of illegal rare bird eggs died in 2006 when he fell 12m from a larch tree whilst taking wildlife photos. Colin Watson, 63, was prosecuted five times, most notably for taking a chainsaw to the tree that contained an osprey nest, and stealing two golden eagle eggs.

SNAKES ALIVE, MAN DEAD

The advice of America's Humane Society is not to own a python as a pet. It is a shame William Boyd Henderson, 19, of New Jersey did not take this advice in 1999, as his 4m long Burmese Python mistook him for food, leaving his dead body to be found in his apartment block hallway with the snake coiled tightly around it.

SNAKES ALIVE, WOMAN DEAD

Fortune teller Nirat Woenglukiaet kept a Reticulated Python for divination purposes in her village in Northern Thailand. Shame it did not help her divine that one day in 1989 her husband would come home to find it wrapped around her neck and that by the time he had chopped its head off, she would already be dead.

SMOKING KILLS IX – THE HUMAN TORCH

Jordan Kilkenny, 49, was being treated for a skin condition at a Florida hospital in 1995 when he tried to circumnavigate the establishment's strict no-smoking policy by taking a smoke on a fire escape. Regrettably, Kilkenny did not realize the gel smeared all over him as part of the treatment was flammable, and when he lit his cigarette, he turned himself into a human torch, dying hours later from massive burn injuries.

MICROWAVE MURDER

Whilst death by being choked by sausage sets a high bar of ridiculous murder, being beaten to death with a microwave after refusing to heat up your boyfriend's sandwiches is good competition. Unfortunately, this tragic fate is exactly what happened to Sally Redfern, 58, from Colorado in 2006. An investigating police officer said: 'Anything in the home can become a deadly weapon when domestic disputes turn this ugly.'

DEATH SUCKS

Another challenger to the killer sausage is the killer vacuum cleaner. Kentucky woman Avril Mae Dudley, 32, strangled her husband Dean, 36, with the hose of her vacuum cleaner in 2006 and then beat him with its accessories until he was clean dead.

HEAD LIFTED OFF

If you are ever fixing an elevator, here is a tip: do not stick your head into the shaft unless you are certain the lift will not come crashing down on it. This is the fatal mistake made by Emil Keller in 1994 whilst attempting to fix an elevator in Bonn, Germany. The moment he forced open the lift doors and looked up, was the exact moment the lift fell, decapitating him.

DEATH DIET

Many men will have a degree of sympathy for the death of Taiwanese man Hsu Tai-yang in 2006. The 37-year-old was thrown out of his family home by his wife, and decamped to an Internet café in Tamsu which, unable to afford a hotel, he made his home. Unfortunately, after three months, the diet of cigarette smoke, instant noodles, coffee and betel nuts began to take a toll on his health and he died from a heart attack. A fellow patron of the cafe said: 'He had nowhere else to go and it is not good to eat only noodles and drink coffee all the time.' A coroner agreed, citing his café diet and lack of sleep as reasons for the cardiac kill.

SNAKES ALIVE, MAN DEAD II

In some parts of the world, gangsters do bling rather than keeping a low profile. As part of his bling, Albanian mobster Betin Koçi kept a 3.6m Burmese Python which he had won in a card game. In 1999, he was found dead in his home with fang marks on his head and hands, and the snake firmly wrapped around his throat.

LETHAL LAVA

The volcanic pools of the Azores attract tourists, photographers and death. In 2009, German Gerhard Kuster was attempting to get all of one in shot when he stepped further back and took a tumble into a pool of bubbling lava. He was engulfed by a sulphur cloud, meaning his companions could not see him for a few seconds and by the time they pulled him free, he was already dead.

YOU CAN RUN, BUT YOU CAN'T LIVE

On February 3, 2003, narcotics cops in Atlanta pulled over a suspect they had been trailing all day. Knowing his crooked game was up, the man fled on foot and tried to jump off a raised section of road onto a building below. However, he misjudged his bid for freedom, plunging 11m and decapitating himself on the spike of a wrought-iron fence below.

MIRROR MALADY

London pensioner Lisa Mumford died in 2012 when she fell down stairs at a lingerie shop after becoming disoriented by the boutique's mirrors. An inquest heard the arrangement of a mirror wall at the top of the stairs had led to confusion amongst many patrons and had caused Mumford's fatal tumble.

HE WHO PLAYS THE PIPER

Scottish piper Gordon Stubbs was killed by a fellow member of his pipe band in 2005 after he criticized the playing of John Hickman. Their band had played in a competition in the previous week and been placed badly, leading Stubbs to point out flaws in Hickman's skills, at which point Hickman threw a chair across the practice hall at Stubbs and began to punch and kick him. A fellow band member said: 'Hickman had apologized for his poor playing at the competition – he had cold fingers and was on medication – but he just snapped at the criticism.'

PICTURE NOT PERFECT

When something you have seen in an old slapstick comedy film happens for real, the consequences are almost always tragic. English tourist Pamela Brookes plunged to her death from the ramparts of Fort Carré on the French Riviera in 2011 as she posed for a photograph. She climbed up onto the sixteenth-century walls, only to tumble backwards as she tried to strike the stance suggested by her boyfriend.

DEATH BY DENTOPHOBIA

Fear often leads to death. Londoner Claire Harper had such strong dentophobia – fear of dentists – that she refused to go to a dentist despite three weeks of intense pain. By the time she finally relented in March 2003, she had contracted septicaemia from an abscess in her mouth due to tooth decay. The septicaemia claimed her life and an inquest heard that her fear of dentists was so strong she had not had a check-up for a decade.

ROCKING OUT

In 2006, a Singapore coroner found that Li Xiao Meng, 16, got so into playing guitar whilst jumping up and down on his bed that he became somewhat insensible to his surroundings. He was so carried away using his bed as a rock trampoline that he took a huge bounce off the bed and shot out of the third-floor window of his dormitory to his death below.

NOT EXACTLY LOVE BITES

When frail 65-year-old Ron Godley refused his 45-year-old wife Nancy's demands for sex, she pinned him down and viciously bit him several times. After the savage attack, Ron managed to dial 911 and to explain his situation to the police in his home state of Oregon, who took Nancy into custody, but Ron died six days later from an infection from one of the bites.

JUST DESSERTS? II

A burglar who climbed into the elevator shaft of a block of flats to escape from the police was crushed by the lift's weights as it travelled up from the ground floor. Londoner Joseph Nyaberi was crushed as the weights pressed down on his chest while he was hiding in 2006. If the police had caught him, Nyaberi would have at worst had a few months' jail time, not a death sentence.

VODKA AND LADDERS

Polish builder Ryszard Karpuc died after falling off a ladder after drinking vodka to keep warm whilst working in Kent in 2012. He and three co-workers had drunk at least five bottles of vodka between them before he slipped and landed on his back. When his fellow workers could not feel a pulse, they loaded Karpuc's dead body into their van and, in a bit of very illegal and inappropriate fly-tipping, drove to some woods and dumped it. They later claimed they did not have good enough English to call an ambulance. Karpuc's sister Eva replied to that saying: 'They had good enough English to buy alcohol.'

SMOKING KILLS X – NO SMOKING IN THE HOUSE

London pensioner Alesandra Alampi died from smoking after she leant out of her bedroom window to enjoy a cigarette. An inquest in 2011 heard how her body was found 6m below. When police investigated further they found an ashtray, cigarette lighter, a packet of Benson & Hedges and a footstool she used to stand on in the room, and a large pile of discarded cigarette butts where Alampi's body fell to ground.

NO ESCAPING DEATH

As this book has shown, fleeing from the police often turns fatal. It certainly did for crook Robbie Carew when he ran from police officers trying to arrest him for burglary straight out into a busy Blackpool road in 2010. He dodged one car, but was then struck by the taxi. An autopsy found his body was full with near toxic levels of the drugs Dehydrocodeine and Diazepam. The coroner was told: 'It is a miracle that he could even stand, let alone run with what he had in his system.'

CRIMINAL TRAIN PAIN

Whilst using quad bikes to make your criminal getaway might put some distance between you and the law, they are no good for outrunning the Grim Reaper, as thieves Owen Harper and Roy Hurst found out in 2010. The pair used the all-terrain quad bikes to make their way across rough country after breaking into a warehouse, but both were struck and killed by a high speed train as they used the bikes to cross train tracks on the outskirts of London.

ON THE HEAD, SON!

Blackburn Rovers football fan Mark Reid, 30, drank so much at a football match at Stoke City's Britannia Stadium that when a 11kg metal bin was thrown at him, he headed it as if it were a football. Not surprisingly, Reid died of head trauma.

TOP 10 RIDICULOUS WORK-RELATED DEATHS – YOU WORK AND THEN YOU DIE

10. Swiss conductor Carl Robert Helg, 66, died whilst rehearsing for a gala performance at the Baden State Theatre in Germany. He climbed up into the venue's lights to get a better of view of his choir, lost his grip whilst gesticulating wildly as he gave orders to his singers, and fell to his death.

9. Cubicle offices are dehumanizing places. Proof? Auditor Felicity Orton, 51, dropped dead at her work station in a Los Angeles office one Friday afternoon in 2011. None of her co-workers noticed and it took more than 24 hours for a security guard to realize something was wrong.

8. Raymond Segura Jr, 56, was crushed to death at the Kelley Bean Company facility in Colorado in March 2012, when a 6m high pile of pinto beans collapsed on top of him. Rescue workers and inmates from the county jail dug frantically to save him, but when his bean-bashed body was found he had been dead for an hour.

7. Paulo Jackson's first day at work in 2002 at a major brewing company in Georgia ended up being his last when a colleague accidentally switched on a palletizing robot whilst Jackson swept up broken glass from under it. Not being able to tell the difference between a pallet to stack and a human, the robot crushed him to death.

6. Bumble Bee Tuna worker Jose Melana died when he became trapped in a steaming machine at the company's Santa Fe Springs plant in October 2012. Melana's job was to place baskets of tuna into a giant pressure cooker, but he became stuck in the machine whilst filling it and could not escape being cooked.

5. Belgian Farmer Axel Mertens was clearly a bit behind when feeding his barn full of chickens in 1987. After slipping and breaking his thigh, Mertens was apparently unable to haul himself to safety from the clutch of ravenous chickens. When his body was discovered the next day, the foul fowl had pecked so much of Mertens away he had to be positively identified through dental records.

4. Team-building days are usually a vile waste of time. For Danny Garrick, his accountancy firm's idea of improving its employees' morale by taking them on a gruelling survival course turned awry. Poor Danny developed hypothermia on a Welsh hillside in 1995 and in a state of delirium, stumbled into a stream where he drowned in 15m of water. Way to go, bosses!

3. A tour guide at Yellowstone Park had the worst first day at work possible in June 2012 when she got lost on a hiking trail and walked too close to the edge of a canyon with a 457m drop. The rock she was standing on suddenly gave way and she plummeted to her death.

2. Here is a tip: whilst at work on a building site, work – and do not play games like walk the plank. Baltimore construction worker 'Big' Jimmy Malick became 'Dead' Jimmy Malick when he and his colleagues decided to re-enact a scene they had witnessed in the film *Pirates of the Caribbean: Curse of the Black Pearl* in 2003. As they did not have a galleon or ocean, they used a plank suspended over an eight-storey drop. The wood broke under Malick's weight sending him not to a watery but a very certain grave.

1. Poor 22-year-old Juan Baten had the worst possible end to any work day in January 2011 – death. During his shift at Tortilleria Chinantla tortilla factory in Brooklyn, Baten reached into a mixing machine to press the dough in an attempt to speed up the mixing process. He reached down too far, became snagged on the mixer's mechanical arms and was pulled into the vat of dough, where his body was fatally kneaded into the tortilla mix.

PATHETIC PRANK

Alcohol not only boosts stupidity, it makes some things funny when they really are not. In 2008, Harry Borden snuck out of a Northumbria pub he and hiking companion Chris Small were drinking in whilst Small was in the lavatory. Borden then scaled a fence and embankment to climb onto a railway bridge so he could surprise Small by shouting at him as he walked under the bridge. He had explained his plan to fellow drinkers, who had not seen the funny side. Nor did Chris Small when instead of being surprised by Harry shouting, he was surprised when he heard Harry screaming as he fell from the bridge whilst trying to avoid an oncoming train.

READ THE BLOODY MANUAL

A collapsing crane in London killed two people – Bobby Monroe, 23, who was washing his car nearby and the crane's operator, John Lundy, 37. However, an inquest in 2010 found the tragic accident could have been avoided if the crane's owners had actually had the correct manual for the model of crane being used instead of one for a different crane, which had several missing pages. If they had, they might not have overloaded it by four tonnes, causing its 50m length of steel to topple backwards.

DUCKING THE SHRIMP OF DEATH

The family of a Californian man who hurt his neck whilst ducking to avoid a shrimp thrown by a chef at a steakhouse launched a multi-million dollar lawsuit for compensation when he died in 2001. They asserted he had died from complications months after sustaining the original injury at the restaurant. Their case was rejected, although the restaurant admitted that throwing of shrimp and other food for diners to catch was part of 'the show performance of cooking'.

ANCHOR AWAY

Anieli Gekas was standing next to a three-tonne ship's anchor which had been mounted in concrete as a landmark at a port 26km outside Athens in 1978. However, as he leant against it and posed for a photo, the mass of rusted metal collapsed down and crushed Gekas, killing him instantly.

NO COOL HAND CAITLIN
When eating eggs, most of us worry only about raising our cholesterol. There are worse things to worry about. Caitlin Matthews, 54, died whilst taking part in a hard-boiled egg eating competition at her local pub in Shropshire in 2013 – even though she did not like eggs. However, Caitlin was no Cool Hand Luke and choked on one of the eggs and began to turn blue. Despite being rushed to hospital, Ms. Matthews died two days later.

WHEEL OF DEATH
William Sheen attended a party in Norfolk in 2010 and, when leaving, thought that the night could only be made better by climbing over a fence and plunging into the water feeding a historic mill. Sheen became caught in the steel waterwheel and was crushed to death, his body found on the wheel the next morning. Unsurprisingly, the level of alcohol in his blood was more than three times over the drink-drive limit.

THE BIG ONE
In 1931, German Guntram Schultz from Hamburg was so shocked when the last bit of his treble bet on trotting races came in at 10/1 and he won £119, that the 70-year-old dropped dead from a heart attack.

50 SHADES OF DEAD III
If you are going to choose to die kinky, you might as well make it absurd. Kord Färber from Krefeld, Germany, was found handcuffed by one wrist to a radiator in his house in 1978. He was surrounded by hardcore pornographic magazines, a football pump, several lipsticks and a selection of candles. He'd smeared margarine onto his genitals and dripped wax onto his chest. Police believe he died from dehydration after leaving the key to the handcuffs out of reach in the pocket of his discarded trousers.

DEATH AT FIRST SIGHT

Death by dangerous driving is so commonplace as not to be ridiculous, but death by seeing a car still counts as somewhat absurd. Back in 1921, cars in some parts of the world were a bit of a rarity. The fast approach of one through the Warwickshire village of Burton Dasset caused such alarm to 70-year-old Ralph Hislop that he collapsed from a heart attack and fell into the path of the oncoming car. An inquest heard it was the first time Ralph had seen an automobile.

DAMNED IF YOU DO

Dangerous driving is nothing new. In 1936, motorist Bill Morgan sped across the main railway crossing in Creswick, Australia to beat an oncoming train. However, he skidded as he went over the rails, the car spinning out of control and hitting a post, shattering the windscreen. Morgan died from a small wound to his neck where a shard of glass severed his jugular.

DAMNED IF YOU DON'T

It is strange how some death spots seem to echo across the years. In 1938, Brian Crilley pulled up in his car at the main railway crossing in Creswick, Australia and waited for a train to pass. As it did, a chip of stone was thrown up from the tracks, hit the windscreen, shattering it. Crilley, like Morgan two years before, then died from a severed jugular.

DEATH WISH FULFILLED

Be careful what you wish for. Jane Smith told her mother she did not wear a seatbelt because 'I would rather be dead than a cabbage.' An inquest in 2011 heard that it was Smith's decision not to wear a belt whilst driving that led to her being catapulted through her windscreen after a collision with a truck on a winding country road in Norfolk, England. Had she been wearing a seatbelt, it is likely she would have survived the crash with only minor injuries.

SMOKING KILLS XI – LISTEN TO YOUR MOTHER

Phil Powell, 20, was banned by his mother from smoking in her home whilst living there, so had taken to sitting on the windowsill of his first-floor bedroom to have a cigarette. His mother had also told him to stop doing this. It turns out Phil should have listened to his mum, because one Friday night in 2012, he fell to his death from the sill. An autopsy showed that he had a blood alcohol concentration twice the legal drive limit at the time of his tumble.

CAUGHT NAPPING

Professor John Stiller, 58, pulled into a service station of the M4 motorway in 1982 to catch a short snooze after five hours of driving, thinking nothing of being parked behind a two-deck car transporter. Unfortunately, as he slept in his car, one of the vehicles above broke free and crashed down onto Stiller's car, killing him instantly. At the subsequent inquest his wife said: 'You can get away with murder in England if you call it an accident.'

CAT WOMAN VS. PIGEON MAN

Shropshire neighbours Jenny Elton and Bobby Veneruso had a long-running dispute over their pets – he kept pigeons and she cats. In 2005, Bobby's pigeon loft was burned down and in what was seen as retaliation, Mrs. Elton found one of her kittens had been poisoned. Ironically, pigeon fancier Veneruso was also a keen clay pigeon shooter and in a drunken row over who had done what to each other's animals, he shot and killed Elton with his shotgun.

FELLED BY A TREE

No man should be an island, but disabled Tim Dorkin lived like one on a small island off the coast of Washington State. When a storm brought down a tree on his trailer, trapping him inside it in 1992, he thought he had no means of raising help and no nearby neighbours to stumble on him. Fearing a long and painful death due to starvation, Dorkin shot himself in the head. Ironically, the gunshot alerted a visitor to his wooded bit of the island, and they discovered his body.

MOORE NOT MERRIER

This book has reinforced in me the idea that the universe is a web of strange coincidence. In the first volume, we wrote about an English librarian called Moore who committed suicide with homemade bombs. At the same time, on the other side of the Atlantic, David Moore was also killing himself with an overly complex system of a homemade guillotine and a series of hard-wired Molotov cocktails that were meant to turn his bedroom into a funeral pyre. Regrettably, whilst his bombs failed to go off, his barbed wire and saw blade guillotine worked all too well.

BOVINE BASTARDS

A Welsh farmer was run over by his own quad bike in 2008 when it was forced forward by cows eager to be fed. Bryn Morgan was found with the quad bike, engine still running, on his crushed body whilst around him a herd of cow enjoyed two bales of hay he had been taking to the herd. An inquest decided that he had been knocked unconscious by cows in a feeding frenzy before the herd had forced the bike over him.

SMOKE IN THE WATER

Londoner Alice Yates, 19, died after a night out clubbing when she experienced a rare, but deadly, allergic reaction to the glycol and water mixture of 'smoke' pumped out across the dance floor. She began to experience breathing difficulties in the club after dancing, and collapsed outside, dying in hospital four days later.

TUBE OF DEATH

Not all hazards from smoke machines are based around inhalation. In film-making, the 'tube of death' is a long, self-inflating tube attached to a smoke machine that can be stretched over long distances, with holes in it wherever you want dispersing smoke. In 2008, a horror film was being shot in Hungary. For one scene, set in a foggy wood at night, a tube of death was used. It proved a bit too effective at making a convincing fog, with extra Balázs Szabados not seeing it in the artificial mist, tripping over it as he ran and tumbling down a 9m embankment to his death.

IN THE SHIT

Brian Black was working in the sewers below Sydney in 1926, helping to expand the network. As he walked across a plank to try to avoid stepping into the sewage below him, he lost his footing and began to slip in. This caused Black to panic and thrust up the metal bar he had been carrying straight into the electric wire on the roof of the tunnel. Electrocution was instantaneous.

BEAR-ING UP STOICALLY

If I had lost my son to being savaged by a bear, I am not sure I could be as stoic as Jan Kundera. His son was mauled to death by one of the bears he trained after he slipped on the water he was using to clean its cage. At an inquest in 1938, the old circus performer said: 'When my boy fell the bear no longer recognized him. He was used to seeing him standing by him. On the ground he was something strange and foreign; something frightening; something dangerous. This is the natural way of things.'

THE ELEPHANTS WERE RUNNING TWO BY TWO

George Branner was so shocked to see two elephants running along the road in Pennsylvania in May 1951, that he became distracted and fatally crashed his car into a telegraph pole. The elephants had escaped from a circus trailer that had broken down 6km away from the spot where Branner met his end.

NO LAUGHING MATTER

Tempting fate can be fatal. Lion tamer Madame Rachid had been mauled by her lions in front of an audience before, so she well knew the dangers of her act. However, in 1949, in an attempt to spice it up she tried to introduce dogs into the routine. Whilst she was trying to accustom the big cats and little dogs to each other, her daughter was watching and began to laugh. Rachid turned to her and scolded: 'This is no laughing matter!' How right she was. With her back turned, one of the lions, agitated by the dogs, struck out at her, killing her instantly.

PACHYDERM PERIL I

An elephant can be a dangerous enough beast at the best of times, but a drunk elephant is someone's death waiting to happen. In 2010, a 70-strong herd of binge-drinking elephants got high on a West Bengal village's supply of fermented rice hooch and began a drunken rampage. After trampling crops, smashing homes and killing three villagers, the elephants either staggered off or fell asleep. Sounds like someone needs to invent elephant-proof hooch jars.

PACHYDERM PERIL II

Elephants do not have to be drunk to be deadly. An elephant brought to participate in rituals at a temple in Vallamkulam, India in 1956 did not like its duties and ran amok. It overturned two cars, a truck, smashed several stalls and uprooted a tree, with which it swatted and killed three men who were trying to subdue it. Way to go, Nelly.

PACHYDERM PERIL III

Given the propensity for pachyderms to run amok during religious rites in India, it is somewhat surprising that it took until 2013 for one of them to be given bail for a murder charged. Thechikottukavu 'Raman' Ramachandran, the tallest 'domestic' elephant in India, killed three women at a temple festival in Perumbavoor in January 2013 and became the first pachyderm in Indian legal history to be charged with murder and then make bail.

DEADLY ENEMA I

The world of self-administered medicine is often strange. The sort of people who think they automatically know better than trained medical professionals will often do ridiculous things. Amongst these might be coffee enemas. Despite little evidence, some people believe them to be good at both relieving constipation and curing cancer. Californian Michelle Dryden administered one to her husband Ron in 2007. It did not cure his cancer, but it did end his pain by causing an electrolyte imbalance that led to a fatal heart attack.

DEADLY ENEMA II

Oklahoman Ella Morgan, 40, was suffering from extreme constipation in 2009. Rather than go to a doctor, she consulted the Internet and bought a kit for administering coffee enemas. She soon became addicted to them, taking them four times a day. This turned out to be the worst type of caffeine addiction. On her death, an autopsy showed that the enemas had led not only to ulcers but to septicaemia and an abscess in the brain, which eventually killed her.

CREAM CRACKERED

In 1978, a pub in Burton, England ran a cream cracker-eating contest in which competitors had to attempt to eat six crackers without a drink in one minute. If they succeeded, they won a pint of ale. Holidaymaker Bill Cunningham visited the pub and took part, but on his fourth cracker, began to choke. Before anyone could help him, he passed out and died.

BUSTED!

A Texas steak and rib restaurant offered a free meal and a T-shirt to anyone who could finish its Bronco Gut-Buster, featuring a slab of ribs, 12 wings, steak omelette, a pound of chili fries, a pound of onion rings and a 900g Bronco burger. It certainly busted the gut of John Brandon Everett Jr in 1989. He died whilst three-quarters of the way through the challenge from a heart attack, thought by a medical examiner to have been partially brought on by the stress of eating so much.

BYPASS BURGER MAN BUYS THE BIG ONE

Unofficial spokesman for the Las Vegas restaurant the Heart Attack Grill, Jon Basso, 52, died in February 2013, from a heart attack whilst waiting for a bus in front of the restaurant he loved. The Grill is infamous for serving Flatliner Fries and the 9,982-calorie, 1.3kg Quadruple Bypass Burger, which is described on the menu as a 'Taste worth dying for'. Anyone who wants to try an eating challenge should give the restaurant a go. Just tell them David from 1001 *Ridiculous Ways to Die* sent you.

HIPPO HELL I

Despite what animal apologists say, you cannot trust some creatures. Badgers are bastards. Dolphins, sex pests. Llamas, lethal. And as for hippos, they kill so often in Africa that they need to be regarded as much more dangerous than crocodiles or lions. I could fill this book with tales of absurd deaths caused by hippos, but I should restrict myself only to the most ridiculous. Top candidate for that spot is held by 41-year-old South African Marius Els. He was killed by his pet hippo – Humphrey – who Els used to ride like a horse and swim with on his farm. Els used to tell people the 1,200kg hippo was like a son to him – a son that bit him to death in 2011. Els had previously told a newspaper: 'I trust him with my heart that he will not harm anybody.' This would be the heart that Humphrey ate, I am guessing.

LETHAL LLAMA

Former coroner Florence Lanahan died in 2012 after hitting her head when her pet llama – Baby Doll – rushed to greet her, slipped on the wet pavement and knocked Lanahan down. A local veterinarian said: 'There was no evidence the llama was acting maliciously.' I am not so sure. Llamas are vicious, hoofing, spitting beasts and if some idiot called me Baby Doll, I would bloody well want to kill them.

DANGER! DOLPHIN!

In 1994, a solitary male Bottlenose Dolphin known to locals of São Sebastião do Alto, in Brazil, as Tião attacked two men who attempted to swim with it. Joao Paulo Moreira, 33, died from internal haemorrhaging and Wilson Reis Pedroso, 41, suffered a broken rib after being butted by the dolphin. A marine biologist who was monitoring Tião said: 'People don't follow our instructions that they should not ride on top of the dolphin and that they should wait for him to take the initiative. I have told them that he prefers women to men, but they do not listen.'

TUNNEL VISION

Many metal thieves die due to electrocution, so it makes a change to hear of one whose combination of thieving and tunnelling did not work out too well. When Griff Evans went into a steelworks service tunnel to steal copper, he was well-equipped, taking a cable cutter, head torch and a walkie talkie to keep in touch with his look-out on the surface. Unfortunately, Evans did not take what he really needed – breathing apparatus – as in the enclosed tunnel he was overcome by the fumes from his petrol-driven cutter and soon passed out and died.

BASTARD BADGERS

In 2007, the British Army in Basra had to release an official statement that it had not released 'man-eating badgers' into the area as a weapon of war. That would have been ridiculous: all the vicious badgers stay in Britain, guarding the home front. Whilst badgers killing people is rare, it does happen. Badger-baiting scum and hunters have died from bites, but the death of innocents is much rarer. However, in 2003, an unprovoked rogue badger in Evesham, England, attacked five people in a 48-hour period. One victim of the bastard badger had to be hospitalized for skin grafts and whilst there, developed multidrug-resistant *Staphylococcus aureus* (MRSA) and died.

HIPPO HELL II

In 1995, preacher James Emmanoel was illustrating Christ's relationship with fishermen and urging his flock to 'Get in the boat with Jesus' by delivering his sermon from a boat in Lake Victoria, Uganda. He had just begun to speak about 'demons coming in many forms' when a hippo overturned the craft he was in, bit a huge chunk from his torso and then dragged him underwater to his death. Ironically, locals believe that hippos on nearby Rusinga Island are under the control of witchdoctors, who can command them to kill their enemies.

GIRAFFE NOT HAVING A LAUGH

South African woman Merike Engelbrecht was walking her dogs in a game park in the north of the country in 2010 when her pets spooked a giraffe with her calf, panicking the long-necked beast. As Merike scooped down to pick up her dog, the giraffe kicked her on the back of the head, killing her instantly.

BAKED ALIVE

Gruesome killings are not in themselves usually ridiculous. Vile, horrid and tragic, yes. Ridiculous, no. However, the small details in the following murder case from 1910 make it absurd. A baker from Ploesti, Romania, called Moraru, returned to his bakery drunk and sent home his apprentices, whom he blamed for spoiling his bread. His wife scolded him for being too drunk to work and tried to take the bread out of the oven before it burnt. This so angered Moraru that he pushed his wife into the oven and closed the door on her. Her screams brought the apprentices back, but Moraru attacked them with a rolling pin and they could do nothing to save her. The local police chief said: 'This crime is like a fairytale come to life which will haunt us all.'

PETTICOAT PERIL

At some levels, the modern world has eradicated many dangers. It is certainly less likely that the tragic but absurd end which befell Mrs Edna Hall in Combaning, Australia in 1896 is likely to happen now. Whilst visiting her husband who was working at a local mine, 'a gale of wind blew a spark from a fire into her voluminous dress and petticoats igniting them, and she was burned to death.'

GHOST OF A CHANCE I

In his wonderful book *Real Christmas Ghost Stories*, author M. J. Wayland uncovered the true story of the ridiculous death of Robert Mitchell in 1856. The 15-year-old visited friends at a Derbyshire farmhouse, where talk turned to ghost stories. As Mitchell left, one of his friends dressed in a white cloth approached and gave a groan before running off. The impact of this left the suggestible Mitchell in a state of shock. He refused to eat, raved about ghosts and after two days in bed, died. His practical joke-playing friend was later charged with manslaughter for frightening him to death.

GHOST OF A CHANCE II

Another true story of being scared to death by a 'ghost' occurred in 1894, when Elizabeth Bishop of Somerset thought she'd seen the spirit of a captain who had died when his ship sunk in the Bristol Channel. Whatever she saw, Elizabeth became delirious with fear and after three days was dead. An inquest determined that she had died due to heart failure brought on by extreme fright.

WHAT A BOOBY

Canadian Luc Dupont, 75, felt so threatened by the possibility of having his home in Vancouver robbed that he set up a rifle with a string that ran across the floor of his bedroom. Unfortunately, one morning in October 2010, Dupont accidentally triggered his own booby-trap, fatally shooting himself. A police spokeswoman said: 'He was a victim of his own fear.'

HAM-FISTED WAY TO GO

Ham radio is a wonderful hobby and that given one of my favourite cousins is a keen amateur radio operator, I would never say a bad word about ham radio hobbyists.

However, it is hard to fathom the lack of common sense displayed by American ham radio operator Brian Moore, 55, his wife Lizzy and 15-year-old son Marvin in 2009. They tried to raise a 9m radio antenna close to a power line carrying 13,000 volts, lost control of the antenna, hit the power line and were all fatally electrocuted.

FLAT FOR SALE, ALL AMENITIES INCLUDING CORPSE

When Ethel Winterton drank herself to death in her London flat in 2010, she died on her sofa. This fact did not register with estate agent Simon Glover, who continued to show a couple around the £800,000 home despite her being dead in the living room. It was only after the couple had left that it occurred to him that something might be amiss and the yellow colour she had turned might suggest she was doing something other than just sleeping.

BIG DAY, BIG BANG

Sicilian wedding photographer Calogero Scimera made a mistake when he asked a happy couple to pose with hunting rifles in July 2010. One of the .22 calibre guns went off as Scimera was taking a photo, fatally hitting him in the head.

HEART HORROR

In scenes that seem to have come straight out of a video game, Californian cage fighter Jarrod Wyatt, 26, ripped the heart from his friend and training partner Taylor Powell, 21, whilst under the influence of a hallucinogenic drink. Wyatt was convicted of murder in 2010 and Taylor's death was recorded as due to blood loss.

DO NOT DISTURB

Dutchman Rishi de Jong, 50, had such a bad temper that when he went to bed with a headache at his home in Den Haag in 2006, his brother and sister who lived with him were too scared to break his last command that they must not disturb him. For four years, they thought he was eating out at night and his dead body was discovered only when workmen came to the apartment to measure it for new windows.

SNORE NO MORE

Few things can wind someone up like a loud and persistent snore. Chinese student Guo Liwei, 24, was so enraged by his roommate Zhao Zan's constant, deafening snoring that one night in March 2010, he stabbed him in the chest, killing him. Guo had previously complained to the authorities of the Jilin Agricultural University about Zhao's snoring and even posted a video of it to the university's website.

HIJAB HORROR

A Muslim woman was strangled to death whilst enjoying a go-karting session in Sydney in 2010. The unfortunate woman's hijab became tangled in the wheels of her kart as she took a corner on the circuit. The garment quickly tightened around her neck before she had any hope of stopping.

HEADSCARF HORROR
It is not just the hijab which can be a fatal hazard when go-karting. In 2008, an 18-year-old from Surrey, England was strangled when her headscarf became caught around the rear wheel axle of a go-kart. Despite being airlifted to hospital, she tragically died from the injuries sustained during the tangle.

HITLER HORROR
I have always believed Nazism was a form of mental illness. The actions of a 22-year-old Neo-Nazi from Chernihiv in the Ukraine do nothing to dispel this impression. On April 20, 2010, the vile miscreant decided to celebrate the anniversary of Hitler's birth with a killing spree, beheading three people with a spade. A local policeman told me: 'The manner of their deaths was horrible, but to be killed for Hitler's birthday makes it even worse.'

MAGICAL MORT XV
A Bangladeshi bricklayer was beheaded in 2010 by four men acting on the orders of a brickyard owner. He had been told by a fortune teller that the way to turn his bricks red was to indulge in a spot of human sacrifice and put the poor victim's head in the kiln next time a batch of bricks was being made.

CLUE IN THE TITLE
Murder is never justified. It is sometimes, despite it awfulness, somewhat ridiculous. In 2010, a 40-year-old Norwegian man killed his mother and cut her up into small cubes after she refused to read a book he recommended to her. Mother possibly should have started running when she saw the book her son was so keen on was *Girl In The Cellar* about kidnap victim Natascha Kampusch.

MORE THAN A BIT FISHY

Fish sauce – traditionally made from fermenting fish and salt for up to a year in 3m-high wood vats – is a key ingredient in much of Asian cuisine. In 2009, three Vietnamese men suffocated in a vat of fish sauce being made in a factory at Carn Ranh. One worker had gone in to fix a pipe and become overcome by the fumes, his two colleagues then succumbed to suffocation after being overpowered by the fermenting fish gunk.

OH, THE IRONY XI – UNGRATEFUL PET

Careful what you wish for. Winning is not always the best thing that can happen to you. Canadian Norman Buwalda fought and won a long legal battle with the authorities for the right to keep a tiger at his rural Ontario home. In January 2010, a few months after his victory, his 299kg pet tiger mauled him to death.

DOGS – NOT MAN'S BEST FRIEND I

A 52-year-old Slovenian doctor fought a four-year legal battle to save his three bullmastiffs from being put down. In 2010, he won his fight and got his pets back from custody, where they had been placed after they attacked a passer-by. However, his joy was short-lived, as the released dogs turned on their owner, mauling him to death in his garden.

BLESS YOU! I

Gordon Styles, 79, died at a residential home in Surrey, England in 2010 after he sneezed so violently it caused his brain to bleed. The coroner said it was the first 'death by sneezing case' he had overseen, but far from the first one he had come across.

BLESS YOU! II

Death by sneezing may seem ridiculous, but there is a long history of it. When King Charles II was taken violently ill in 1685, he asked his successor to look after his mistress and apologized to his courtiers saying: 'I am sorry, gentlemen, for being such a time dying.' After this, his physicians hastened his death by administering a potion made from cowslips and ammonia 'to promote sneezing' to cause the coup de grâce and end the King's suffering by lingering on the liminal line between life and death.

BLESS YOU! III

Danny Ennis, 19, from London, died after a sneezing fit in 1992 whilst at work on a building site. The fit of sneezing brought about a fatal brain haemorrhage. At the inquest into his death, the coroner's court heard from one of Danny's co-workers: 'He did a massive sneeze, I said "Bless you", then he sneezed again, clutched at his ears and went.' The inquest decided that an undiagnosed condition – neurofibromatosis – played a central role in Danny's death from sneezing.

KILLER KARAOKE V

Ely Dignadice's rendition of the popular Filipino love song "Remember Me" so upset patrons at a Manila nightclub in 1998 that after he had finished, 10 men who had seen him perform beat him to death with beer bottles and wooden clubs.

KILLER KARAOKE VI

A Thai property tycoon hogged the microphone at a Bangkok karaoke bar for three hours in 1992, compounding his irritation factor by singing "Candle in the Wind" three times. When a bar patron objected to the third rendition, the tycoon had one of his bodyguard's shoot and kill the man spoiling his fun. At the subsequent murder trial the tycoon defended his three-hour stint by saying: 'Everyone was transfixed by the beauty of my voice.'

KILLER KARAOKE VII

Karaoke has led to killings in nations across the world. Whilst the majority are concentrated in Thailand and the Philippines, it is not uncommon in any country with both karaoke and loose gun control to see a singing-related shooting. Even Canada suffered a karaoke killing in 1992 when a man singing a Vietnamese version of "My Way" thought audience members were laughing at his performance. He flung down his microphone and shot two of them, hitting Tan Ngoc Le in the head and instantly killing him. A waiter who witnessed the killing said: 'No one was laughing, his version was good. He just thought the smiles of liking were laughter.'

FOREVER BLOWING BUBBLES

In April 2009, Mr Dieudonne Masha and a neighbour were walking on the shore of Lake Kivu in Democratic Republic of Congo when they spotted a military patrol. Lacking his ID card and fearing reprisals, Masha ran away. Unfortunately, Lake Kivu has vast reservoirs of carbon dioxide – known in Swahili as *mazuku* (evil wind) – and Masha ran straight into a huge bubble of carbon dioxide that suffocated him.

THE COSMIC JOKER STRIKES AGAIN V

Austrian Catholic Gunther Link, 45, died when he attended a church to give thanks to God for being rescued from an elevator. He embraced a pillar supporting an 390kg stone monument to a saint at Weinhaus Church, bringing the massive piece of masonry down on top of him.

HOW NOT TO PICK A WINNER

Tony Baxter, 63, from Swansea died after picking his nose. An inquest in 2009 heard how his nose picking led to a nosebleed which Baxter was too drunk to either notice or tackle, leading to his eventual death from loss of blood.

BORED BOAR BLUNDER

German hunter Gerold Barth, 56, was shot by three friends who were hunting with him in a forest outside of Freiburg. Barth had gone off by himself and was scrabbling through undergrowth when his alleged friends mistook him as a wild boar.

KEEPERS – BEE-WARE!

Welsh beekeeper Alun Evans, 46, died in 1999 after he was stung feeding his bees. Due to the hot August weather he had not worn any protective clothing and was stung on his head, chest and arms. The venom in the stings led to a heart attack four hours later, whilst he was being treated in hospital. His wife said: 'Alun thought he had built up an immunity like other beekeepers because he had been stung so many times before.'

A RUBBISH WAY TO GO VI

Dave Maynard died in 2009 after being crushed by the mountains of rubbish he had acquired across a decade of emptying his neighbours' dustbins into his flat in London. His council had removed his hoard of rotting rubbish in 1998 and spent £250,000 refurbishing it for him, but had done nothing since to tackle Maynard's hoarding behaviour.

A RUBBISH WAY TO GO VII

Police searched for Billie Jean James, 67, for four months before her husband eventually found her body under mounds of rubbish at her Las Vegas home in August 2009. Police with sniffer dogs had searched the property three times, but had been unable to find her amid mountains of clothes and empty fast food boxes. A police spokesman told me: 'We could not find her, as the rotting smell overpowered the dogs. Everyone's best guess is she had a stroke and became disorientated in the maze of passageways she used to navigate through the house due to all the rubbish.'

JUST SHOCKING

You would think a metal thief trying to steal copper from an electricity pylon might have done some basic research on electricity. That was not the case for Englishman Adam Shuttleworth, who was electrocuted in 2009 as he stood on a 9m metal ladder as he tried to steal metal from a pylon carrying 33,000 volts.

A SPOT OF DEATH

Tragic Tony Gissing, 14, died after he was prescribed Sebomin for his acne. The coroner at his inquest said: 'I have researched this, but there are no other deaths involving this tablet anywhere in the world. Tragically, Tony's reaction seems truly unique.'

A BATTY WAY TO GO I

In 2006, a health-worker in Peru died from rabies carried in the bite of a vampire bat. Ironically, he had been working to try to prevent rabies deaths from bat bites among the indigenous communities in the north-eastern Peruvian Amazon.

TOP 10 RIDICULOUS DEATHS FROM AUSTRALIA – STREWTH (NOT SO) ALIVE!

10. DIY tree felling is rarely a good idea. Bobby Grange from the Northern Territory turned himself to toast in 2010 when he cut down a Carpentaria palm in his garden. One of its branches came down on a power line and he electrocuted himself when he tried to dislodge it.

9. William Birley of Montrose, Victoria, had made it to the ripe old age of 94 when he was done in by his pipe-smoking habit in July 1940. It was not cancer that felled the old trooper but a simple fall whilst at home, which forced the stem of the pipe into his throat, causing him to choke to death.

8. Orchard hand William Joseph Williamson, 22, met his end in October 1937 in Borenore, NSW, due to his smoking habit. Williamson had been spraying trees with lead arsenate and not paying attention when making his roll ups. He transferred enough of the insecticide into his smokes that when he lit up on a break, he killed himself with a fatal dose of arsenic.

7. I am married to a wonderful Aussie lass, so I have come to learn how important betting is to the culture of some Australians. Therefore it makes perfect sense to learn that in 1951, Augustus Fisk of Condobolin, NSW, was so excited when his greyhound won a race that he ran straight out onto the track. Forgetting his own safety, he ran in front of an ongoing race and was fatally knocked over by a pack of greyhounds running at a speed of nearly 60km/h.

6. In September 1911, 18-year-old dentist's assistant Kenneth Stewart was lying on his bed playing a mouth organ when he swallowed his dental plate containing a false tooth, which his boss had specially made for him. The plate lodged in his throat and poor Kenneth died from the results of the operation to remove it.

5. Cindy Firman, 42, tied her husband Brian's arms to the overhead lamps of a Sydney hotel room in 1986 and proceeded to climb on top. During the throws of passion, Brian managed to pull on his restraints so hard he brought the light fitting crashing down onto his head, fatally smashing his skull.

4. Elinor Hunter was a character. Born in Philadelphia and formerly known as Prairie Rose, she had toured the States with Will Rogers as his common-law wife and assistant in a knife-throwing act before the cowboy actor made it in Hollywood. She had become a nurse during World War I, met an Australian soldier and moved to Sydney. In 1939, and now a 51-year-old widow, Hunter was making her morning coffee when she tripped, catching her dressing robe on the stove's gas tap and knocking it on whilst simultaneously suspending herself on the stove. Helpless because she was trapped in her gown, she died from gas poisoning.

3. The gods seem very cruel. Barry Burton, 64, from Adelaide was suffering from Parkinson's disease when he died in 1945. The cause of death was Parkinson's-related – Barry had toothache and decided to rinse his mouth with eucalyptus. However, a spasm of paralysis struck his arm as he raised the bottle to his mouth and forced him to drink more than a cupful of eucalyptus, which proved fatal. Poor bugger.

2. In July 1942, whilst the world was at war, Mrs Pearl Mavis, 35, met her end due to her fondness for imitating the calls of wildlife. Whilst calling out to emus in the scrubland near her home in Yanco, NSW, Mavis was accidentally shot her by husband who thought she was one of the large birds. Although police were initially suspicious, a coroner's enquiry found him to be totally innocent given his wife was well known locally for hiding herself in bushes and pretending to be various birds and other animals.

1. There was a period when Oz led the world in the sport of dwarf tossing, but it seems to have fallen somewhat out of favour, even in its former strongholds such as Western Australia. Whatever the reasons for its decline, the sport has done its bit for ridiculous deaths across the years. In 1989, Bob 'Big Blue' Hoxton, 48, died from a heart attack at a bar in Kalgoorlie when he strained to pick up a dwarf called Barney O'Leary. Friends at the time said: 'Barney was just a bit too much for the Big Blue. He'd been working flat out all day and was just too exhausted to toss the little chap.'

BARRIER BARMY

George Smith, 54, died in 2007 whilst trying to get his car out of a London car park that had closed for the night. He used a hacksaw to cut off the padlocks on a height restriction barrier and wedged a recycling bin under it to lever it up. Unfortunately, he hit the bin as he exited, causing the barrier to smash through his roof and kill him.

BOWLED OVER

A 1974 cricket match between two Kent teams in Meopham was marred when Bill Jameson, 44, was hit by a ball whilst attempting to take a catch at the boundary. Jameson shook off his injury, despite a large bump on his head. However, back in the clubhouse, sandwich in one hand and a pint of beer in the other, he suddenly collapsed and died due to a brain haemorrhage.

CYCLIST PIPPED BY THE LAMP POST

John Latimer was crushed to death by a falling lamp post as he cycled along a road in Thorpe Bay, Essex. The lamp post came down on him after it had been hit by a car with enough force to snap it in two. The coroner presiding over the inquest into Latimer's death said: 'It was a million-to-one bit of bad luck he was pedalling in that spot at that time.'

FOOTBALL FAN'S FREAK FALL

Keen Liverpool Football Club fan Mark Taylor, 40, got into a scuffle with former lodger Stephen Millard and was pushed onto his beloved model of the home of LFC, Anfield stadium. Unfortunately, the fall not only broke his model but left Taylor with three broken ribs, a collapsed lung and internal bleeding, which led to his death. Home Office pathologist Dr. Basil Purdue said: 'The plaster model was a very strong object with lots of jagged bits and some were broken. I don't think he would have been aware he was mortally injured. It was sheer ill luck. With prompt treatment he may have survived.'

HANGED OUT TO DRY

A 40-year-old man from Southend, Essex fell down the basement steps outside his home in 2004. The chap, who had been drinking, managed to get his jacket caught on the steps' metal railing and accidentally hanged himself.

OWN GOAL

Young footballer, Damian West, 19, was returning to his home in Kent after an all-day drinking session, during which he had drunk nine pints of beer. Whilst crossing a road, he stumbled and fell into the middle of it, remaining there lying on his side. Regrettably, a driver ran straight over him, killing him instantly. A police forensic officer investigating the accident said: 'It seems not unusual for young people who are intoxicated to lay in the road, and I cannot give an explanation for that behaviour.'

YOUNG, DUMB AND DEAD DRUNK

Bristol teenager Tony Carr was given a bottle of vodka for his 18th birthday in 1993 and bet £50 by the friend who gave it to him that he could not drink it all by the end of the party being held for him. What a pal. Tony drank three-quarters of the one litre bottle and collapsed. Before an ambulance arrived, he choked to death on his own vomit. He was four times over the drink-drive limit at the point he died.

PIRATE PLONKER

One of the local landmarks of my childhood was a water tower near my home town of Hadleigh. I always longed to climb up it. I still do. However, unlike Andy Cowan, 24, I would never think of doing it whilst trying to haul a rucksack filled with an aerial and transmitter for broadcasting a pirate radio station. The extra weight caused him to lose his grip and tumble 18m to his death in 2004. Since then, I have never been able to look at the tower in the same light.

BEARD BURNING BLUNDER

Johnny Cairn, 53, of Canterbury, England was a heavy smoker and a heavy drinker. He also had a very bushy beard. These three things combined in 2008 to cause a ridiculous and painful death when, whilst heavily under the influence of alcohol, Cairn managed to set fire to his beard, but was too drunk to put it out. Workers at the housing project where he lived, rushed into his apartment when the fire alarm was set off, but though he was doused with an extinguisher, he died from 40 per cent burns to his body.

ALL AT SEA AND IN THE SOUP

The high seas can be a dangerous place. Samuel Whesker was a cook on the Scottish Shire Liner the *Argyllshire*. On a voyage between London and Melbourne in July 1923, Whesker was lifting a cauldron of boiling oxtail soup just as a wave crashed through the port hole in the kitchen, causing him to slip and spill the soup all over himself, dying from the scalds he received.

CROSSING GATES TO PEARLY GATES

Mrs Gertrude Mary Allen, 50, was the attendant at the Kitchener railway gates in Tamworth, Australia in 1937. One day, as she was closing a gate for an approaching train, a horse slipped into it, causing the gate to swing backwards, flinging Gertrude unconscious onto the tracks and the path of the train. Although the train managed to stop just inches from her prone body, she died from a fractured skull.

STRICTLY COME DYING

Think outrageous legal compensation claims are a new blight on society? Think again. In September 1944, Parkes Municipal Council in Australia was sued for compensation by the sister of Mrs Mary A. Jordan after she had died while collecting her ration book by slipping on the highly polished floor of a dance hall. A barrister for Jordan's sister claimed the council were responsible for making her have to go to the Protestant Hall to get her new book.

DANCE OF DEATH

Never rile a man with a loaded gun. In June 1895, teenager Fred Pormeroy, 16, from Cobar, Australia, began to dance in front of William Crow, who had been out hunting. Pormeroy began to taunt Crow that he would never be able to hit anything, that he could not hit his dancing feet. Crow was so annoyed, he took aim and shot Pormeroy in the shoulder, killing him.

CAREFUL OF THAT SHEEP, MATE

Sheep can be tricky and lethal buggers. In August 1926, Thomas Stewart was trying to get a mob of sheep into a pen when one refused to go through the rails at a ranch near Gundagai, Australia. Stewart then spooked the errant sheep so much, it ran blindly at him, butting him so hard in the abdomen that he died from peritonitis.

A FOUR-LEGGED FRIEND? HARDLY!

After downing drinks one December in 1912 at the Lanboyd Hotel in New South Wales, Australia, John H. Barlow tried to untie his horse, which was tethered to a rail in front of the hotel. In his inebriated state, he spooked the animal, which took fright and pulled the whole rail away. Unfortunately for Barlow, the rail swung and struck him on the back of the head, killing him instantly.

SLEEPWALKING TO DEATH

New Zealander Trevor Gerard, 25, sleepwalked to his death in April 1938. The Auckland man walked out of his house and put an outstretched arm through a neighbour's window, severing an artery. The window smash alerted help, but it was too late for Gerard, who died from blood loss.

NOT THE SHARPEST TOOL

My wife is an Australian. When she pointed out this story to me, which happened in her home city of Sydney in June 1937, she simply said: 'What sort of idiot sharpens a revolver?' Quite. The answer to that question is John Patch, 20, who was sharpening the barrel of his revolver on an emery wheel when the gun exploded and a piece of the weapon penetrated his stomach, killing him. It was thought the barrel was plugged with gunpowder, but no one ever quite worked out why he was sharpening it.

MORE THAN A CHIP OFF THE OLD BLOCK

Elaborate suicides are tragic, but never escape the taint of ridiculousness. In May 1938, the 26-year-old son of timber merchant John Kolar, took his life by attaching himself to the conveyor in his father's sawmill and allowing it to carry him towards the electric circular saw, decapitating himself.

GOING OUT WITH A BANG

Widow Susan Grace Kelly, 80, died in 1935 at Armidale, Australia during a storm. It was not the lightning which killed her, but the sound of thunder. After one clap unsettled her, she proclaimed: 'That was very close, I don't like it', the next clap breaking overhead caused her to shriek and then die from a heart attack.

BIG TOPPED

In 1927, several circus elephants were being ridden across a level crossing in Illinois when a signal failure meant the troupe was approached by a passenger train bound for Aurora. One elephant was hit by the train, falling and crushing to death its trainer who was riding it. Two other circus workers riding the elephants were also killed when the rest of the troupe stampeded, fatally throwing them to the ground.

THE PERILS OF WATCHING THE BIRDIE

Some journalists like to hype a story up, claiming it is a first. In April 1937, a Brisbane newspaper claimed that the death of Thomas Saunders, 86, in Chesham, England was 'the first case of fatal collision between two pedestrians'. Hardly! Death from bumping into someone on the street has been claiming lives in England for centuries. One particularly ridiculous incident happened in London in 1862 when Charles Mesham bumped into Henry Mason in Dover Street, causing Mason to drop a 'small clock with chimes' he was carrying onto his foot. The resulting wound turned septic and Mason died within a week. Mesham claimed he had not seen Mason when he bumped into him because 'I was chasing a canary belonging to my cousin.'

OUT FOR A DUCK

From the *Wodonga Express* of February 1908 comes this story of 23-year-old twins Sydney and Allison Guest, who were duck-shooting in a salt lake at Tooan in Australia. After they had bagged a few ducks, they de-bagged, stripping and diving into the water to collect their kills. Unfortunately the shock of the cold water caused them both to suffer from heart attacks and drown.

PARKIN'S PYRE

David Parkin, 19, from Bathurst, Australia took a break from his work on a farm by having a sleep atop a haystack he had built. Unfortunately, one of his fellow farmhands was careless with discarding a cigarette and the haystack went up in flames, turning Parkin's bed into his funeral pyre.

PENKNIFE PHYSICIAN

Australian travelling showman Bruce Ashford, 57, died in April 1919, after a bit of ill-advised penknife surgery. Ashford suffered from varicose veins, and noticing a new black mark on one of his legs, decided to try to lance it with his pocket knife. Unsurprisingly, this act caused a lot of bleeding. He called at a farm to get a bucket of water to wash the wound, but instead of stopping to rest, carried on walking. He was found dead on the road by a passer-by. The medical examiner who conducted the autopsy on Ashford said: 'I have never in my years seen a more exsanguinated body. If he had not kept walking he would have easily survived the wound. It is my opinion he walked himself to death.'

GRAFFITI GAFFE

One lesson you might want to take from this book is: Do not run from the law. It rarely seems to work out well. Essex graffiti artists Ben Brand and Adam Greaves were spraying designs on a District Line Tube train at a Barking depot in 2007 when they were spotted by security guards. The pair ran away and were immediately hit by an oncoming train, killing them both instantly.

TAXI TWIT

John Dexter died from injuries sustained after leapt from a moving taxi in 2005. The 18-year-old from Sandwich, Kent jumped from the taxi after its driver attempted to drive him to a police station when his passenger did not have the money for the fare.

MORTAL MOTTO

A teenager who had adopted the motto 'If in doubt, flat out!' died during a high-speed pursuit with police in 2006. Jamie Crawley, 18, from Newhaven, England, drove away from a filling station without paying for his petrol. Crawley put his motto into practice, sending his car to its top speed of 200km/h. Outrunning the police, Crawley switched off his car lights to avoid being seen and was then hit by a truck, a collision with fatal consequences for the young speedster.

LETHAL LOOSE SCREW

A missing screw on a cherry-picker platform used by council workers in Yorkshire to change the bulbs in streetlamps caused John Elgin, 30, to be thrown from the machine's bucket in 2006. An accident investigation found that the bar which supported the platform and kept it level buckled because just one screw was missing. A colleague of the dead worker said: 'John hated going on the machine. He felt it was a bit too much like a fairground ride.'

POACHER TURNED GAME

Some things, such as poaching, are best done in the dark. This makes them inherently dangerous. One poacher not taking any account of this was Billy Forrest. As his friends drove a 4x4 across a field in Lincolnshire without any headlights, Billy hung out of the window to train a torch on his dog as it caught a rabbit. Without lights, the driver could not avoid a large rut which flipped the vehicle on its roof, causing Billy to be thrown clear and onto his shotgun, which then discharged into him.

NOT CUTTING THE MUSTARD

Londoner John McGowan had recently lost his job and suffered a marriage breakdown. However, what pushed him into killing himself in a phone box with its telephone cord in 2006 was a row about a ham and mustard sandwich. The 30-year-old was so upset over the way his girlfriend had made a sandwich for herself – putting mustard on it, he claimed, meant she did not want him to kiss her because he hated mustard – that he stormed out into the night and hanged himself.

50 SHADES OF DEAD IV

Lancashire man Barry Tennant was so keen to indulge in a bit of sexual experimentation that he set an alarm clock early to trick his wife and children into leaving the house. They had a terrible shock when they returned, finding Barry's corpse suspended in a self-created leather harness, wearing women's clothing and with a dog lead around his neck. The coroner recorded a verdict of death by misadventure, feeling it was all about a bit of autoerotic asphyxiation that had 'gone too far.' Far too far.

WHAT'S THE STORY? DEAD TORY

Jim Howard, the steward at a social club in Surrey, died from alcohol poisoning minutes after a shot-drinking contest at the bar of the club. The 62-year-old got into a Jagermeister shot-downing contest with a 22-year-old and lost in the worst way possible, dying from alcohol toxicity after taking just minutes to push himself more than four times over the legal drink drive limit.

BIG SPLASH, BIGGER DICK

Richard Waller's regular trick after several pints imbibed in pubs near his home in Padiham, England, was to jump into the River Calder from a road bridge and emerge on the other side. However, on December 20, 2009, the trick went wrong. Waller was more than three times over the legal drive limit for alcohol, and his friends were so used to him doing the stunt that when they did not see him emerge they thought nothing of it for 10 minutes, by which time it was all over for Waller.

NO RESPECT FOR DOCTOR'S ORDERS

Arguing about politics is enough to raise anyone's blood pressure, but it is an especially bad idea when you have a heart rhythm problem and have stopped taking the beta blockers your doctor prescribed and are trusting in homeopathy instead. It was in exactly these circumstances that Respect Party worker Abu-Bakr Rauf collapsed and died in a Bradford car park in March 2012 after he got into a heated exchange with a fellow campaigner. Wherever you are on the political spectrum, there is a simple lesson here: keep taking the tablets.

HAS BEAN

Lorry driver George Oakley was buried under eight tonnes of animal feed when he backed up his wagon and a stockpile of soyabean meal accidentally poured down on him. Despite being pulled from the pile by colleagues and resuscitated, Oakley died later in hospital from the initial effects of suffocation.

DO AS YOUR MOTHER TELLS YOU

Gracie Collins, 70, had been telling her sons for eight years that she wanted them to fix the drip under the kitchen sink of her Essex bungalow. They should have listened to their mother because one morning in 2009, when Gracie went to make a cup of tea, she was killed when her home exploded in a gigantic ball of flame. A subsequent investigation showed the cause was a gas leak from a wrought-iron gas pipe that had been eroded by a slow-dripping leak from the kitchen sink above it.

COMIC KILLED BY LAUGHING GAS

Respected club comedian Jerry Broughton, 42, was found dead in his bed in his Stoke home in 2009. At the subsequent inquest into his death, it ironically emerged that the man renowned for making others laugh had died after accidentally overdosing on nitrous oxide – laughing gas – whilst watching pornography on his laptop. Nitrous oxide is a known sexual stimulant, but death by toxicity is a risk for anyone using it.

OH, THE IRONY XII – NO LOVER OF LATEX

Student Brian Kahn, 21, died after what a coroner described as a 'freak reaction during a lifesaving operation'. Kahn, from Walsall, died in 2009 after he suffered a rare allergic reaction to the surgeon's latex gloves.

SCONE OF STONE

Birmingham pensioner Barbara Bradley, 75, died after choking on a fruit scone whilst enjoying a day out at the seaside in 2006. After choking on what, according to Bradley after her first mouthful was 'a shamefully dry bit of baking', a piece of the scone became lodged in her lungs, leading to her death.

NOW HE'S WORKING ON THE GHOST TRAIN

Not attempting a spot of maintenance while a rollercoaster is running seems like blinding common sense to you and me, but it seemed to pass by amusement park engineer Mike Boyce, who climbed onto the track of a rollercoaster in England in 2008 to grease the track after earlier problems with the ride. Boyce did not seem to hear the approaching ride nor his colleague's shouted warning and was hit head on by the cart.

DEADLY DODGY SAUSAGE

The family of Southend-on-Sea man Ali Hughes, 28, put his death down to a 'dodgy sausage' he had eaten whilst visiting London to watch a football match. The Tottenham Hotspur fan endured four days of vomiting and diarrhoea before being found dead in his bed. The inquest heard his death was due to food poisoning and would have been avoidable if he had sought medical assistance.

DEADLY SAUSAGE SANDWICH

Christopher Stoke, 44, from Upminster, Essex, died while choking on a sausage sandwich in 2008. Stoke was more than five times over the legal drink-drive limit for alcohol when he wolfed down the sausage sarnie from a 24-hour cafe and began to choke. A post-mortem showed he died from hypoxic brain injury caused by loss of oxygen. The coroner concluded that if he had not been so drunk, he would have been able to save himself.

MOCK THE DEAD AND JOIN THEIR RANKS

It is an insult to get drunk, urinate and then climb on a war memorial. However, that did not stop Kevin Swift of Walsall doing so in 1986. However, he went from mocking the glorious dead of several wars to being ingloriously dead himself when he fell from a height of 3m onto some metal railings, impaling himself. The two friends he was with, who were also drunk, thought his groans were a joke and left him to die from the rupture of his stomach.

GETTING THE BOOT

In 2009, Billy Moyes, 55, was found dead in the boot of his car a week after he crawled into it to sleep off a binge drinking session at a pub in Somerset. A policeman who had been investigating Moyes's disappearance said: 'It appears clear Mr Moyes didn't want to drive while under the influence of drink and so decided to sleep it off in the boot of his car. It is tragic his noble intention turned out this way.'

HOW DO YOU LIKE THEM APPLES?

Yorkshireman Matt Jordan, 46, boasted to friends he could drink 15 litres of cider. In an effort to back up his claim, he challenged several of his friends to drink 1.7 litres of cider more quickly than him. None of them could. However, while repeatedly demonstrating this by taking on all challengers at a party in 2009, Jordan drunk so much that he collapsed, dying from heart failure brought on by alcohol toxicity.

DYING FOR A PEE VI

An English tourist in Spain, Darren Botham, 54, fell to his death while looking for a toilet in a Spanish bar in 1996. Botham was put off from using the toilet in the pavement cafe he had been having a coffee in because the number of computer users inside upset his technophobia. Instead he tried a bar down the street, but not reading any Spanish, went through a storeroom door instead of a toilet and fell down a flight of stone steps to his death.

OH, THE IRONY XIII – CASH DASH SPLASH

A 23-year-old burglar who had just robbed a florist shop, jumped into the River Aire in Scotland in the mistaken belief that the shouts she heard while fleeing from the scene of the crime were police. In fact, it was another group of burglars coincidentally robbing the same premises on the same day. Unfortunately, she was dragged down by the money box she had stolen and died from drowning.

WHAT A COCK

If you keep chickens, you ought to know better than to get between a cock and his hens. Grocer Harry Picker from Mount Gambier, Australia, had kept fowl for years but one day in February 1876, he ignored this simple rule. Picker was attacked by his prize bantam cock, which spurred him so badly he had to retire to bed – from which he never got out of again, as the multiple wounds became infected, leading to his death.

SPURNED BY HIS TRUE LOVE

The pride and joy of Welsh farmer Geraint Lewes was his vintage tractor. According to his wife, 'he spent more time looking after it than he did me', making what happened to Lewes in 1987 more than a little ironic. His machine had a mechanism on its side so the engine could be turned on from outside the cab. As the tractor was in gear when Lewes turned it on, it lurched forward, trapping him underneath, causing the injuries leading to his death. He was still conscious when found, saying over and over: 'I can't believe she has done this to me.'

DRINKING AND ENTERING

Irish farmer Finn McDermott, 56, died after locking himself out of his home in 2009 and becoming trapped when he tried to get back into it through a bathroom window. He had just returned from an annual pilgrimage to Croagh Patrick and was highly inebriated. The window had shut on him as he climbed through, rupturing his liver, breaking his ribs and trapping him halfway in, halfway out. The coroner remarked that if he had drunk less, 'He would almost certainly have been able to free himself.'

HERBAL HEALTH HICCUP

Herbalism is a skill that can take decades to master. It is certainly one poor Connor Farrell did not have. The 21-year-old from the Republic of Ireland bought dozens of specialist herbs from around the world through the Internet. However, his own blend of herbal tea proved lethal, causing his death by cardio-respiratory failure when one of the ingredients he used – Kratom leaves – reacted badly with the other herbs in Connor's cup of home brew.

PAMPER PERIL

Irish woman Heather Geraghty's monthly pamper night turned lethal in 2009. According to her husband, Connor, it was her ritual to 'have a pamper night once a month where she would slap on a face mask, have a bubble bath with candles and drink some wine. I knew better than to ever disturb her during it as did all the kids.' The do not disturb rule had unintended consequences when Heather sank in a drunken stupor under the water and her body was not discovered for more than 12 hours.

PEANUT PERIL

Londoner Damian East died after experiencing an extreme allergic reaction to a takeaway in 2001. Despite suffering from a peanut allergy, he ordered a satay burger smothered in a spicy peanut sauce. The several pints of lager he had consumed earlier may have been a factor in his odd choice. East's body went into anaphylactic shock, his throat swelling to the point he could no longer breathe, long before paramedics had a chance to reach him.

ANIMAL CRACKERS – TOP 10 RIDICULOUS ANIMAL-RELATED DEATHS

10. Never get between a pig and its food. Hungarian farmer Imre Kovac made that mistake in 2010 whilst trying to inspect one of his pigs. The hefty sow, weighing 95kg, decided that if Kovac was going to get in the way of her dinner, she would take a bite out of the farmer. The porker severed Kovac's femoral artery and he bled to death within five minutes.

9. In 2010, Zimbabwean hunter Tamsen Lucius climbed a tree to get a better spear-throwing position whilst hunting wild boar. However, whilst attempting to kill his prey, Lucius fell from the tree and managed to fatally impale himself in the chest with his own spear.

8. Arvid Ahlberg, 70, was cross-country skiing in 2010 when he was shot and killed by hunter Iris Blom. It was not that Ms. Blom had poor aim, it was just that the bullet she fired, ricocheted off the elk she shot at and it hurtled into poor Ahlberg's skull.

7. Lynne Hinds was so scared of mice that when she saw one in her London kitchen in 1993, she climbed onto a work surface to put as much distance between herself and the rodent. Unfortunately for Lynne, whilst standing on a cupboard, she slipped and fell, smashing her skull on a cooker on the way down. At the inquest her husband said: 'I had told her if she saw one to hit it with a broom, but her phobia must have got the better of her.'

6. Chinese fisherman Huang Wu, 58, was dragged to his death when he hooked a giant sturgeon with his rod in March 2013. Friends fishing with him saw him wade into the river to retrieve his rod after the fish pulled it from his hands. When he grabbed it again, the fish dragged him and the rod 46m out into the river, before pulling Huang under the water. A friend said: 'He had just told us what a big catch he had made and then suddenly the catch had him.'

5. Nepalese living close to the Kali river live in fear of a giant catfish called a goonch. One of the fish – which can grow to 2.4m in length and weigh 82kg – developed a taste for human flesh after feasting on the burnt flesh left over from funeral pyres placed in the river. In 2008, the fish snatched 18-year-old Yash Barral as he waded into the river to cool down, whilst in 2009, it dragged fisherman Shushant Dangol to his death. In 2010, farmer Bikash Guri attempted to rescue a goat from the river, only to be bitten and then dragged into the water by the giant goonch. Perhaps it is no surprise the river is named after Kali, the Hindu goddess of time, destruction and death.

4. Jane Smith, 25, from Atlanta was strangled by her pet python Diablo after he got agitated by her attempts to feed it some medication in October 2008. Her husband found the snake coiled around her throat and a syringe Jane used to administer Diablo's drug, still gripped in her dead hand.

3. Vir Nakai was painting a tower block in Mumbai in 2012, when he fell 68m to his death after an eagle attacked him for damaging its nest. There is a life lesson there: where eagles dare, men should not go disturbing things.

2. Exercise turned deadly for Candice Berner when she went jogging near the settlement of Chignik in Alaska in 2010. She became the first person to be killed by wolves in the United States in 50 years. A local policeman said: 'She had no reason to expect that her run was going to turn out that way.' Funny that, because if I knew I was going to be attacked by wolves, I would be sure not to go out jogging, either.

1. Bolivian police claimed that 18-year-old fisherman Oscar Barbosa committed 'suicide by piranha' when he jumped out of his canoe in the Yata river and allowed the flesh-eating fish to devour him. A local police officer said: 'He was drunk, but knew the river was full of red piranhas at this time of year. He knew what they would do if he went in the water. Death was certain. This was suicide by piranha.'

PRATFALL

English rugby player Jerry Cartwright, 25, died in 2005 after becoming drunk at his club's annual black tie dinner and attempting to perform a bizarre tradition of the club in which members tried to leap from the roof of the clubhouse into a nearby tree. An inquest heard he was more than twice the legal drink drive limit when he misjudged his leap and plummeted to the ground, fracturing his skull.

HIGH HEELS HELL I

Catherine Reese, 27, from Bradford, died after falling over in her high heels during a night out in 1997. She was taken to the accident and emergency department of the local hospital, but sent home after her swollen knee appeared free of any fracture. However, a blood clot formed, which travelled to her brain and killed her the next day. At a subsequent inquest, a friend of Catherine's said: 'Her heels were three-and-a-half inches high. She was walking on them OK at the start of the evening, but at the end she was struggling as she had drunk quite a bit. She was petite and would never dream of going out for the night without wearing heels.'

HIGH HEELS HELL II

New York lawyer John Gordamo had a fetish for being trampled on by women wearing nothing other than stockings and high heels. In 1985, he paid a prostitute to walk over him and kick him whilst she wore a pair of stilettos. This kinky sex session ended with him having several cuts, abrasions and wounds around his groin and thighs. Despite the injuries becoming infected, Gordamo was too ashamed to seek medical help and ended up dying from heart failure.

THE LAST TRAIN

Londoner Mark Lester, 34, died after becoming trapped on a deserted Tube train in 1986. In what sounds like a nightmare or start of a horror film, Lester had fallen asleep on the last train home. He woke up to find himself alone, the lights off and the train stopped in a tunnel. He then attempted to climb out of the train by the interconnecting doors of its carriages, when it began moving from its position in the siding, fatally crushing him against a tunnel wall.

PECKISH FOR A POP UP

Worry over debt is a terrible thing, but not everyone reacts like Louise Bellman from Birmingham. The 37-year-old librarian died after eating the circuit board and wiring from her broken toaster. Despite being rushed to hospital, her bizarre actions cost her life. However, at least she denied her creditors the chance to get their pound of flesh.

DOGS – NOT MAN'S BEST FRIEND II

Welsh businessman Gregory Dyke died when he waded into the sea at Aberdaron in 1989 to retrieve a ball he had thrown for his pet Dalmatian when the dog proved too lazy to get it. However, he fell into the surf, his clothes becoming so waterlogged and heavy that he could not stand up again. Dyke's last words before he drowned were: 'I can't get up. That bloody dog!'

FAILURE BURSTS BUSINESSMAN'S BALLOON

English businessman Simon George from Stroud was so proud of never having failed an exam in his 40-year life, that he could not deal with the failure of not passing an IT exam in programming in 1997. He reacted to flunking by buying a canister of helium gas designed to inflate balloons and inhaling it all, killing himself.

FROM RUSSIA WITH DEATH – TOP 10 RIDICULOUS DEATHS FROM RUSSIA

10. A Muscovite mother allowed her 21-year-old son, his uncle and a friend of the family to drink 1 litre of pure alcohol mixed with snow in her home. She even joined in the binge. Bad mistake. She was too inebriated to stop her son getting into a drunken argument with the other two men about the existence of God. When they refused to deny he did not exist, the son stabbed them both to death.

9. Nikon Filipov died in 1998 after he made a drunken bet with two friends that he could survive for an hour naked in the -27°C temperature of a winter night in Irkutsk, Siberia. Filipov stripped naked and went and stood in an alley beside a bar, and when his friends went to check on him after 20 minutes, he was already dead.

8. Two Russian businessmen from Kirov died in 2010 after diving from a steam room, to a plunge pool. Instead of it being ice cold to cool them down, the pool had accidentally been heated to boiling point. A third man who was with them was unable to pull them to safety before they were boiled to death.

7. In July 2012, Arseni Zolnerowich from Saint Petersburg drunk far too much vodka and in an argument with his wife, refused to get off the folding couch and come to bed to sleep it off. In frustration at his refusal, his wife kicked the handle of the couch on her way out of the lounge. This activated the mechanism that folded it against the wall to save space. Arseni was then trapped between the mattress and wall and, in his drunken state, could not escape. When his wife checked on him three hours later, she discovered Arseni had suffocated.

6. Saint Petersburg citizen Yelena Pushnoy, 57, died in 2008 when she got out of her car and suddenly found herself falling into a pit of boiling water. One of the ageing pipes used to heat the city had ruptured and caused the ground above it to give way at exactly the spot Pushnoy had parked.

5. Saint Petersburg seems to be an unsafe city. In August 2012, Ilari Denisov was walking along one of the city's residential roads when a car wheel was thrown from the window of an apartment block. Although the wheel did not hit him directly, Denisov stood still and watched it bounce right up to the moment it bounced into his face, breaking his jaw and dealing him such a massive head trauma he died two days later. Police were unable to determine which apartment the wheel came from.

4. In Russia, vodka and ridiculous death have a very close relationship. Drunk mugger Pasha Bukin held a knife out to pensioner Lilya Kulakov in the town of Beloyarsky in 1998 and demanded money for vodka. Lilya responded by pulling out her husband's prosthetic leg she was carrying in her shopping basket and hit Bukin on the head with it. Bukin lost his footing in the assault and fell fatally onto his knife.

3. Foma Shmelev from Krasnoyarsk developed a dangerous addiction to getting high by drinking petrol. Death, when it came to Shmelev, was not from the damage his addiction was doing to his central nervous system and major organs, but from a secondary bad habit – smoking. Shmelev slashed a pipe at a filling station to get his fix and after escaping from the scene of the crime, lit up a cigarette and himself thanks to his careless gulping having splashed his clothes with fuel.

2. A Russian ice-skating bear, dressed in a tutu, attacked and killed circus director Dmitry Potapov whilst he made the bear rehearse for a show in Bishek in 2009. The bear dragged Potapov across the ice rink by his neck whilst on the skates. Local experts blamed the bear's aggressive behaviour on malnourishment. Personally I blame it on the cruelty of making it skate and wear a bloody tutu!

1. In 2006, Nastya Horina, 15, rang police in the Russian city of Pskov to tell them she had killed her aunt. The teenager told them her missing pet dog had come to her in a dream and asked her to punish the person who had caused its death. When her aunt confessed to selling the dog to a barbecue shop for a bottle of vodka, Nastya, together with a group of younger friends, forced her aunt to a gravel pit ,where they beat her and then buried her alive. Nastya returned the next day and when she confirmed she had avenged her barbecued pooch with her aunt's death, rang the cops to confess.

NEEDING DRUGS LIKE A HOLE IN THE HEAD

Englishwoman Heather Perry, 41, achieved a degree of infamy when she appeared on live television in 1992 and drilled a hole in her own head – a process known as trepanning – in an attempt to cure her depression. It obviously did not work as, 10 years after having to be rushed to hospital after she pushed an electric drill into her head too far, she died from a drug overdose. After an inquest into her death, her brother said: 'She thought the trepanning would be the answer to all her problems of depression and addiction – but obviously it wasn't. I do wonder whether it actually had an effect on her brain and led to what happened later.'

CROSSING A LINE NO FRIEND SHOULD DO

Nasty piece of work Julian MacLeod sent spoof love texts to his friend James Harrison pretending to be from James's ex-lover, with whom he had cheated on his wife. Harrison was so distraught when he got the series of texts across two weeks in 2012 that he walked onto a level crossing and was hit by a high-speed train travelling from Paddington to Worcestershire. At an inquest into Harrison's death, the coroner attacked the 'remarkably juvenile' actions of MacLeod. With friends like that, who needs enemies?

A ROD FOR HIS OWN BACK

When Gary Lowe was accidentally locked in a third-floor bedsit by his brother Jake in 2012, he decided to use a wire curtain rod attached to the window to try to lower himself to the ground. Bad idea. The rod broke and Gary fatally fell some 9m to the concrete below. An inquest into his death heard, unsurprisingly, that both Lowe brothers had been drinking heavily before the incident.

THERE'S A RAT IN MY KITCHEN

Slim Londoner Ashlyn Barton, 29, fell into a narrow 25cm gap behind a kitchen unit while trying to resolve a problem with rats in her kitchen in 2001. She became trapped behind the unit and suffocated after she attempted to retrieve some rat poison whilst inebriated. A pathologist who examined her concluded her death was from 'positional asphyxia caused due to alcohol intoxication.'

KILLER PAPER CHASE

Roadsweeper Bobby Baker chased a paper bag blown by wind down a road in Yorkshire in 1994 and slipped, fracturing his ankle. However, what should have been a non-threatening injury ended up killing Baker when a blood clot caused by the fall travelled to his lungs. One of his colleagues commented: 'It is hard to believe chasing a bag could end up killing anyone. It's a sad and ridiculous way to go.'

ROLLOVER

In 1929, George Winch of Prahan, Australia was flattened to death whilst at work. George was a flagman, giving warning of the approach of a steamroller. Winch was waiting for a car to pass and failed to notice that the steamroller was only a couple of yards behind him. He attempted to jump clear, but failed, the roller crushing him from feet to hips before it could stop. Ouch.

REVENGE OF THE SNAKE

Ken Webb, 16, of Leongatha, Australia went for a bicycle ride with his pals – it is what the cool youth did in 1936. While cycling, the group of lads found a snake crossing the road and young Ken found a stick and beat the snake to death. Within a minute of doing this, he collapsed and died himself. The coroner at the inquest in Webb's death ruled he had died from a heart attack brought on by the exertion and excitement of killing the snake.

BLAST OFF!

Construction worker James McGregor, 63, of Nowra, Australia was so tired after a hard day working and long night drinking that he went to bed fully dressed. Unfortunately, McGregor forgot to take the detonators out his pockets and during the night he fell out of bed, causing one of the detonators to explode, fatally injuring him.

HEAD IN THE WRONG PLACE

In March 1926, Australian Nurse Lena McLenan, 27, put her head into a Melbourne hospital's lift to gossip with some of her colleagues. Regrettably, she was so carried away in conversation that she forgot to move her head when the lift began to move down. The lift trapped her and snapped her neck.

THE COSMIC JOKER STRIKES AGAIN VI

Australian Barber James Marr was giving a customer a shave in his Perth barbershop one morning in November 1925, when the client collapsed in the chair. Marr then rushed him home in his car. When he returned and reopened his shop, he told the next customer what had happened, and as he said: 'He collapsed just like that!', Marr himself collapsed, suffering from a massive fatal heart attack.

SUICIDE FRENCH STYLE

I am a huge Francophile. There is no denying the French have style; even some of their suicidal citizens take their lives with a tasteful nonchalance that is world-leading. On January 13, 1914, a certain Monsieur Guilloman, 61, of Alfortville, Paris selected a quiet spot on the River Seine, lit the fuse of the stick of dynamite he was holding and then sat down, calmly smoking a cigarette and waiting until he was blown to pieces.

HEALTH AND SAFETY NIGHTMARE MAN

Robert Gallantine, 50, would have been any health and safety expert's worst nightmare. One day in August 1938, the New Zealander from Wellington decided to clean a clock. He filled a basin with petrol to soak the mechanism in, then, deciding the room was insufficiently lit, climbed a ladder to open a wooden shutter. The ladder slipped and in jumping to save himself from injury, Gallantine knocked over the basin, spilling petrol onto his clothes, which ignited because he had been working with a lit cigarette in his mouth the whole time. Turned into a human torch, Gallantine then stumbled over a 9-litre can of petrol, which exploded and killed him.

SHEARER SHAGGED OUT BY DOPE

Drug taking in sport is not new. Doping has been going on since the nineteenth century. Even my beloved team, Arsenal, were popping pills to win matches in 1925. However, it is truly shocking to learn that even in 1955 and the world of competitive sheep shearing, some people would stoop to taking performance-enhancing drugs. Australian Charles Ernest Oliver was going for the world-shearing record that year and dosed himself up on the amphetamine Benzedrine. Unfortunately he took so much that not only was his attempt on the record unsuccessful due to his irrationality, but he also managed to fatally poison himself. Cheating idiot.

NO LAUGHING MATTER

English comedian Joe Dixon was a huge hit in the variety theatres of Great Britain after World War I. Unfortunately the constant performing took its toll on Dixon's voice and, self-medicating, he began to gargle with potassium chlorate – sometimes used as a disinfectant, but also used in safety matches, fireworks and explosives. Dixon was found dying in the toilets of a Leeds railway station in 1922, when he overdid the gargling, swallowing enough potassium chloride to poison himself. The coroner believed that Dixon had: 'an unknown, but terrible susceptibility to the substance he turned to in hopes of alleviating his problems.'

WE WERE ONLY FOLLOWING HOLY ORDERS

In September 1925, several followers of a sadhu – a Hindu ascetic – were brought before a judge in the Indian city of Barabanki. The sadhu had decided to perform a religious rite by having himself buried and they had been arrested for their role in first digging and then filling in his grave. When instead of emerging from the grave cleansed and enlightened after several days, the sadhu died in it, they were arrested. The judge freed them when he heard that as his disciples, they were afraid he would beat them or cause them bad luck if they did not do as he ordered. I am not sure that is a defence I would recommend if you find yourself in court actions.

LAIDLAW LAID LOW

Australian detectives were set a puzzle in January 1947, when the 1.8m tall body of 40-year-old farmer Claude Laidlaw was found in a tank of water less than 1.4m deep on his farm near Terang. They eventually pieced together Laidlow's last moments, concluding that he had been repairing a windmill on his property when one of the blades struck him on the head, knocking him unconscious and throwing him from the windmill and into the tank.

KILLED BY DEATH XI – DAISY DEATH

Englishwoman Annie Boyd, 29, from Whitehaven, was in her father's greenhouse in 1907 to pick flowers for her aunt's funeral wreath when she slipped on some ice and the stalk of a Michaelmas Daisy went into her wrist. A piece of the stem remained in the wound and Annie died from lockjaw 11 days later.

DOING MORE THAN SPLITTING HAIRS

Killing yourself is not always an easy business. Yet in September 1938, Thomas Williams from Rockhampton, Australia, made it look simple, offhandedly telling his wife he was going out and would not be back as he was 'going to put an axe in my head.' He was as good as his word, walking into some scrub and then embedding a tomahawk 6cm into his skull.

OUT OF THE FIRE ...

Ronald Robert Wallrodt, 23, crashed his truck in Northam, Australia, in December 1952 when the smoke from a bushfire obscured the road. Volunteer firefighters had to be called to cut him from the wreck, but as they attempted to get him free, the truck burst into flames, forcing them to douse the vehicle with their hoses. Unfortunately, in trying to save Wallrodt, they actually managed to drown him.

STUNNING MISJUDGMENT BY COPS

Tasers are used by police forces across the world as a non-lethal, life-saving alternative to more drastic use of force. Despite the theory, hundreds of deaths have been reported due to safety issues with tasers. One with the whiff of ridiculousness about it was that of 56-year-old wheelchair user Gloria Doulton, who was tasered with 50,000 volts for a total of 121 seconds by two police officers in Florida. The police had called at her home, only to be confronted by Doulton in her wheelchair threatening them with a knife and a hammer. Because of her large size, the cops stunned her 10 times when they thought their tasers were not having an effect. However, they certainly did have an effect, triggering a fatal heart attack.

TERRIBLE SLIP-UP

John Bradley, from Birmingham, died in 2009 after slipping on a bar of soap, which caused him to fall onto the plastic spike of a solar-powered garden lamp. An inquest heard that although Bradley had been drinking, it was not a factor in his standing on the soap and falling onto the lamp, which was being stored upside down in a bucket in the garden of his parents' home.

WHEN SAFETY KILLS

There is something ridiculously ironic as well as tragic when a safety device meant to save your life ends up killing you. Charity worker Sally Troughton was giving a lesson to a disabled man on how to use an aerial slide at an outdoor leisure centre in England in 2005 when the strap of her safety helmet strangled her. The helmet got knocked back whilst she was travelling down the zip wire and poor Sally could not relieve the strap's pressure on her throat as her arms were forced up another safety measure – a chest harness.

KILLED BY DEATH XII – DEADLY FUNERAL

James Wise, 23, died after attending a funeral of a friend's grandfather in Liverpool in 2010. Wise argued with the driver of the car taking him home, opening the door and attempting to leave the vehicle whilst it travelled at 32km/h. As he got out, he banged his head. Seemingly OK, the driver took him home, but he was found unconscious the next morning by his girlfriend. Despite being rushed to hospital, he died within hours of brain damage. An inquest heard that Wise had drunk heavily before and after the funeral, where he had also taken cocaine and cannabis.

MOTHER KNOWS BEST

Former banqueting manager Gary Russell, 65, choked to death on a doner kebab because he could not use his new false teeth, as he found them uncomfortable. Londoner Russell choked after a couple of mouthfuls, as he could not chew the meat properly. His 84-year-old mother and a keen vegetarian, Gladys Russell, told an inquest: 'I used to tell him eating meat would kill him.'

DYING FOR A PEE VII

Jenny Dunn, 21, begged her friend Jimmy Clyde to stop his car so that she and her friend Emily Dupont could get out and pee. As the two girls relieved themselves ahead of his car in the dark on an Alabama road at 1am on an August morning in 2005, Clyde thought it would be funny to scare them by pulling away. Unfortunately, he did not know they were squatting in front of him and he hit them both, running over Dunn and killing her. You will not be surprised to learn, Clyde was significantly over the legal drink drive limit at the time of the accident.

BASE-IC MISTAKE V

Since the death of Austrian tailor and inventor Franz Reichelt, who tested his parachute by jumping from the Eiffel Tower to his death in 1912, the managers of the famous landmark have taken a dim view of parachutists jumping off of it. Aside from the stunt carried out for the 1985 James Bond film A View To A Kill, all parachuting attempts have been illegal and usually fatal. In 2005, Norwegian BASE jumper Kjetil Moen managed to sneak his parachute past Eiffel Tower security. However, he was less lucky with his leap when he fatally smashed into the first level of the structure after his parachute got snared and detached from him.

BATTY WAY TO GO II

James Harborne, 66, of Kansas City was accidentally killed by his son-in-law Bobby Franklyn Jr. in 2005 when Bobby swung a sledgehammer in an attempt to hit a bat that had flown into the home they shared. A misjudged blow hit Harborne on the head and he died instantly.

PLANE STUPID

The boss of a Dutch cattle feed company died in 2005 when a stunt meant to impress an employee backfired with deadly results. Ambroos Joosten had intended to fly his ultralight aircraft past the home of Jakob Heyman whilst waving to him and his family. Unfortunately, after waving, Joosten could not get his craft to clear Heyman's farmhouse and he flew straight into it, killing himself and burning down Joosten's property.

FLESH-EATING UFO MONSTERS MADE ME DO IT

In 2004, American crystal meth addict Gary Holden smashed his car into a UPS truck, killing its driver. At a subsequent trial for murder, he claimed his reason for doing it was to escape an alien race called the Hemodrones, who lived inside the Earth and used flying saucers. Holden went on to claim he had to flee because the Hemodrones had been attempting to capture him and put him on a cargo ship bound for China, where he was going to be eaten. Unsurprisingly, Holden's drug-induced story did not get him off the murder charge.

GETTING THE HORN

The one-horned rhinos of India are so rare that unless you travel to Kaziranga national park in the state of Assam – its only remaining natural habitat – you are very unlikely ever to see one. However, this fact makes the death of Sanjiv Baruah in July 2003 even more ridiculous. The villager from the Darrang district of Assam, several leagues away from Kaziranga, was happily minding his own business, gathering grass on a riverbank when he saw a one-horned rhino struggling in the water. It had been washed out of the national park in a flood caused by monsoon rains.

Fascinated by the animal's plight, Baruah called over friends to watch as the 3,000kg rhino struggled to get out of the water. Alerted by the hullabaloo Baruah was making, the first thing the enraged rhino did when it freed itself from the water was charge straight for him. As the one-horned beast thundered forwards, Baruah was suddenly much more endangered than the rare rhino. He slipped in the mud and found that one horn was more than enough for a killer goring.

HYENAS ARE NO LAUGHING MATTER

Anyone who thought those stories about Masai tribesmen killing lions with their bare hands as a rite of passage were the stuff of legendary hogwash might be interested to hear about the death of Moses Lekalau of Kenya. In 2007, the 35-year-old herdsman from Kenya was walking home to his village from the small hillside market town of Maralal when he was attacked by a lion. The king of the beasts pounced on Moses and brought him to the ground, but he fought back, wrestling the cat onto its back.

A passer-by saw Moses fighting barehanded with the lion, but could do nothing to scare the animal off and so ran to get help. When he returned with a local police officer they found the lion dead and Moses still alive but now being attacked by a pack of hyenas. Firing shots at the frenzied carnivores forced them to flee, allowing the dying Moses to tell how he fought the lion to the death for nearly 30 minutes, leaving him too exhausted from the battle to fight the hyenas, which had opportunistically jumped him. They had bitten off his hands and toes, causing the loss of blood which finally killed him.

DEATH FROM ABOVE

When we wrote the original 1001 *Ridiculous Ways To Die*, I got a very snotty letter from a scientist telling me one of our stories was wrong because no one had died from a falling meteorite 'although a dog in Egypt was killed'. Much as I hate to disagree, I did and do with the complaining astronomer. In the 1849 volume of his work *Cosmos*, German scientist Alexander von Humbolt records: 'Several persons had been struck dead by stones falling from heaven, as for instance, a monk at Crema on September 4, 1511, another monk at Milan in 1650 and two Swedish sailors on board a ship in 1674'. Another author, T. L. Phipson, in his 1867 work *Meteors, Aerolites and Falling Stars*, gives more details on these instances, especially the one at Crema. Citing the contemporary accounts in *The Commentary of Surius*, *De Rerum Varietate* and *Opus Epistolarum* he tells how the meteor shower fell across several acres, not only striking and killing a monk but also killing several sheep.

THAT'S ALL VOLKS!

It became clear to me that while researching this book I could have easily written a book called 101 *Ridiculous Deaths Due To Autoerotic Asphyxiation*. From rock stars to politicians to actors, there is no end of idiots who have lost their lives thanks to a fondness for the sexual kink of 'scarfing'. The process of cutting off the air supply is meant to greatly increase the intensity of orgasm. Many of those who tried scarfing swear that, by cutting oxygen at the moment of climax, their pleasure is increased tenfold.

Of all the deaths due to scarfing I have come across, possibly the most ridiculous was first reported in the pages of the *Journal of Forensic Sciences: Autoerotic Fatalities* in 1983. It recorded how one native of the state of New York went to a clearing in woods, got naked and tied one end of a chain to his neck and other to his Volkswagen Beetle. The 40-year-old airline pilot then fixed the car so that it turned in circles, forcing him to jog alongside it, the chain squeezing his neck if he did not keep up.

Unfortunately for the scarfer, the chain got caught around the back axle and he was pulled to the ground. Although he avoided the automobile's wheels as he skidded along, the chain tightened around his neck. Whether it helped him achieve a tenfold orgasm as it choked him to death is just one of life and death's little mysteries, which we are never going to be able to solve.

CASTLEMAINE XXXX

In the 1980s, Australian Castlemaine beer was promoted in the United Kingdom with the slogan: 'Australians wouldn't give a Castlemaine XXXX for anything else'. Somehow that seems an apposite epitaph for Joseph Hartley, who was employed at the Castlemaine Brewery in South Melbourne in 1897. On the nightshift in August, Hartley became dizzy while testing the beer and fell headfirst into a vat of beer 3m in diameter and 3m deep. Reports of the incident at the time seem less interested in Hartley's death, but in the fact that the vat of beer – valued at £140 – 'was shamefully run into the drains of the street by that enemy of happiness which has the official title of Customs officer'.

SPACE ODDITY

On January 7, 1948, Captain Thomas F. Mantell of the USAF became the first person ever recorded to have lost their life pursuing a UFO. Mantell was one of three Air Force pilots to chase an unidentified object from his base at Godman Field, Fort Knox across Kentucky. The other two pilots broke off, but Mantell kept on until, according to the Air Force, he blacked out from lack of oxygen at 7,620m and his plane spiralled down to the ground, crashing at a farm near the Tennessee-Kentucky state line. Adding to a note of ridiculousness, the Air Force claimed Mantell was chasing Venus – an unlikely explanation given the dozens of eyewitness reports and Mantell telling his base that the UFO 'looks metallic and of tremendous size.'

A LOAD OF BULL

Renowned Scottish botanist David Douglas died in 1834 whilst attempting to climb Hawaii's Mauna Kea volcano. Douglas fell into a pit dug by bullock-hunter Edward Gurney. Not seriously harmed, he tried to climb out. He might have made it if a huge bull had not also fallen into the pit, crushing him to death.

THAT SINKING FEELING

Despite what you may have seen in films, it is almost impossible to drown in quicksand. Like everything else on the planet, quicksand obeys the laws of physics, particularly those associated with displacement and buoyancy. One man who did manage to drown, however, was Ròdolfo Fierro in 1915.

Fierro was a key lieutenant of Pancho Villa in the Mexican Revolutionary Wars. As a soldier he displayed great bravery and extreme brutality; not for nothing was he known as Villa's executioner. On October 15, Fierro was at the head of his troops marching on Sonora, when an ill-advised shortcut led to his horse blundering into a patch of quicksand and throwing him. Despite the presence of his men, Fierro sank rapidly, the large amount of gold he had stuffed into his belt giving him negative buoyancy to a fatal extent.

THE ULTIMATE STICKY END

In 1919, molasses was big business in America. As well as being the standard sweetener, it was also the raw material for industrial alcohol, which is why the Purity Distilling Company of Boston had 2.3 million gallons stored in a tank at 529 Commercial St. This tank – 15m high and 27m in diameter – was known to leak at the best of times; to the extent that locals would routinely take pots and pans and help themselves to molasses as it oozed out from weak seams.

On January 15, 1919, however, the tank simply exploded. It is speculated that a sudden rise in temperature during the preceding 24 hours (from -17°C to 5°C) caused the molasses to expand. Since the tank was full to the brim the molasses had nowhere to go, and the tank simply gave way. Witnesses said that the noise of rivets popping sounded like a machine-gun, and that the earth shook. The shockwave sent debris flying through the air and blew a truck into Boston harbour. This was followed by a tidal wave of molasses moving at an estimated 56km/h, with enough force to derail a train.

Twenty-one people died – either struck by debris or overwhelmed by the flood – and a further 150 were injured. The water in the harbour was brown for months and local folklore has it that on hot summer days the area smells of molasses even now.

TRAINWRECK TV

Uruguayan TV show *Challenge To The Heart* rewarded charities if people completed difficult tasks. In 2006, with cash for a hospital up for grabs, a group of competitors were trying to pull a train and two carriages when the vehicles gained speed and ran 20 of them over, severing the limbs of the most severely injured and killing seven. This might explain why I have always preferred unreality TV – it is less dangerous.

HARD TO KILL

In 1933, five small time New York gangsters got homeless drunk Mike Malloy wasted with booze and got him to sign an insurance policy making his life worth $1,790 on his death. The gangsters figured it would be easy to kill off Malloy and collect on their investment. They were wrong. It was ridiculously hard to kill him.

At first they believed they could speed his demise by buying him even more drink, but when that seemed too slow a route to riches they tried poisoning his booze with antifreeze. This did not kill Mike Malloy. Nor did the turpentine they got him to drink, nor the horse liniment or rat poison they mixed into his food. They fed him oysters soaked in methanol. These failed to kill him, as did a sandwich of spoiled sardines mixed with poison and carpet tacks. They got him to pass out with drink, then took him to a park and left him barechested with 19 litres of water poured over him in a night of -26°C temperatures. Still Malloy lived. They then had him run over by a taxi, but despite broken bones, Malloy remained stubbornly alive.

Finally, when Malloy was next passed out drunk, they connected a hose to an apartment's gas jet and put the other end in Malloy's mouth. Although this finally killed him, this form of murder and stories heard in bars across New York of 'Mike the Durable' alerted police to the crime and the five gangsters were convicted of murder, four of them going to the electric chair at the notorious Sing Sing prison.

LIVING THE DREAM AND DYING IN IT

English motorcyclist Andy Stafford was killed in Kazakhstan in 2009 when his bike collided with a cow crossing the road. A Kazakh police inspector said: 'It is more common for cows to be a hazard here than in London, I think. He was not prepared.' According to his friends, Stafford was 'living the dream' by riding across Central Asia. I guess that must be the dream where a cow ends up killing you. I have that one.

THE BANANA SKIN OF FATE

On her deathbed, 73-year-old survivor of Nazi and Communist regimes Ivanka Perko joked: 'I cannot believe after all this time it was a bloody banana that killed me.' Ending her days in Australia in 2006, Perko had a lifelong sense of humour and defiant attitude, which never left her as death approached. Ms. Perko had developed a condition that made her skin delicate and she died from complications that set in when she dropped the pointed end of a banana on her leg, scratching herself. A close friend said: 'She joked about how ridiculous it was to go that way. She was the bravest woman I ever knew.'

GOLD STANDARD IN ANTI-AGEING PRODUCTS

Diane de Poiters died in 1559 at the age of 66. She was mistress to King Henri II of France. Despite being 20 years older than him, she looked his age and was acclaimed for her stunning looks. Many put this down to the elixir she drank everyday to combat the ageing process, containing scorpion oil, spider webs, frogspawn, mercury and gold chloride. This anti-ageing product may have kept her youthful looking, but it also killed her. Recent tests on her hair show her body was poisoned by both the mercury and gold. According to one scientist: 'Chronic gold poisoning leaves you with fragile hair, teeth and bones. It also turns the skin white through anemia. Diane had 500 times more gold in her body than is normal and there is little doubt it killed her in the end.'

CORPSE CLOSET COLLEGE

Amorous James Betts, a student at Corpus Christie College in Cambridge, was sealed in a cupboard by his lover Elizabeth Spencer to conceal him from her father John Spencer, Master of the College, in 1667. Unfortunately, Betts suffocated whilst hidden in the closest.

RILE A WHITE SWAN

I live on a canal, and although I lack common sense, I know not to mess with the two swans that are my neighbours. This makes me smarter than German Albrecht Hirsch. While fishing at a lake in Bavaria in 1938, he began to throw stones at swans to get them to move away, as he claimed they were scaring the fish. One of the swans took exception to this and began to attack Hirsch. According to other anglers, he attempted to make a strategic retreat, getting on his bike and riding away. However, the swan pursued him, constantly diving at him and forcing him to smash his bike and his head into a stone wall. It is alright to laugh loudly at this death, as Hirsch was a card-carrying member of the Nazi party.

THERE, BUT FOR THE GRACE OF GOD

If you have spent most of this book, like me, muttering in your inner voice: 'There, but for the grace of God', you might want to know where the phrase comes from and why it is so apposite for ridiculous deaths. John Bradford was a sixteenth-century English protestant reformer. In 1553, his religious views had him placed in the Tower of London on the trumped up charge of 'stirring up a mob'. Whilst in the Tower, Bradford was convinced he would soon be released and, when he witnessed a group of prisoners being led to their execution, remarked: 'There, but for the grace of God, goes John Bradford.' This was a ridiculous tempting of fate, so it comes as no surprise that Bradford spent the next two years in prison before being burnt at the stake. The phrase was remembered for its irony and survived in the variant: 'There, but for the grace of God, go I.'

IT IS THE WAY THEY TELL THEM

This book is far from novel in its interest in ridiculous deaths. From the days of the great Greek city states, people have been collecting cases of absurd, unlucky, curious and ridiculous deaths. Journalists have always relished the chance to tell the story of a death with some outlandish element. On February 3, 1899 an Australian newspaper for the Northern Territory contained the following story:

'A death of the most unusual character occurred at Howley on Tuesday evening. The night saw a heavy storm which was accompanied by much thunder and lightning across the district. During the progress of the storm the Chinese cook employed by Howley Goldmines Ltd. was standing in the kitchen eating a banana, when a flash of lightning entered the kitchen and struck him dead. The trace of the lightning was left on the side of his face and down the unfortunate man's side. The banana bore no trace of lightning.'

To think some people accuse me of having no taste and decency.

TERMINAL TANGLE

English truck driver Jerry Barnes, 54, smashed his truck into motorcyclist Jamie Grey, 18, when his shoelaces became tangled around the accelerator pedal and he could not get his foot to the brake. The impact on the A338 road in Dorset killed Grey and, at a subsequent trial where he was cleared on any wrongdoing, Barnes told the court: 'I tried to put my foot on the brake to come to a halt and it was like it was handcuffed to the floor. It was awful.'

AND ALL OUR YESTERDAYS HAVE LIGHTED FOOLS THE WAY TO DUSTY DEATH

Little in our world is new. Ridiculous deaths have always been a part of life, just as have absurd superstitions, taboos and ideas about those departed from our physical world. Therefore maybe it is fitting to end on a story that combines a glimpse of both of these from the past.

From the safe distance of the twenty-first century we know that reports of will-o'-the-wisp – also called Jack-o'-lanterns, Pixy-light and in Latin, *ignes fatui* – foolish fire, are likely to be ephemeral balls of fire caused by a mixture of naturally-occurring gases in a swamp or bog. Our ancestors did not have the luxury of such certainty. Where there is mystery, mankind makes stories, and stories can be dangerous things.

In the first survey of Britain written in 1577, historian William Camden referenced what is now Syleham in Suffolk, saying: 'In the low grounds at Sylham, just by Wingfield in Suffolk are the Igne Fatui, commonly called Sylham Lamps, the terror and destruction of travellers and even of the inhabitants, who are frequently misled by them.' Accounts of will-o'-the-wisps or Sylham Lamps leading to deaths are numerous in local records. In one account, two travellers come across a Sylham Lamp and are divided upon what its purpose is. One of them believes it to be a dangerous spirit come to lead them astray, the other, a William of Eye, believes it to be the spirit of his dead father, released from purgatory as a flame to guide them to a church so that he can arrange for a mass to be said. Regrettably, William decides to 'be led by the Lamp', following it off the path, into boggy ground and his death.

Death and the ridiculous are often inseparable. They have always been with us. They always will be. It seems that wherever we are in time, it is not only death and taxes we cannot escape from, it is death, taxes and the ridiculous.

Also available from Prion Books:

ISBN: 978-1-85375-742-6

ISBN: 978-1-85375-708-2

ISBN: 978-1-85375-796-9